AF479261

TAEWON JANG
STAINED GROUND

TAEWON JANG
STAINED GROUND

With an essay by Lyle Rexer and an interview by Suejin Shin

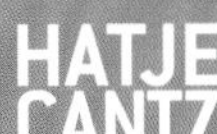

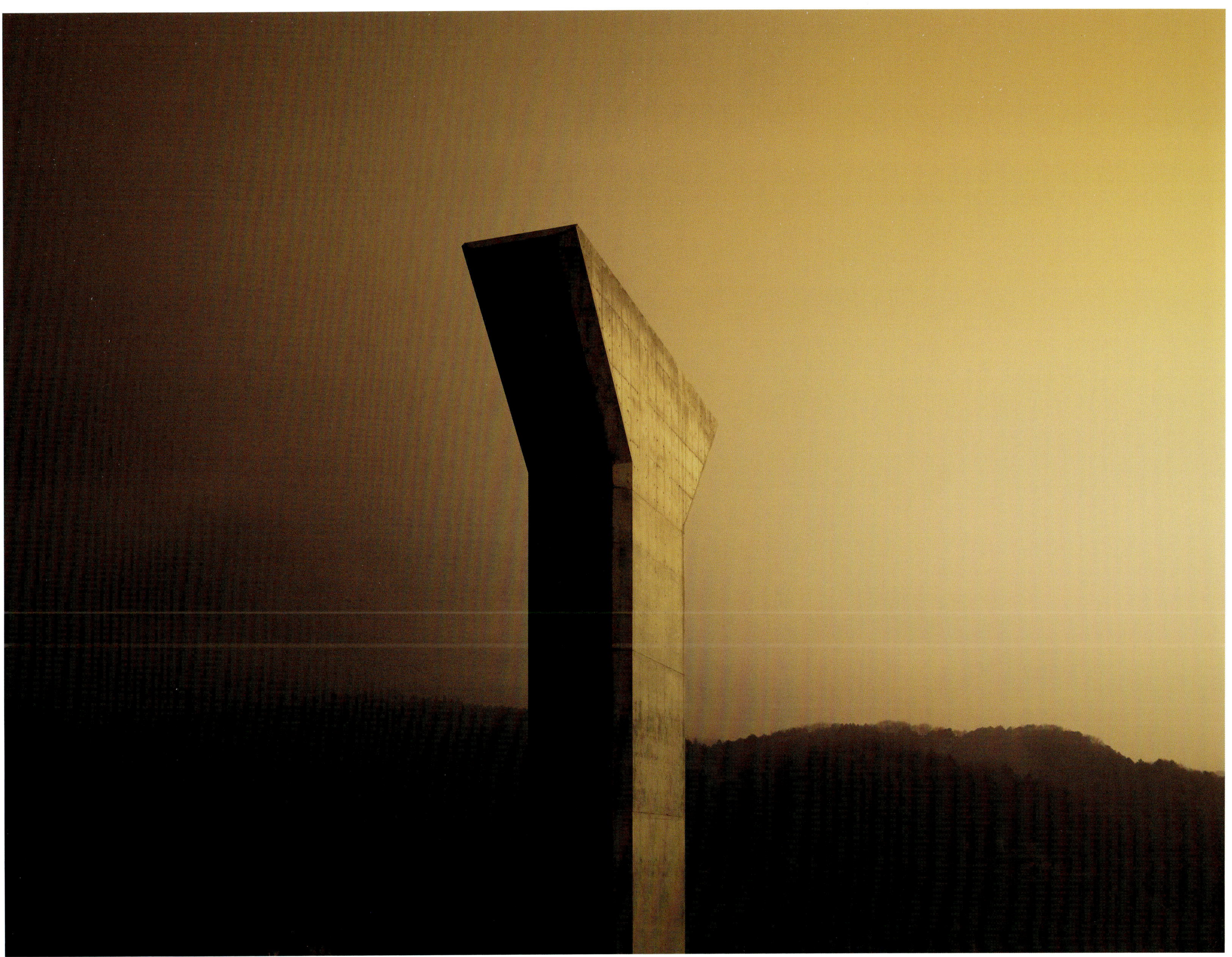

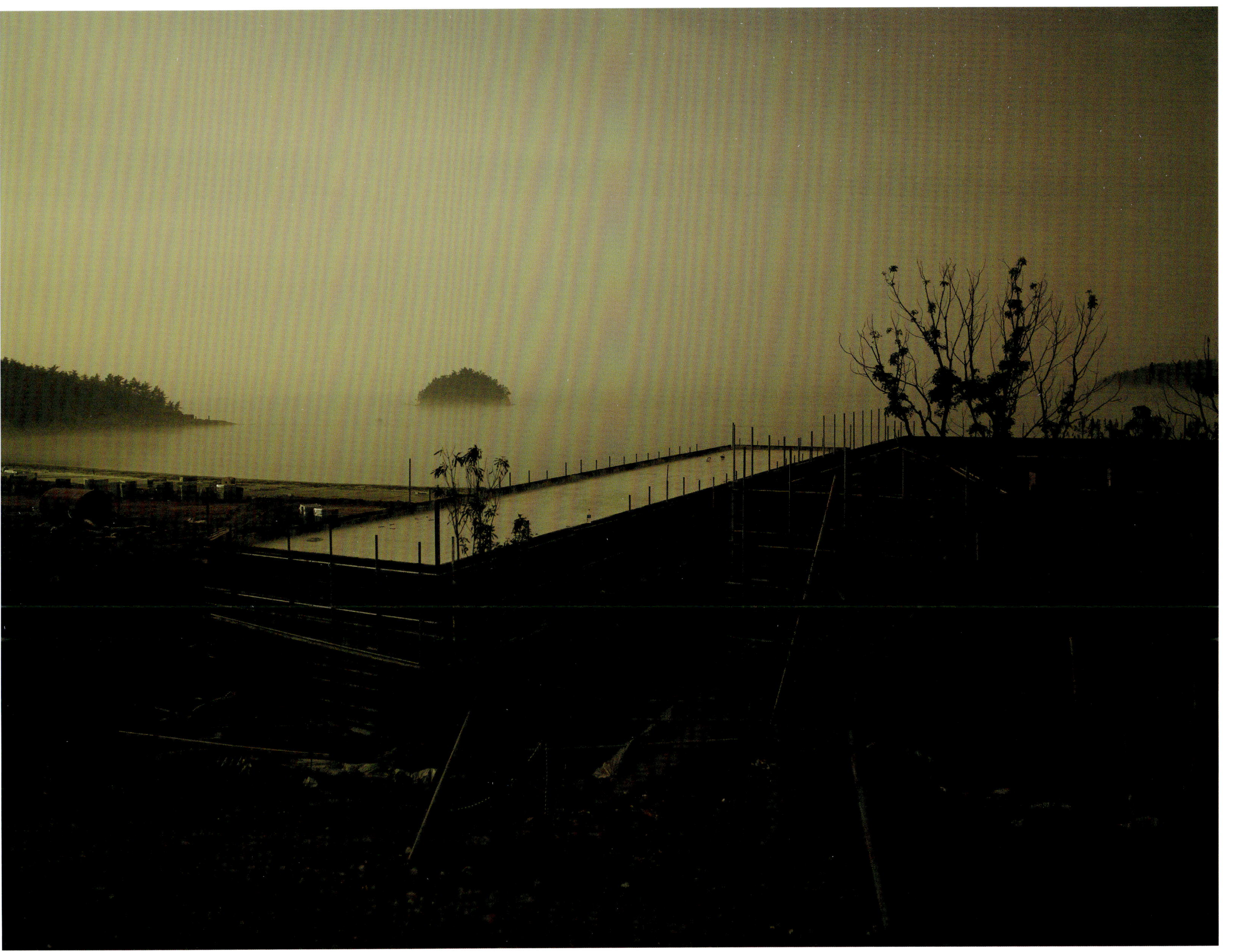

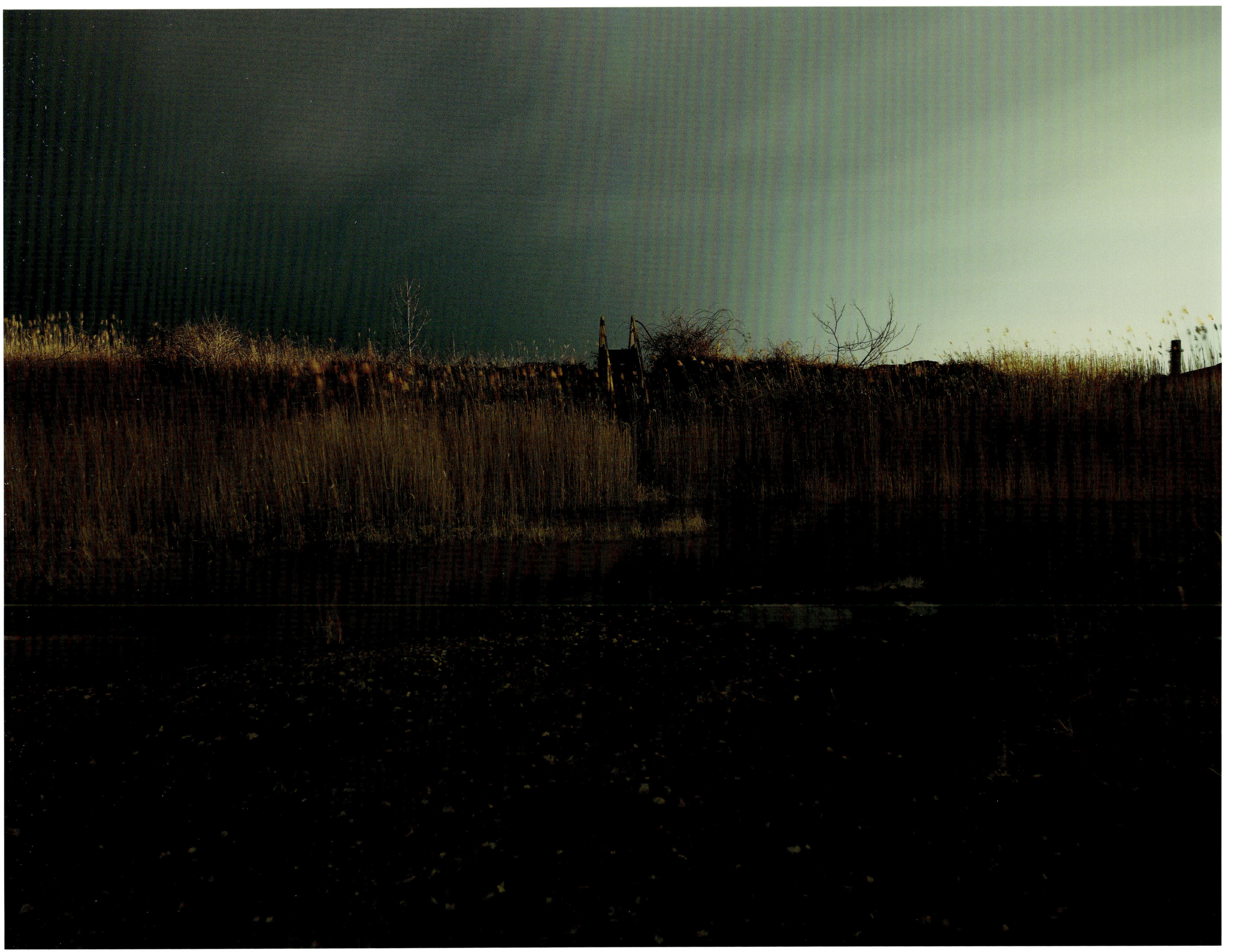

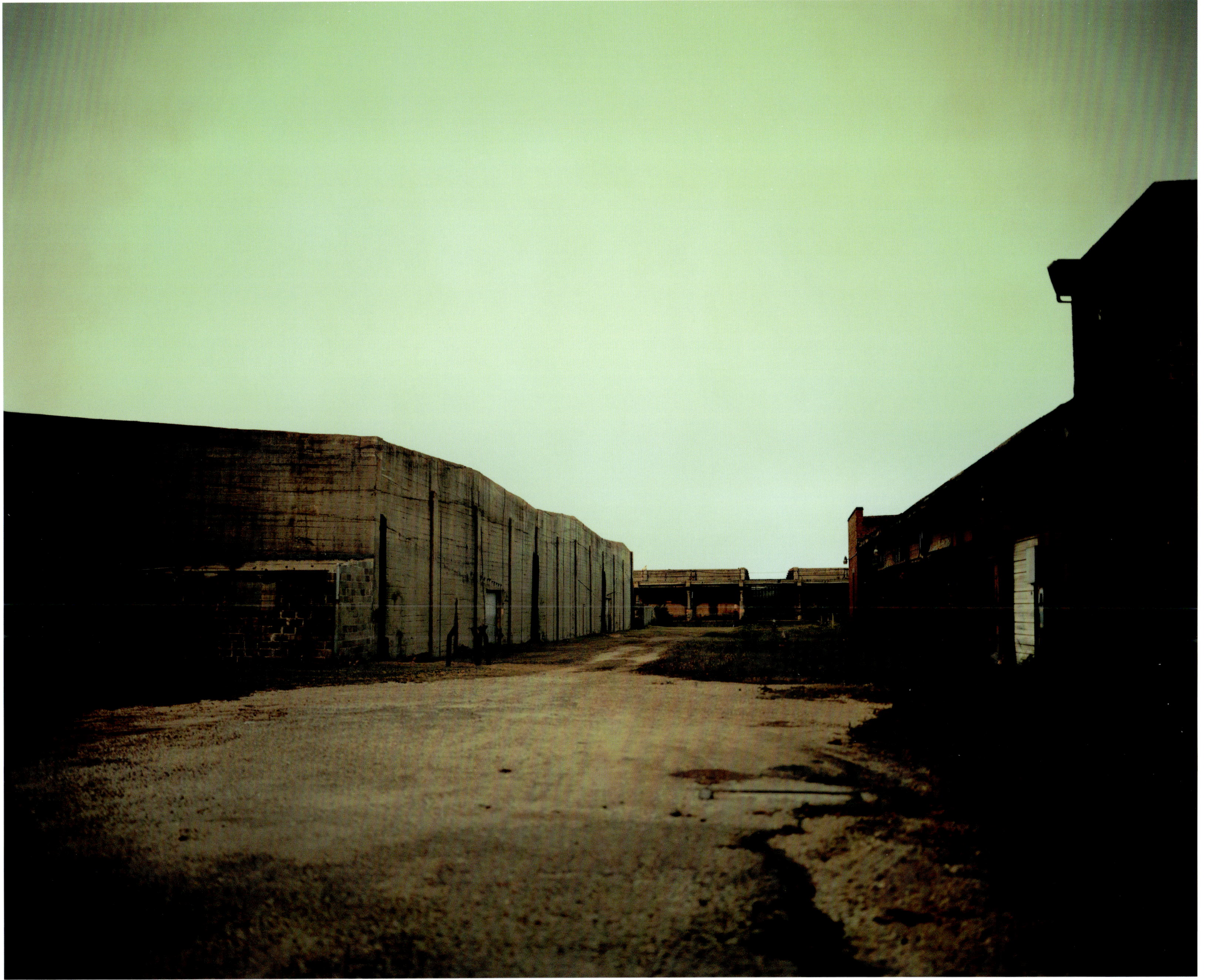

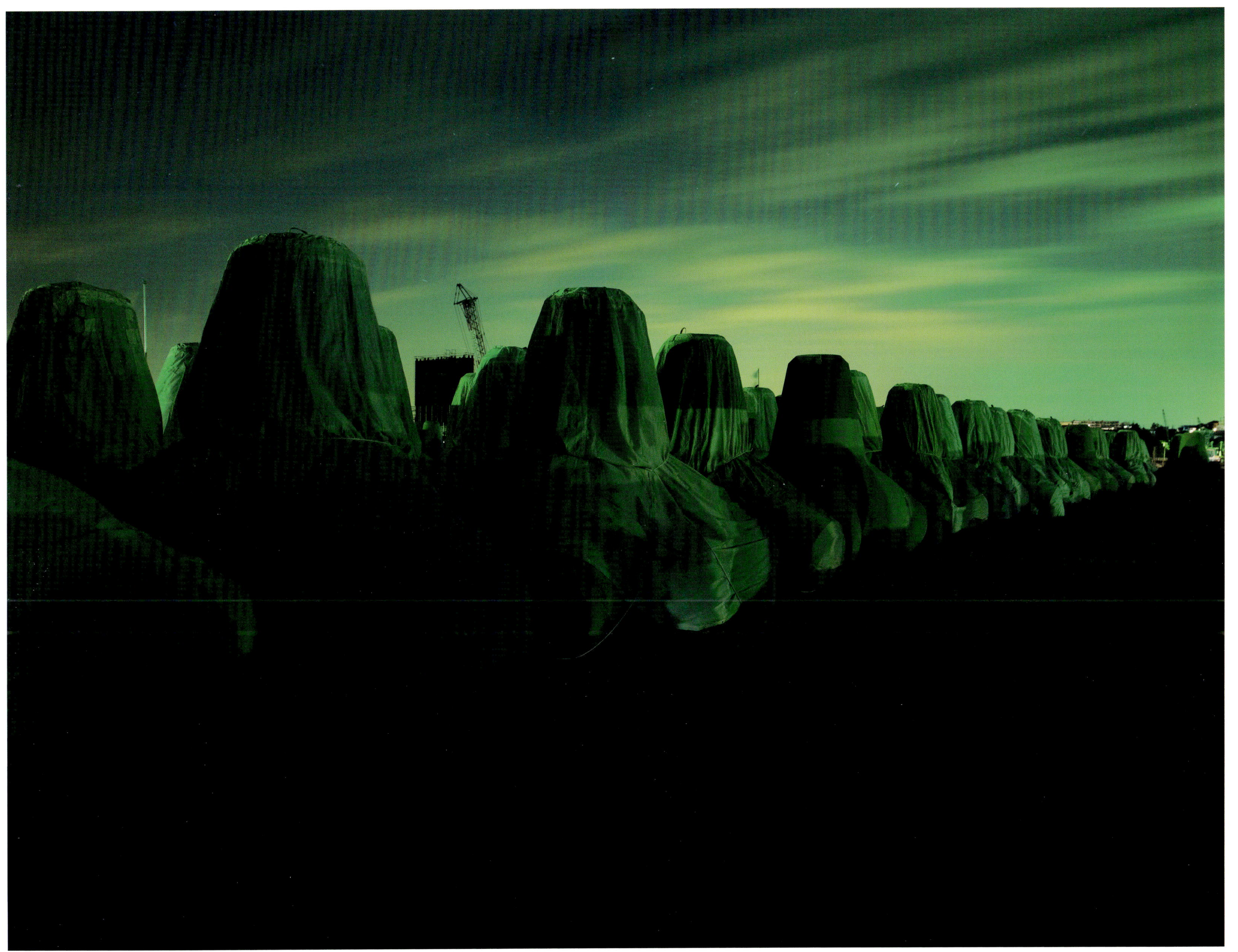

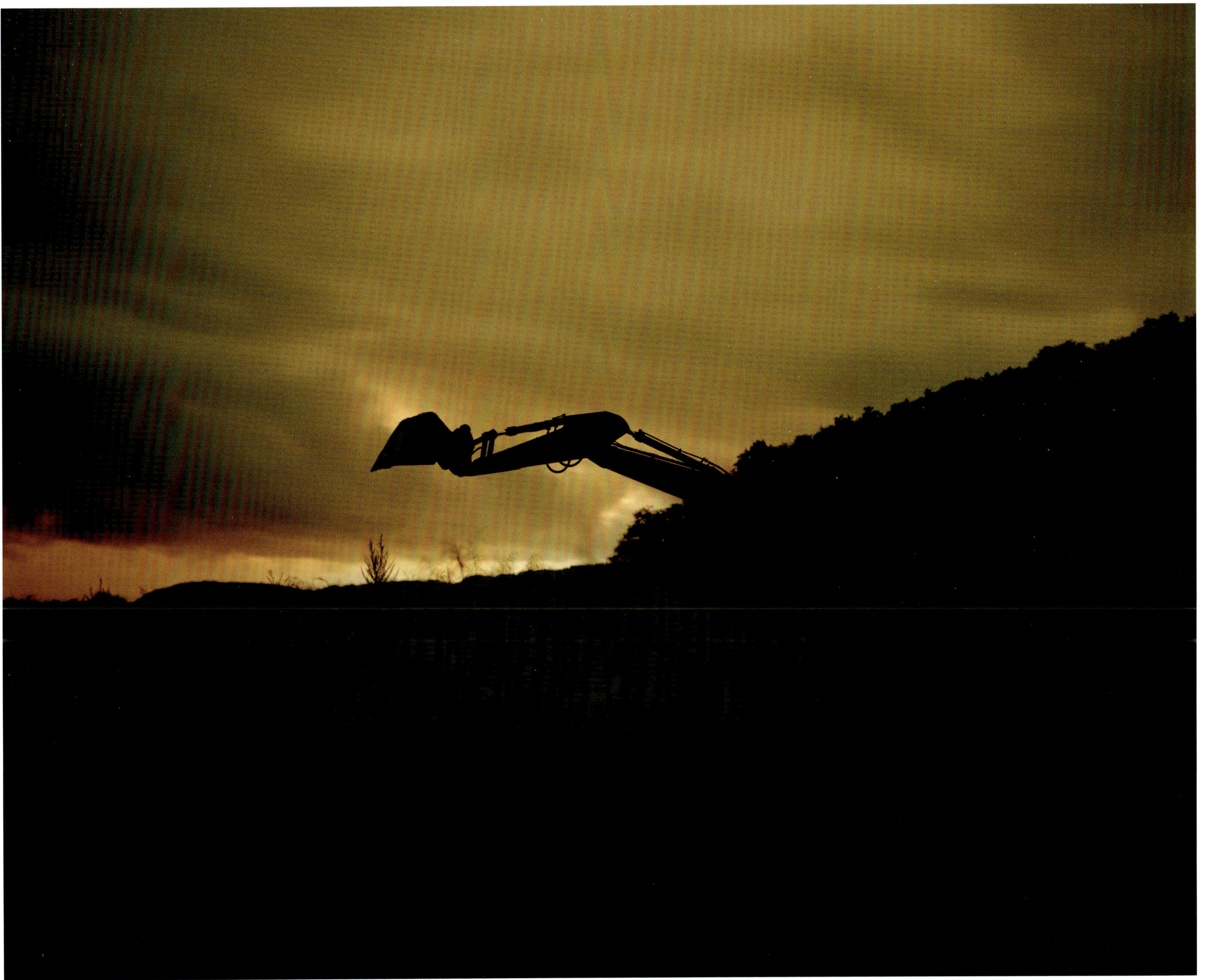

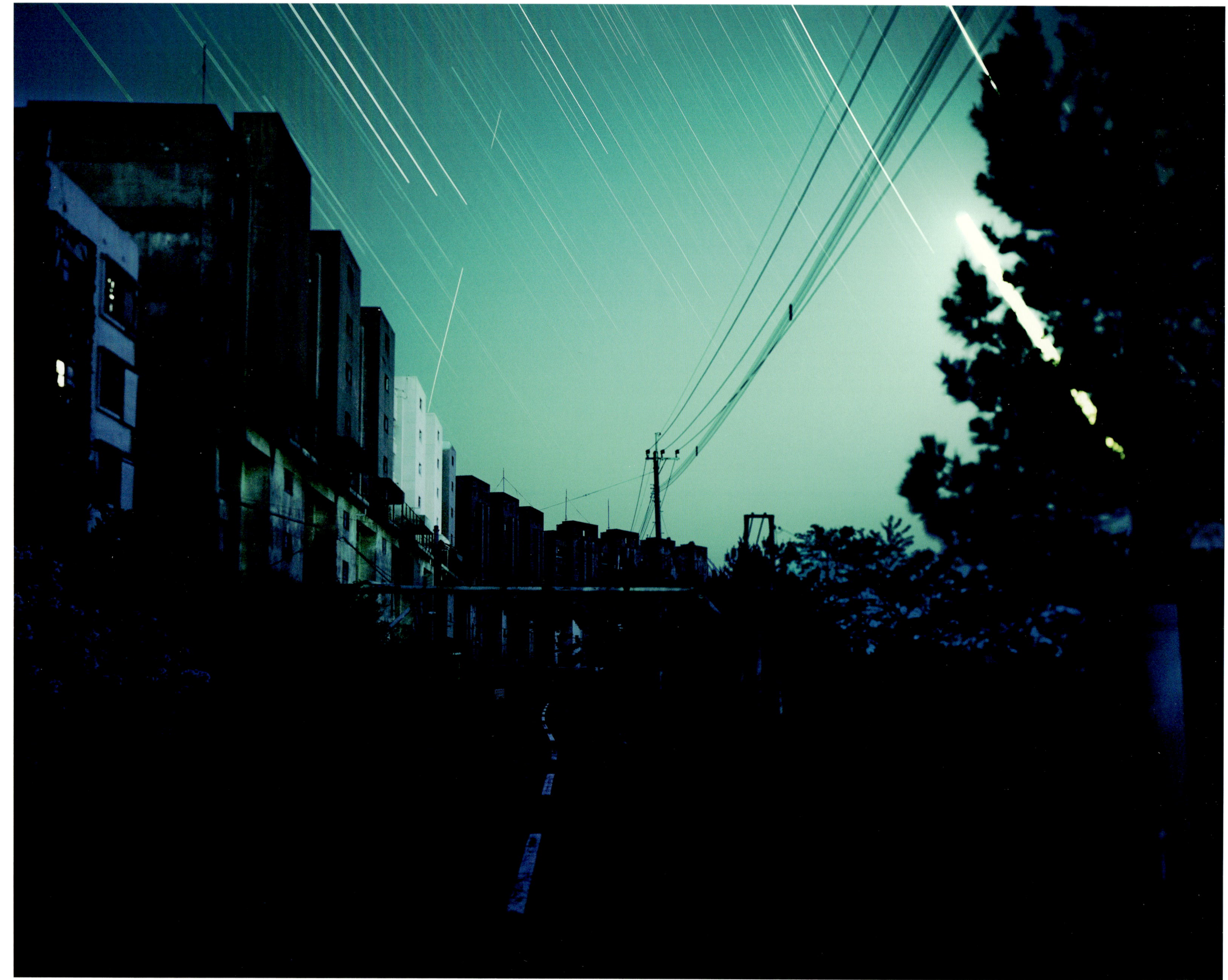

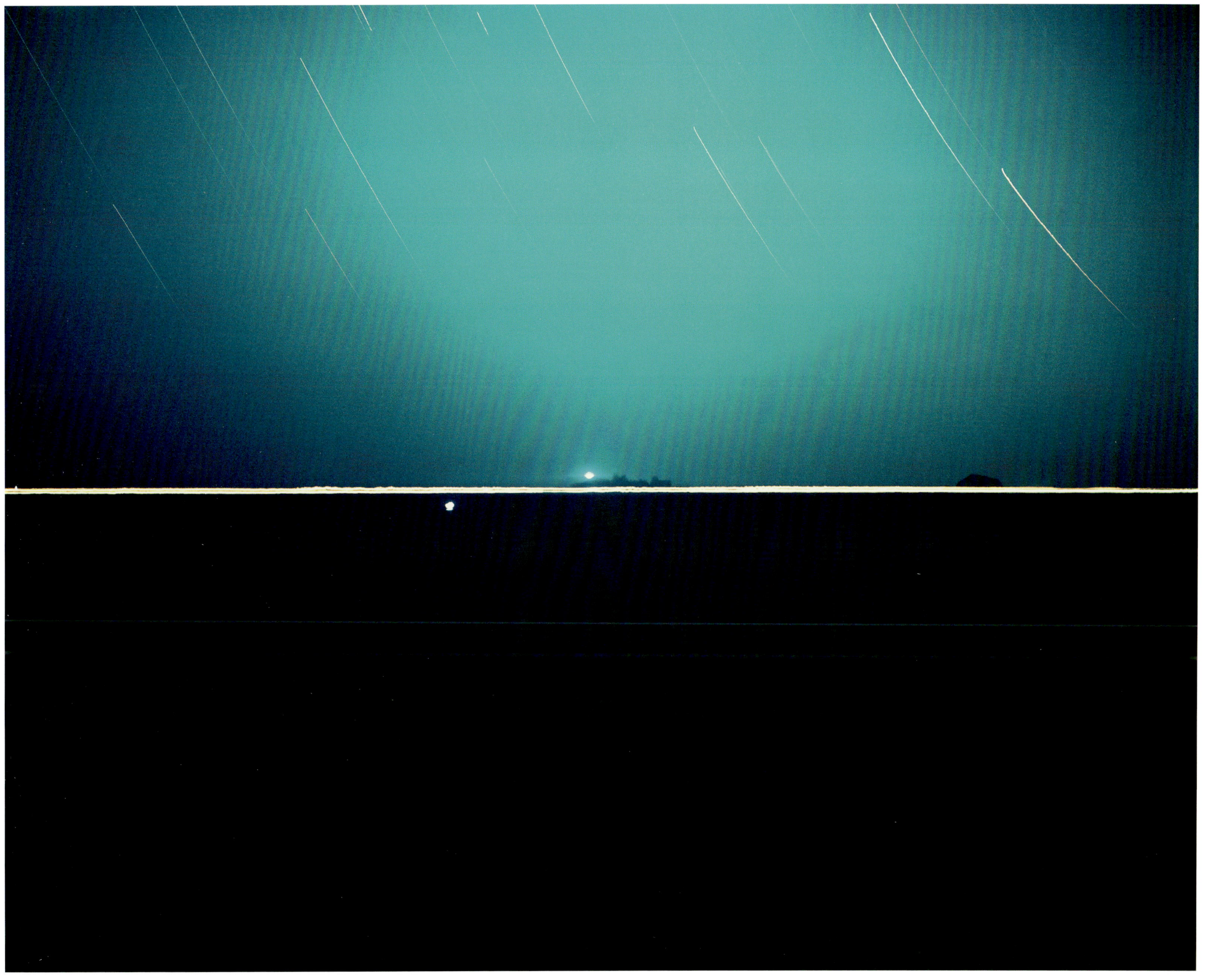

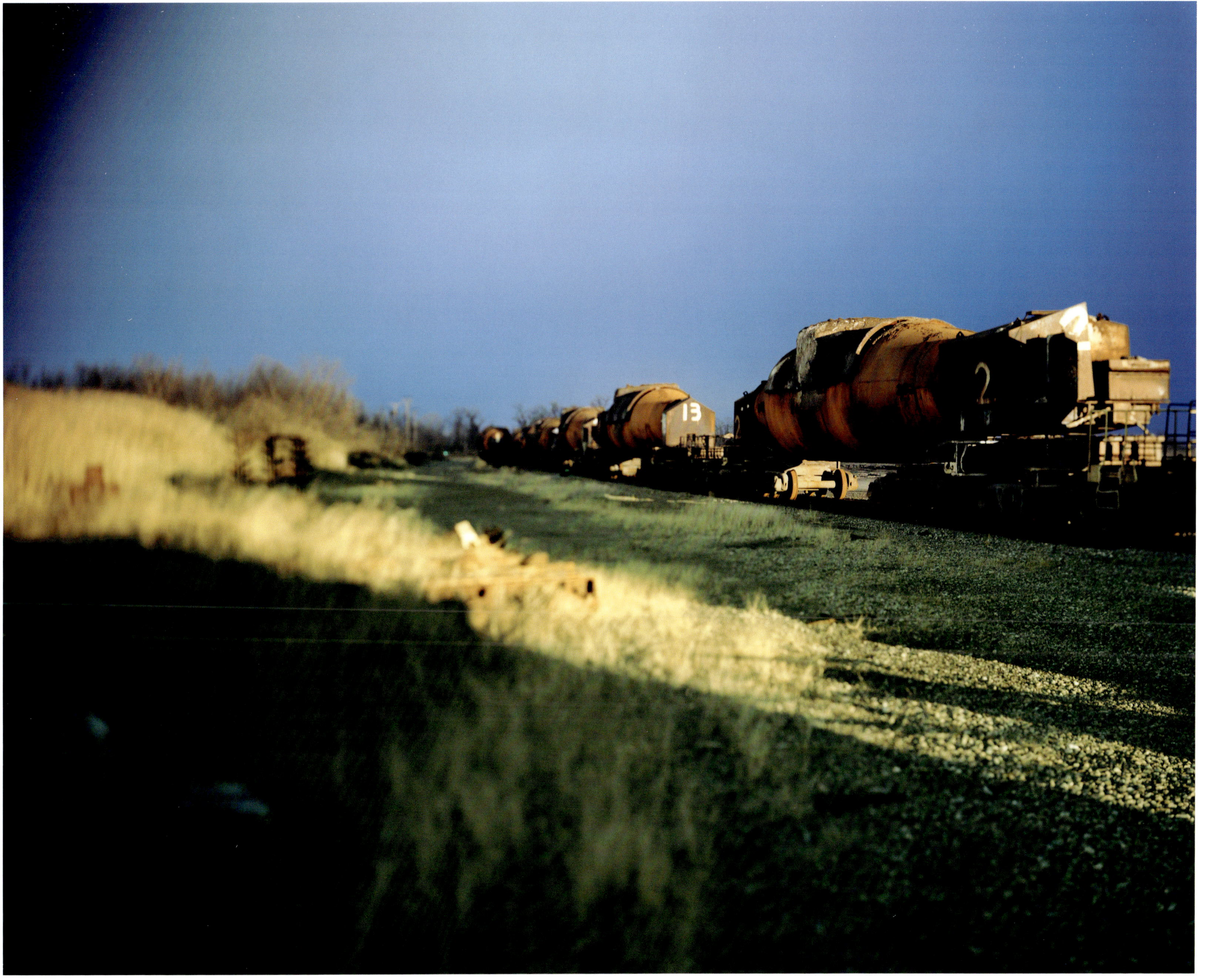
13
2

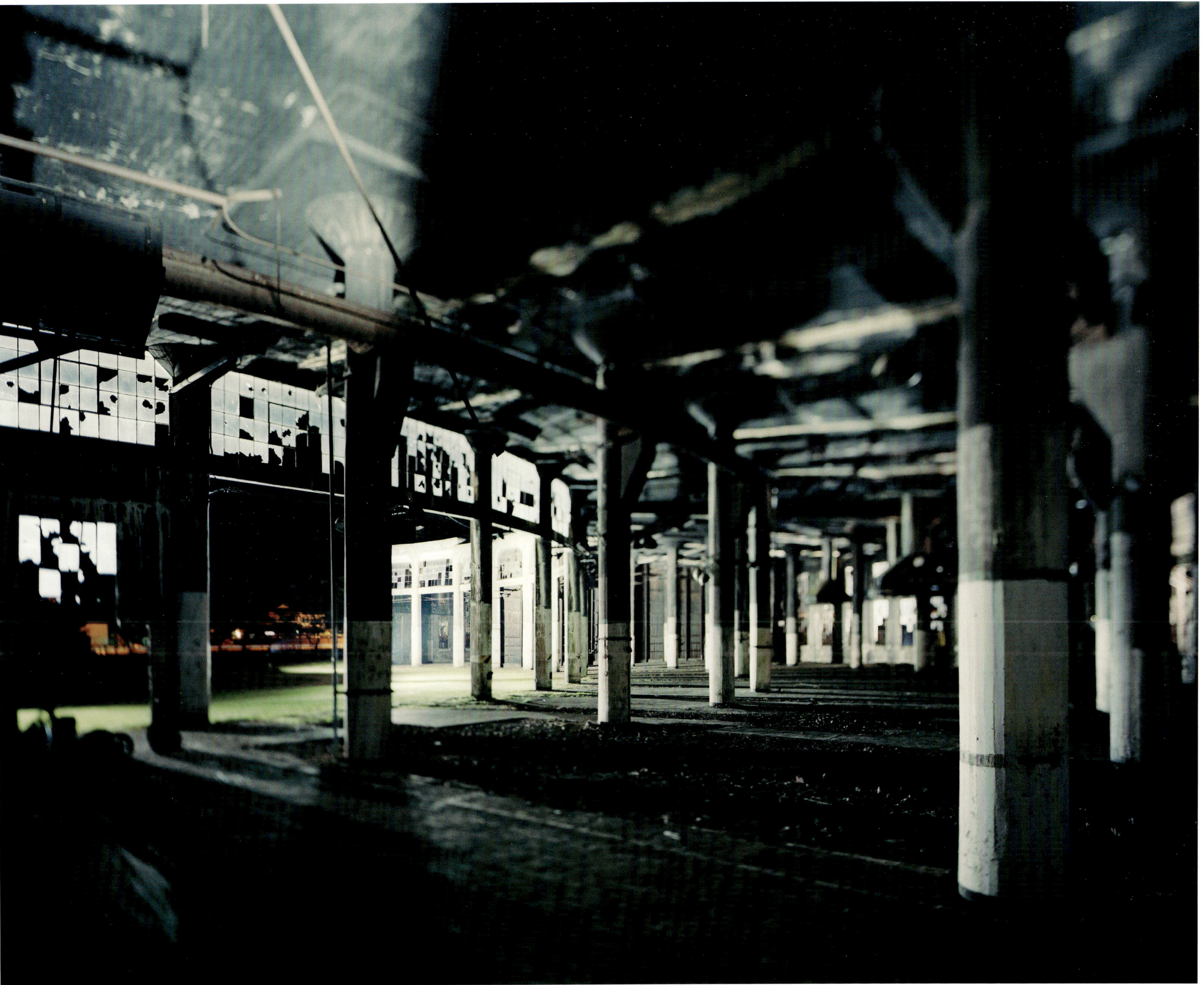

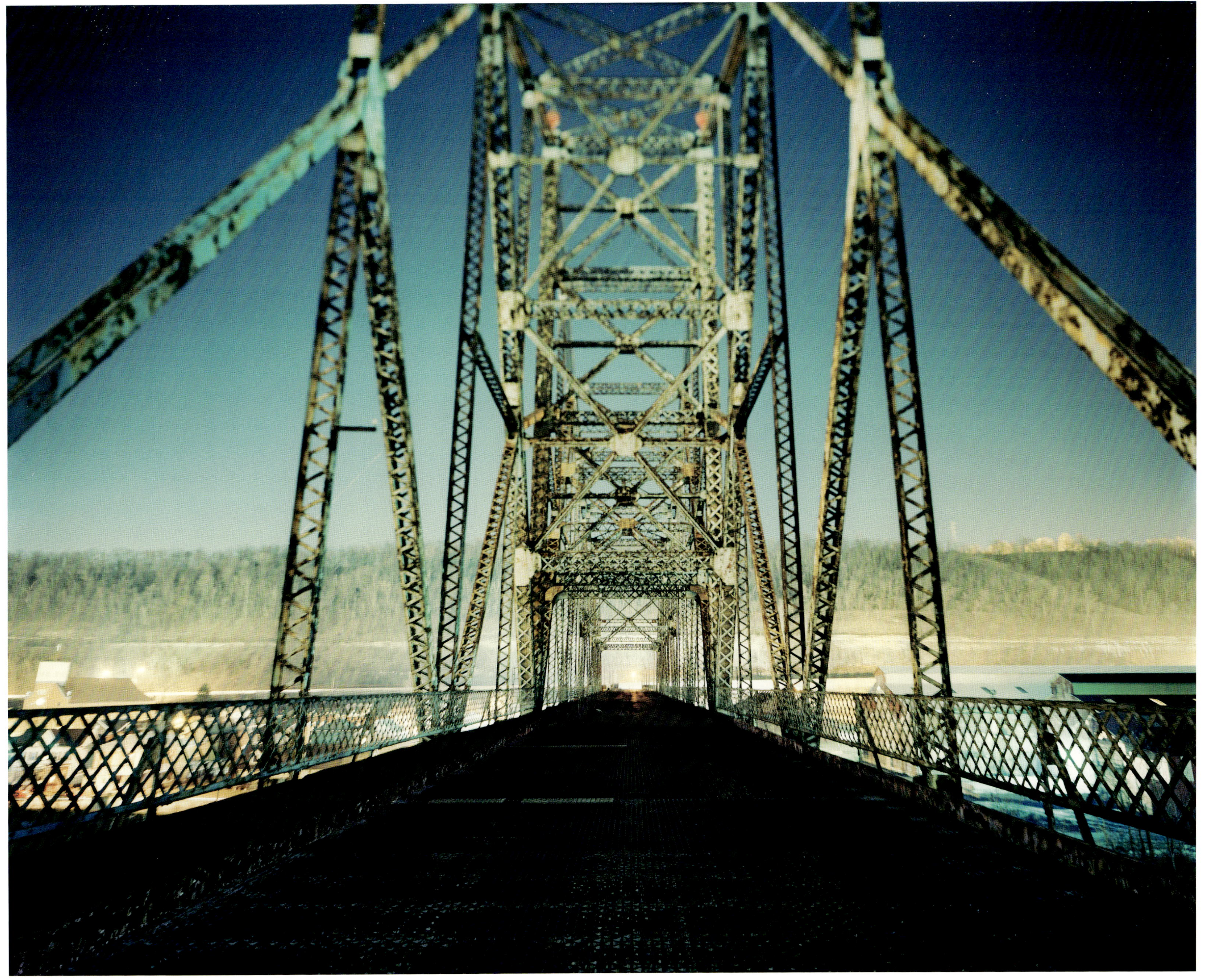

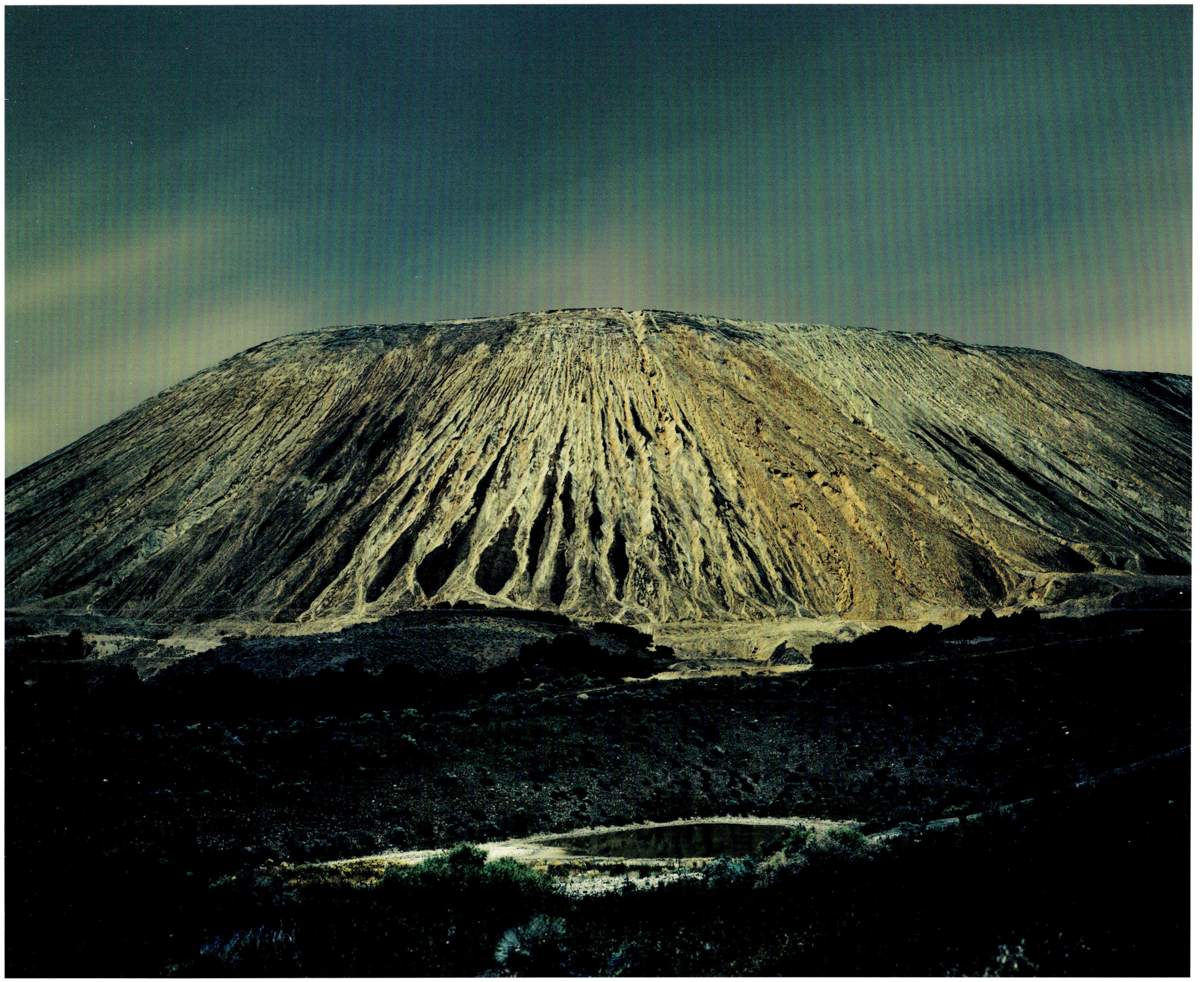

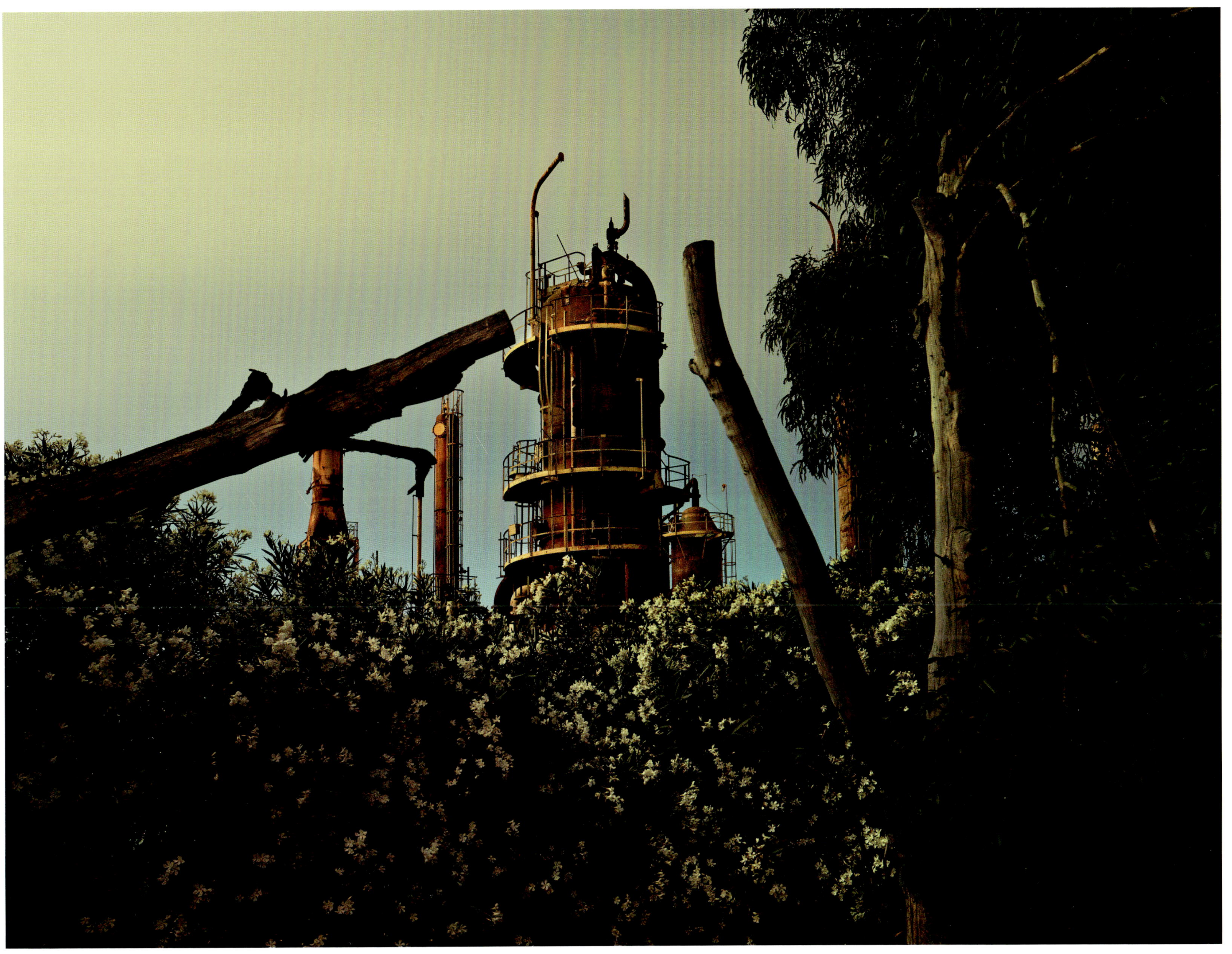

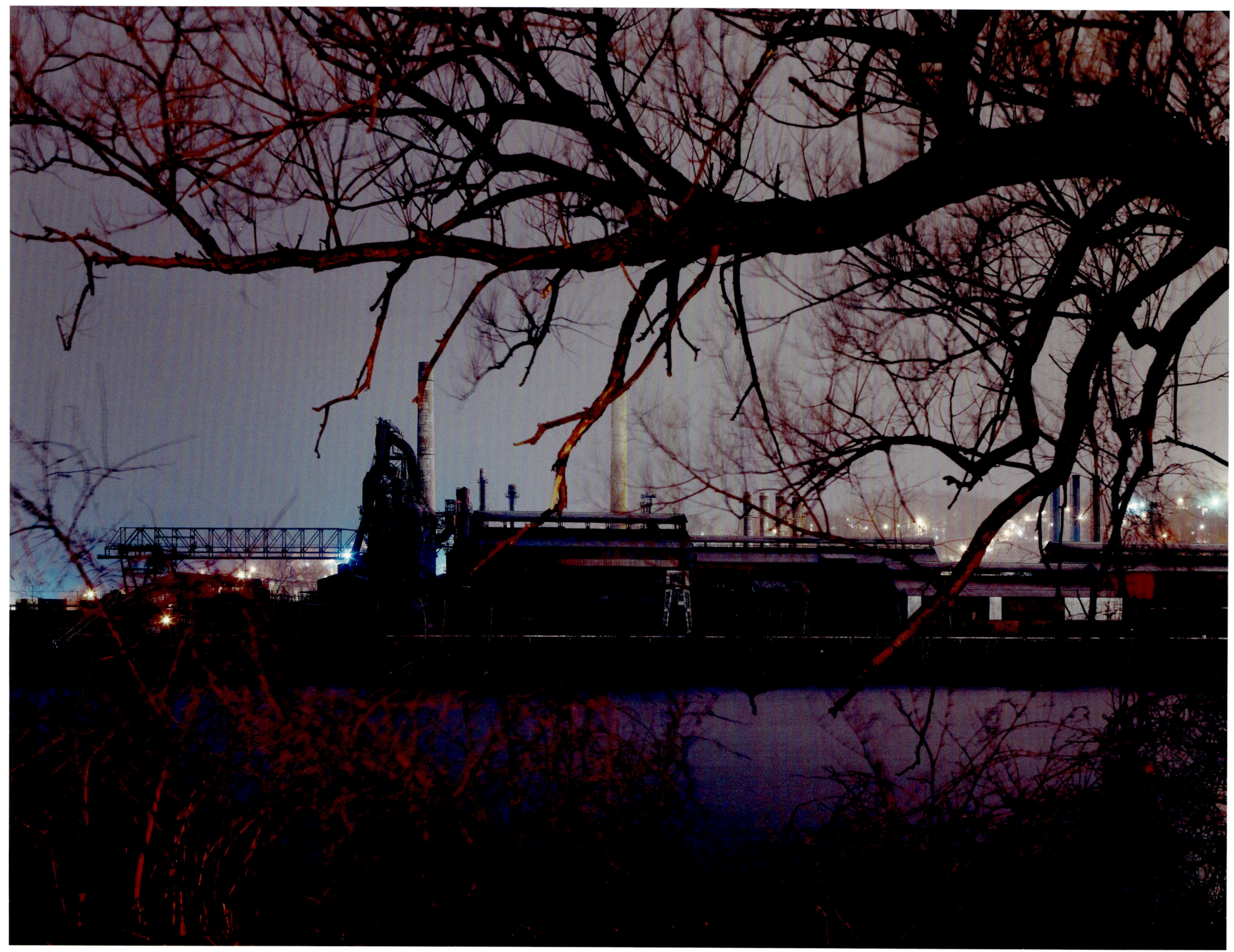

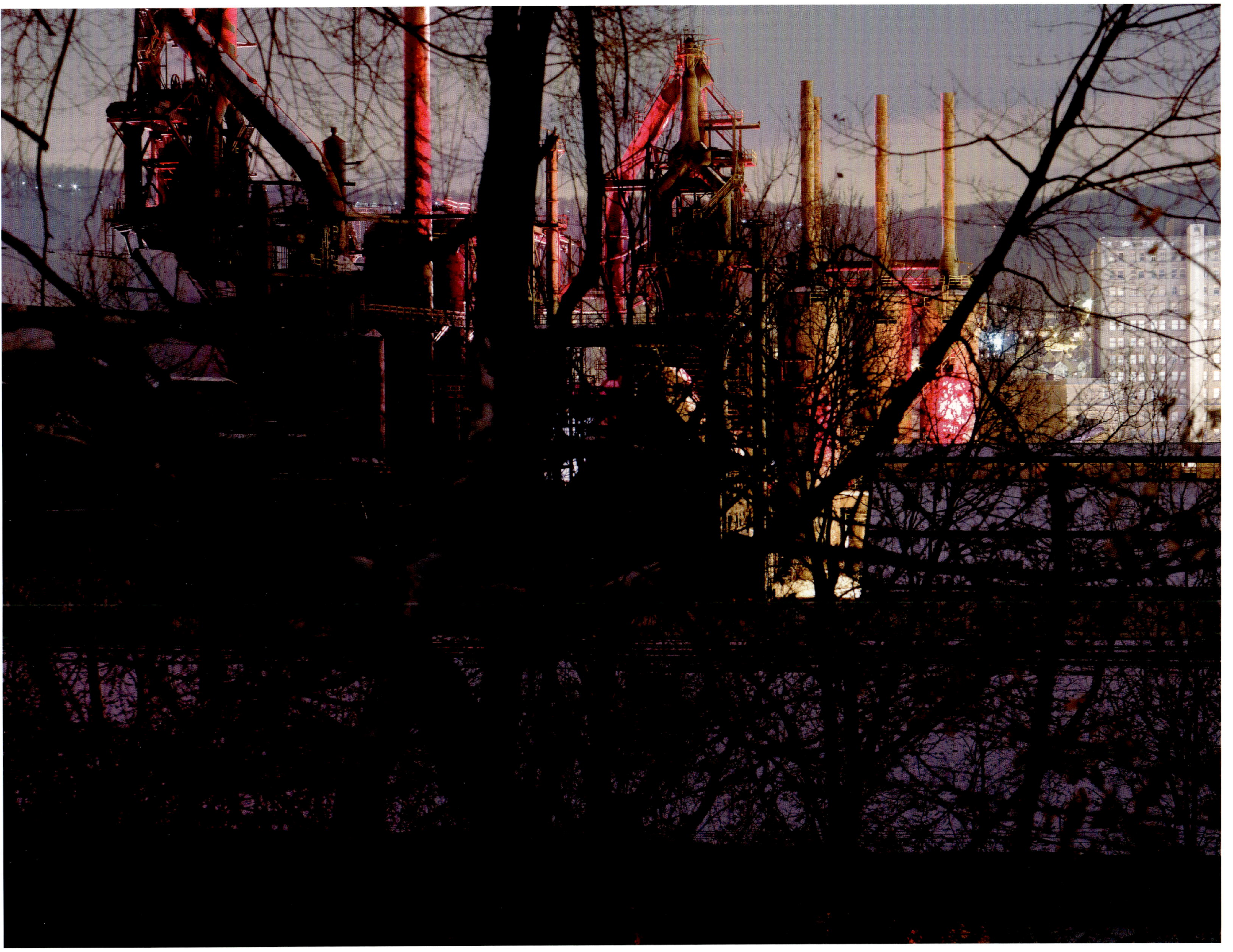

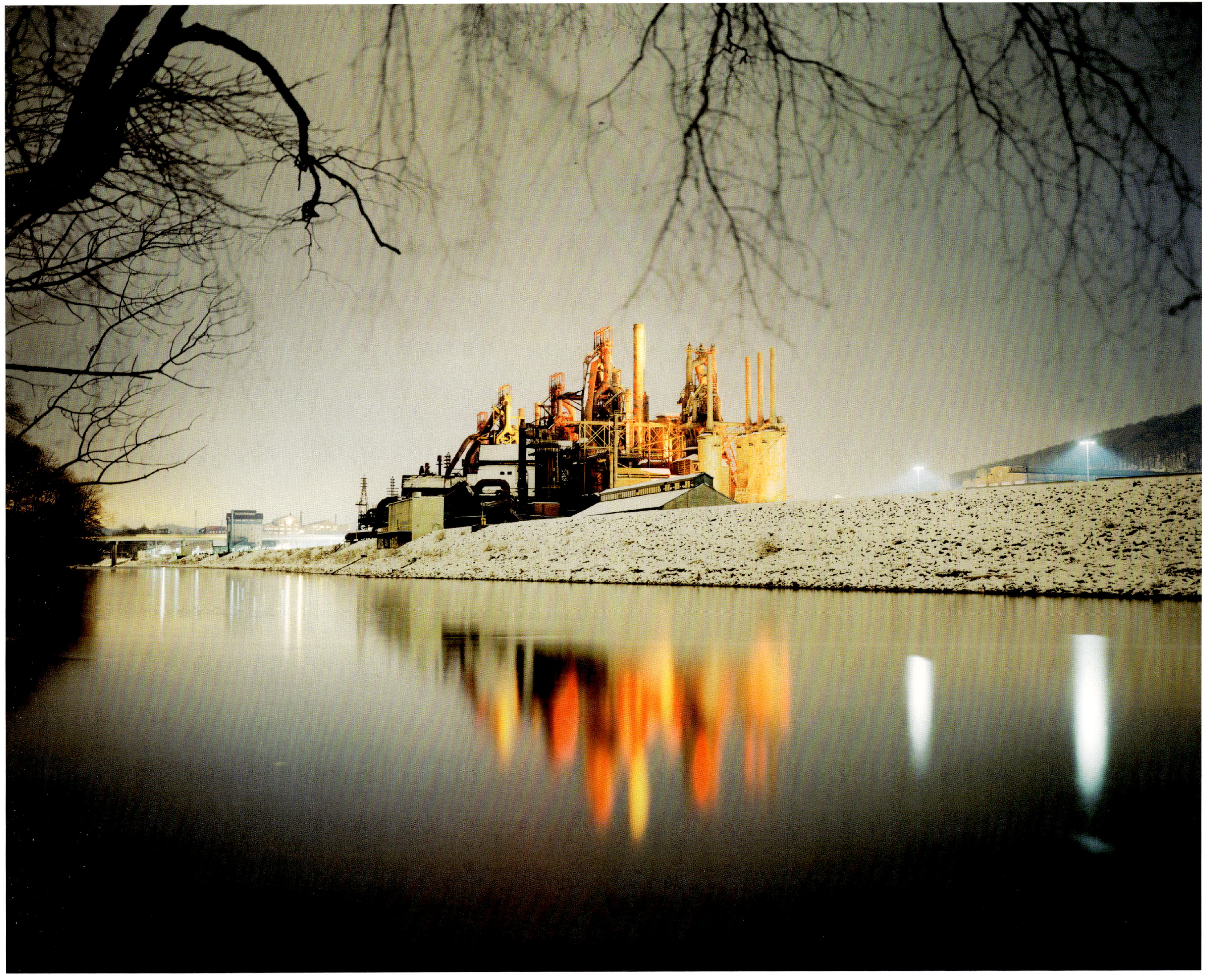

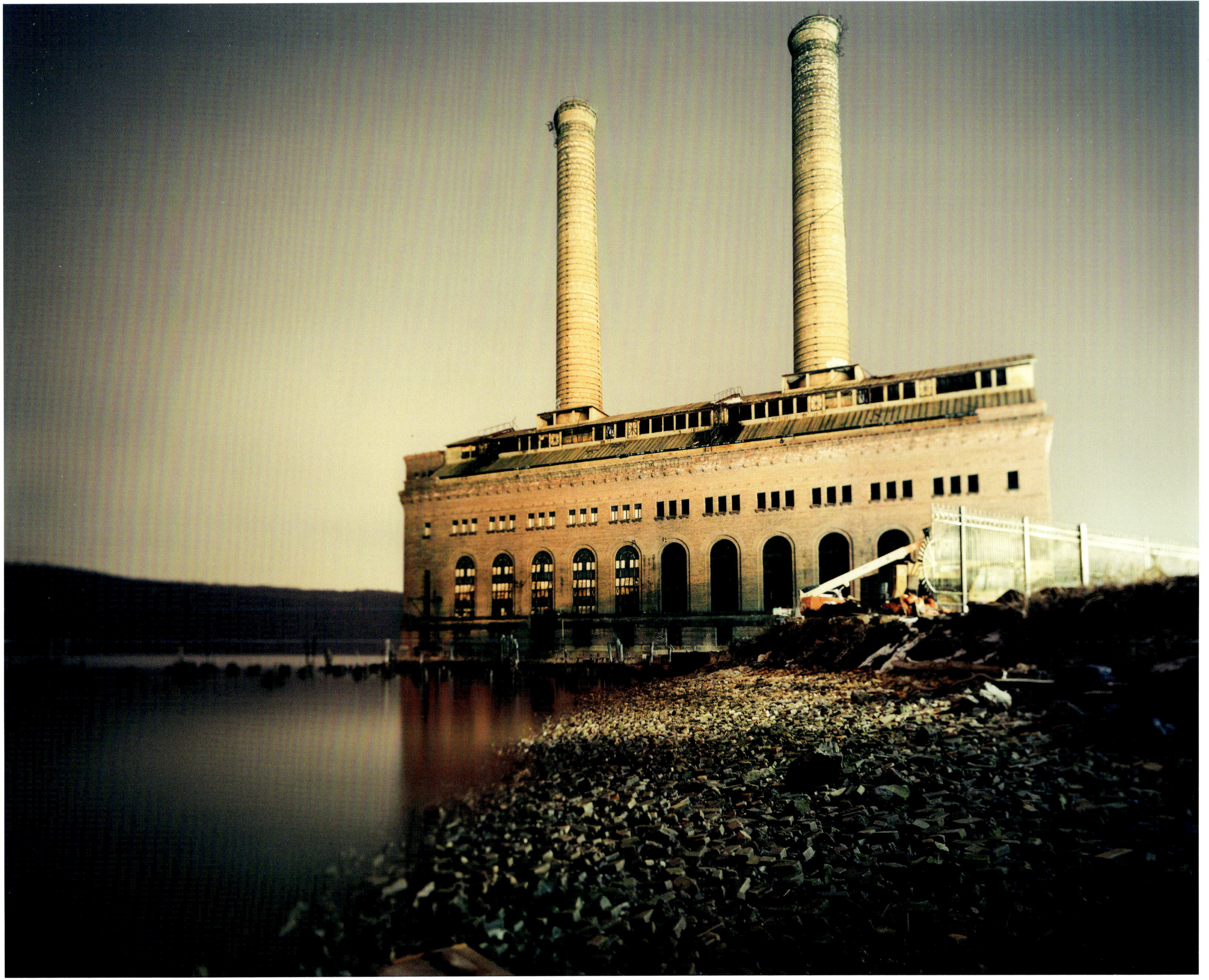

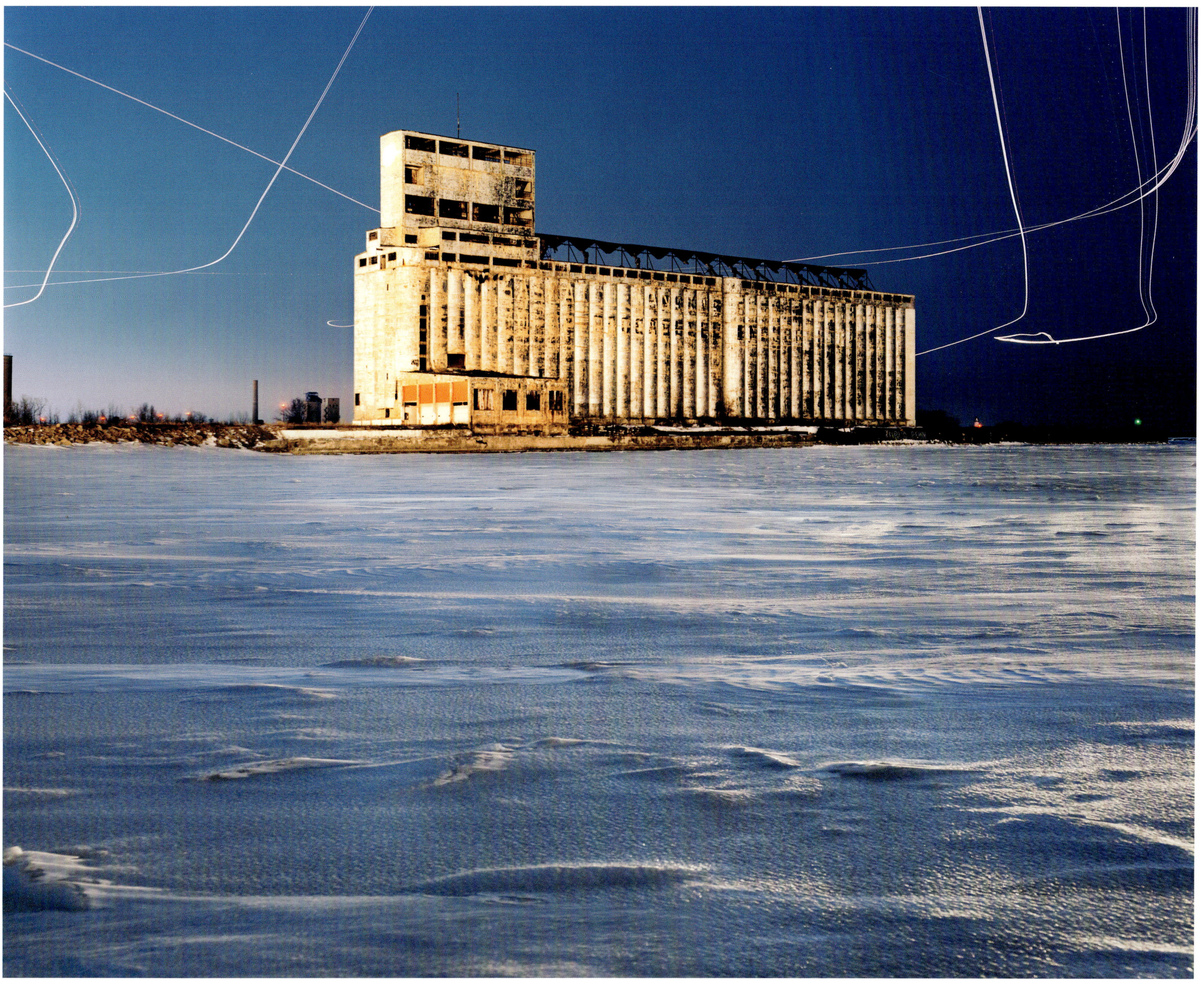

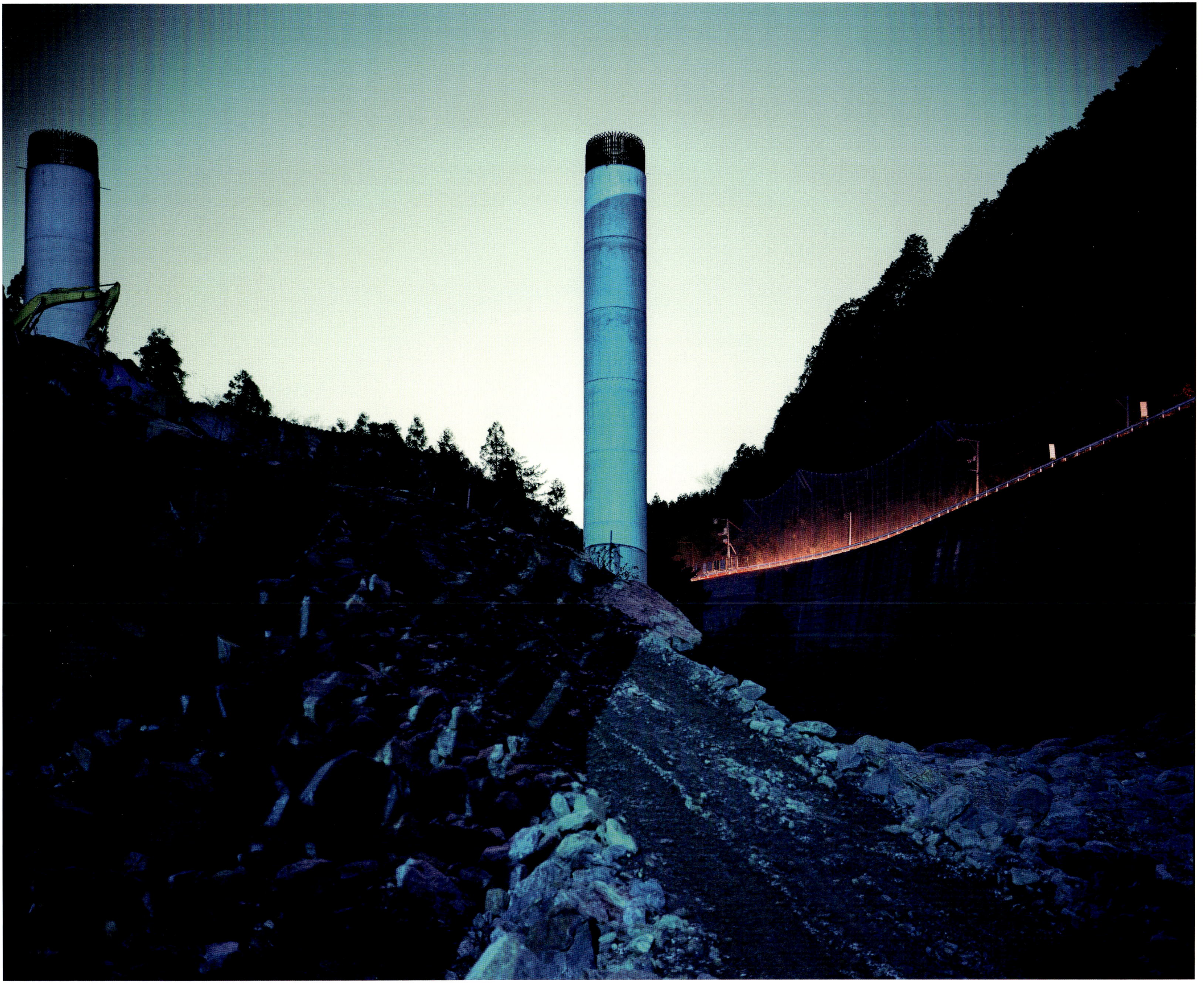

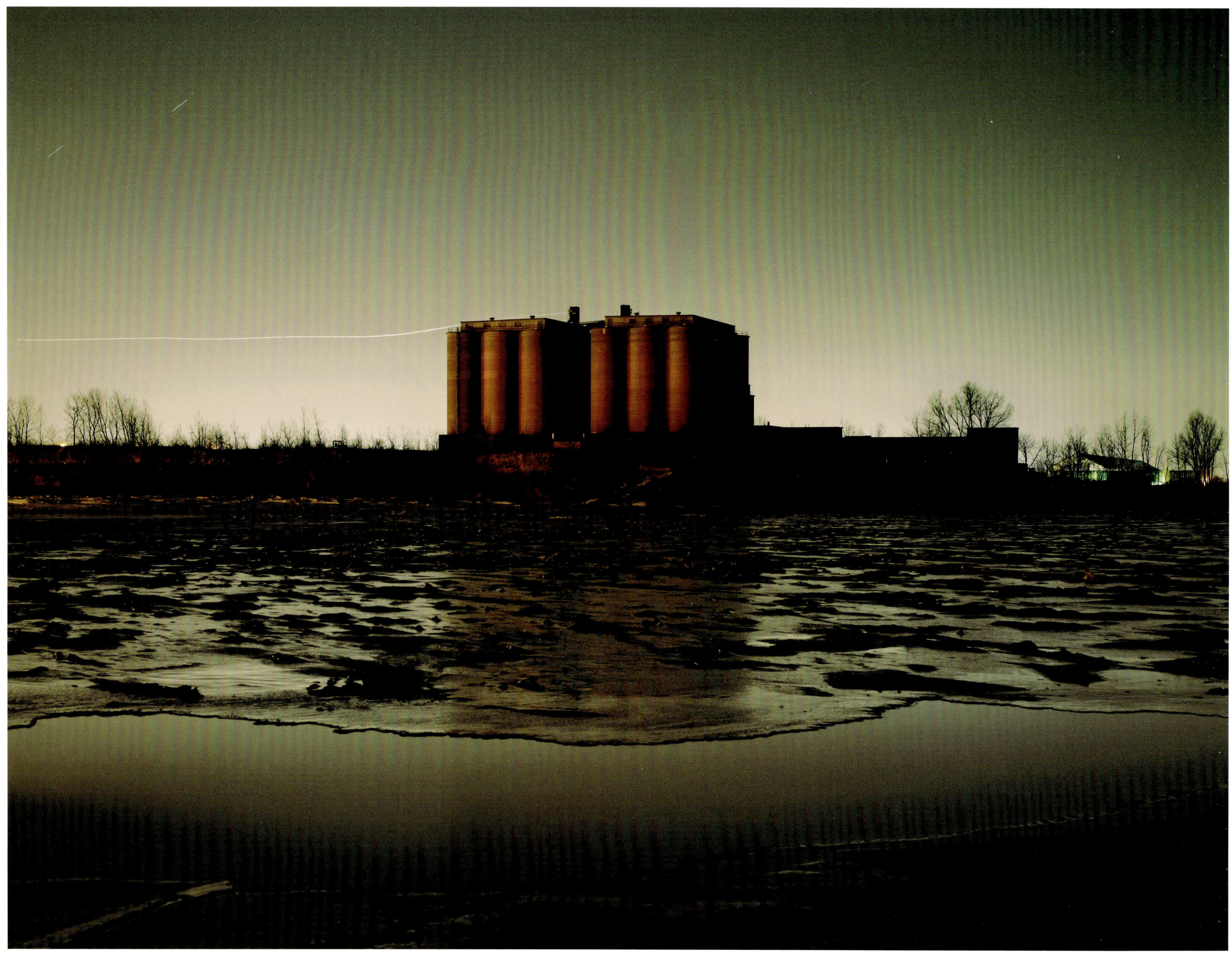

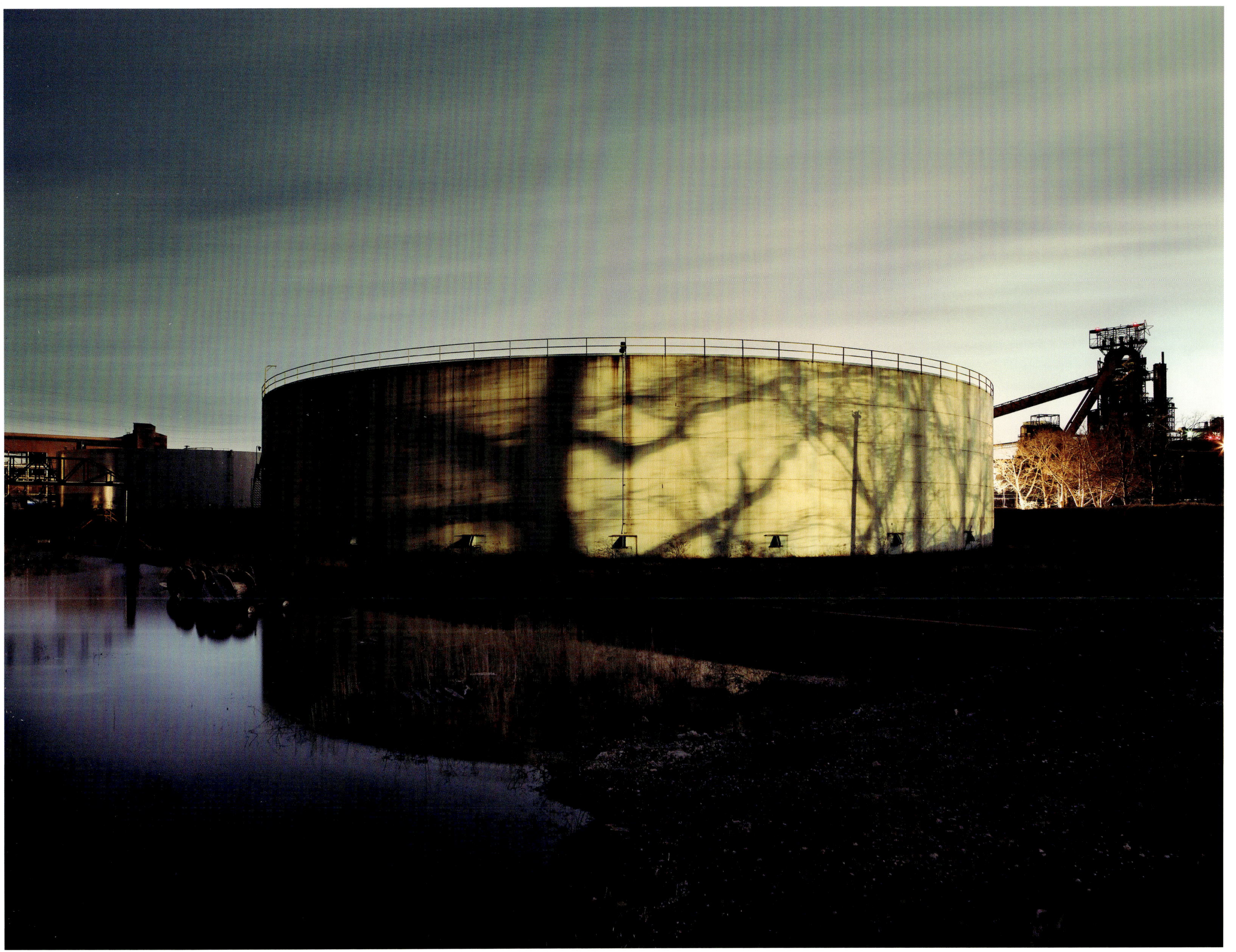

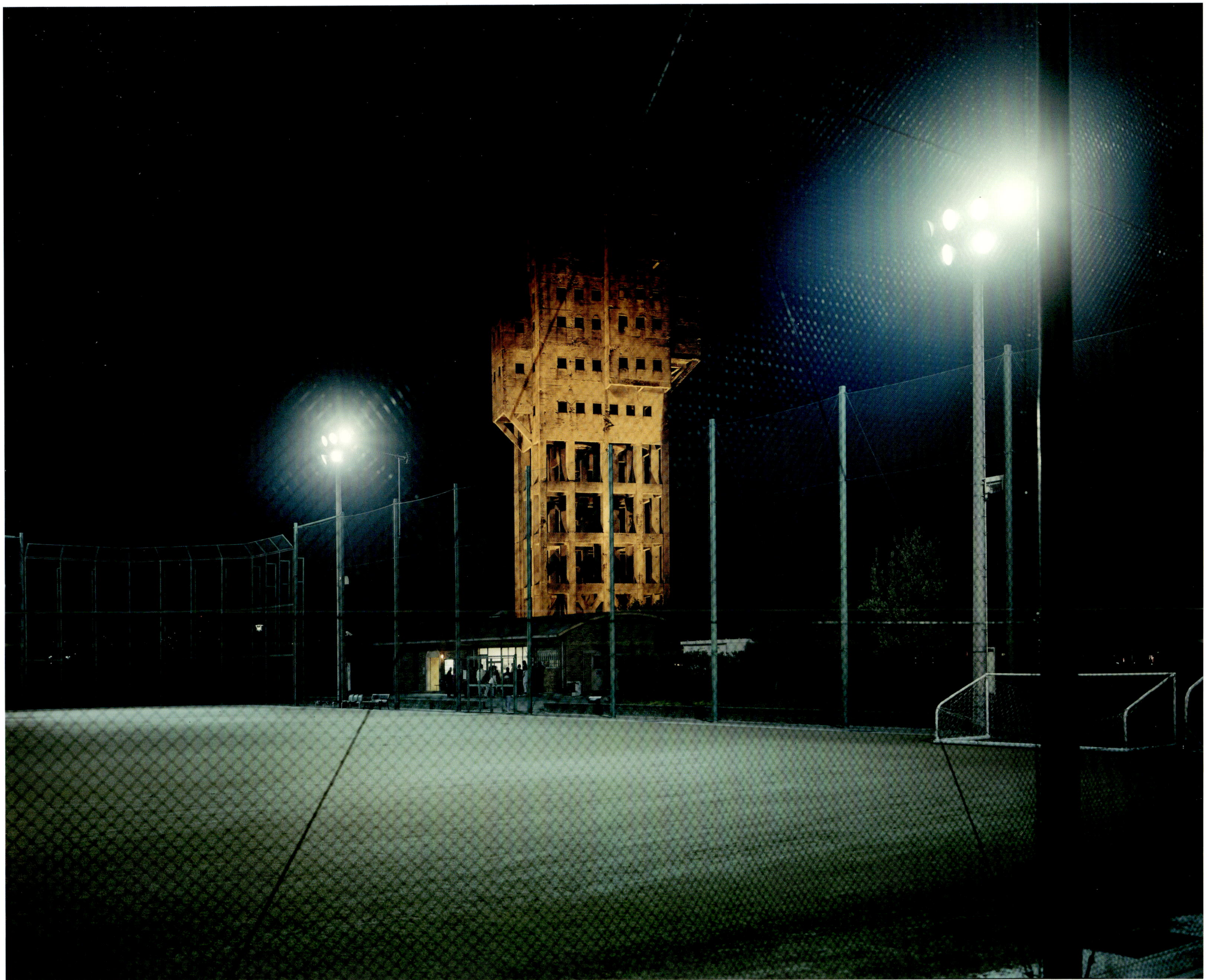

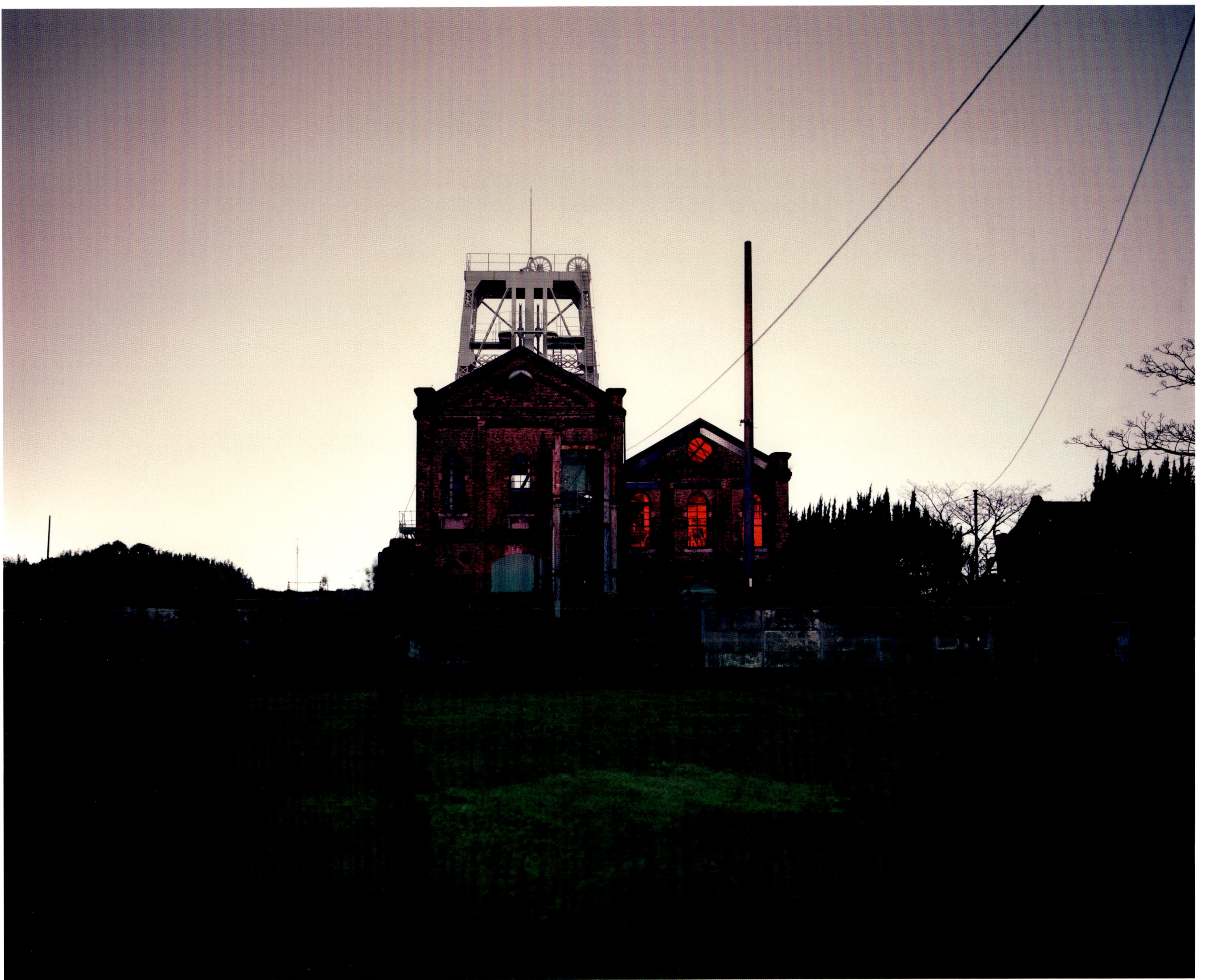

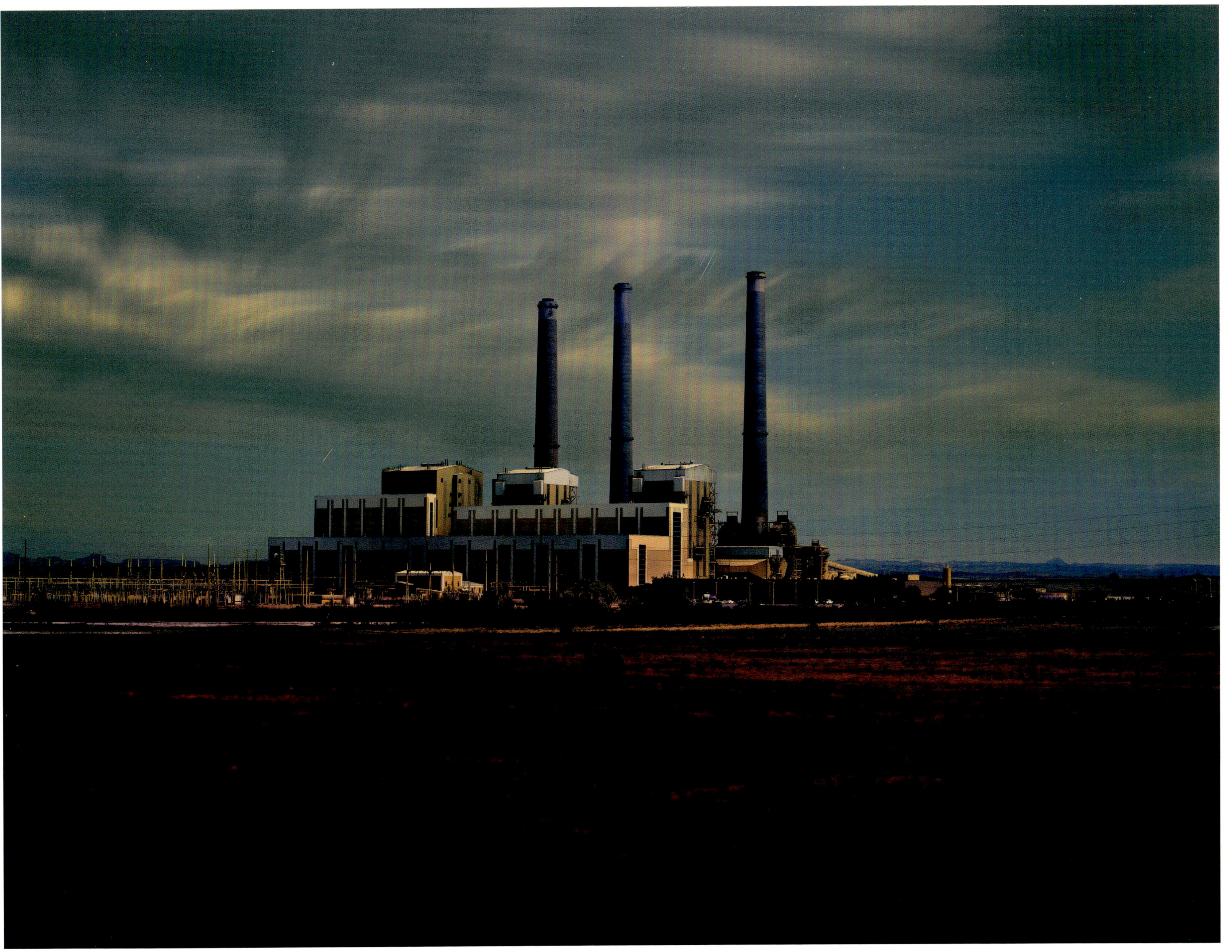

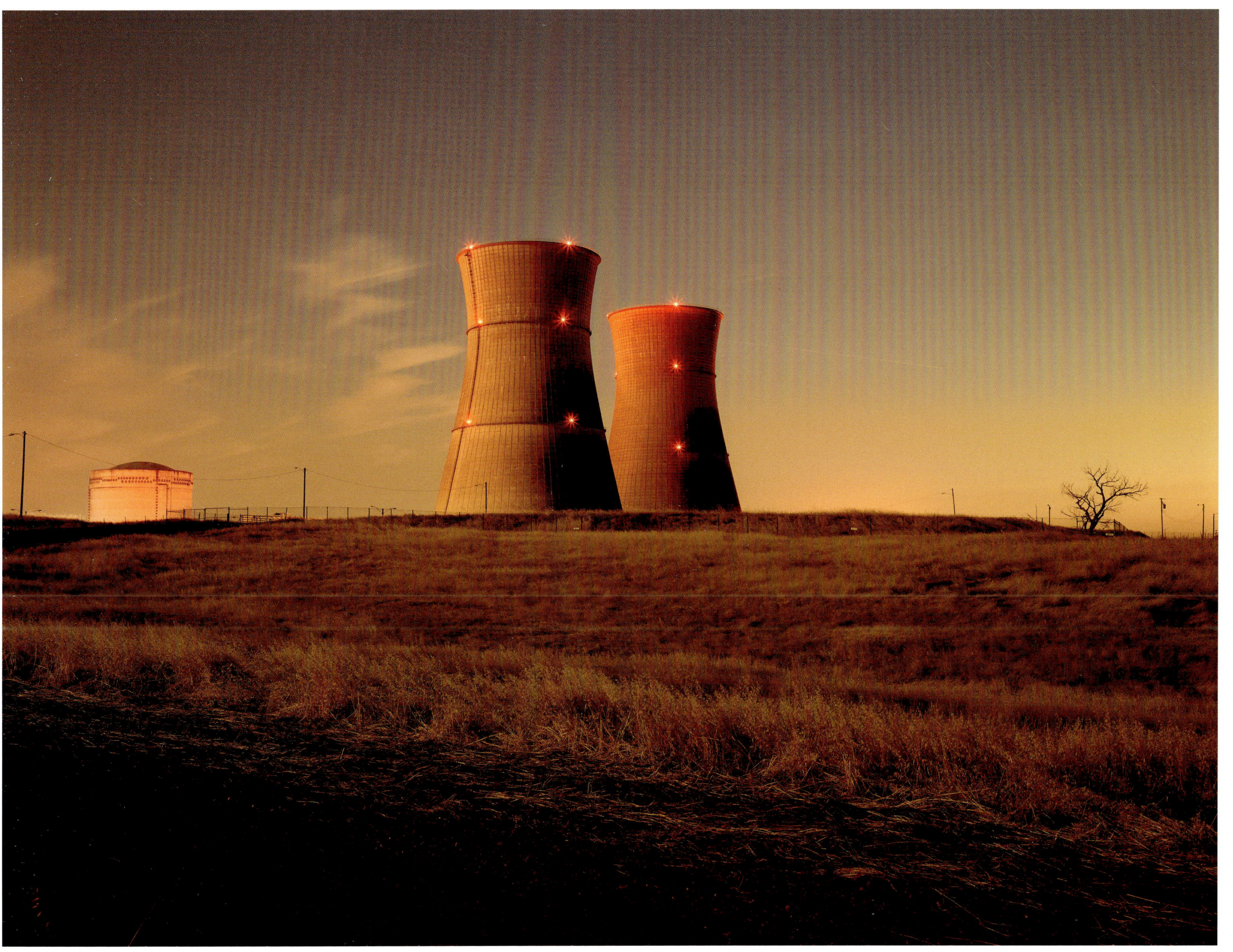

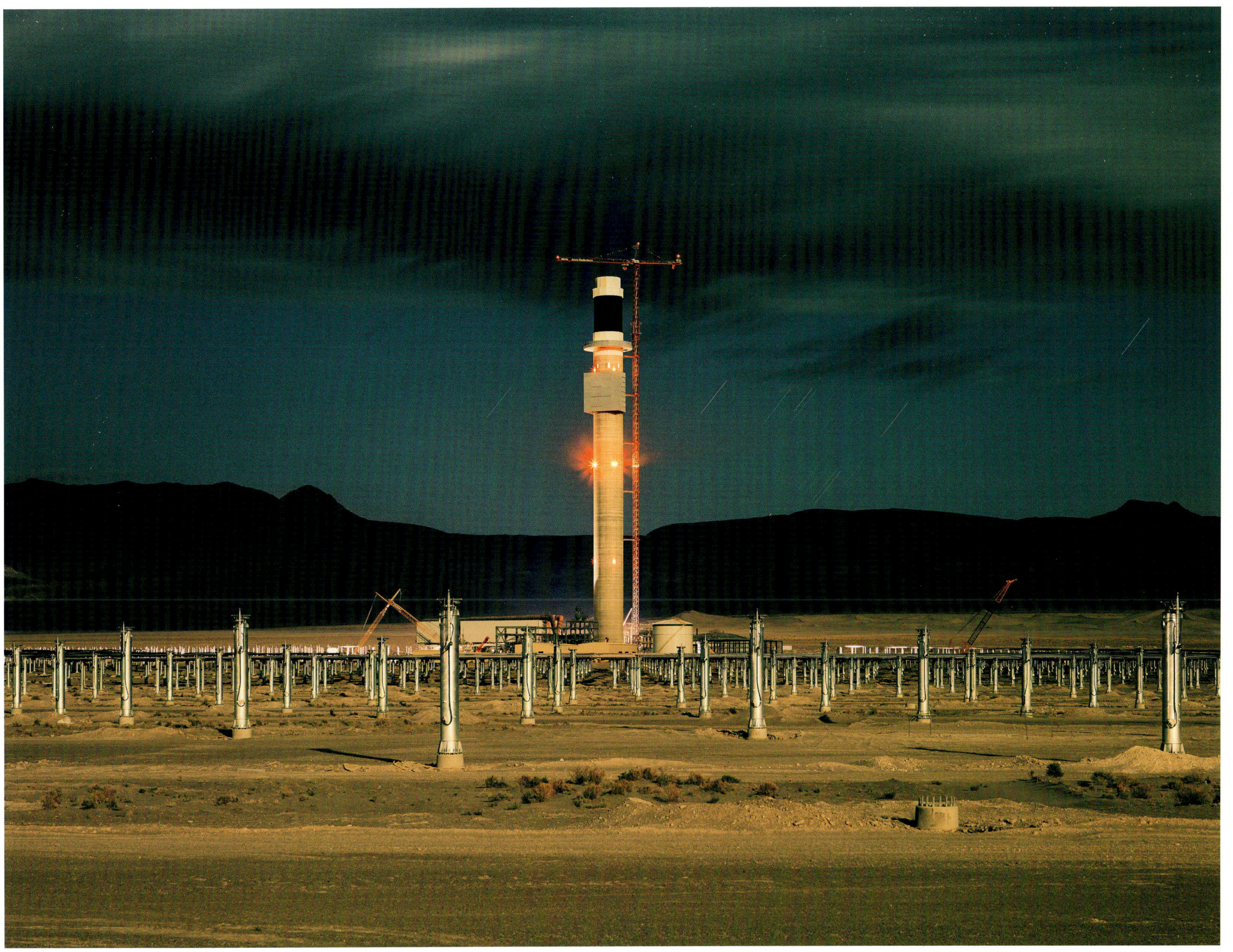

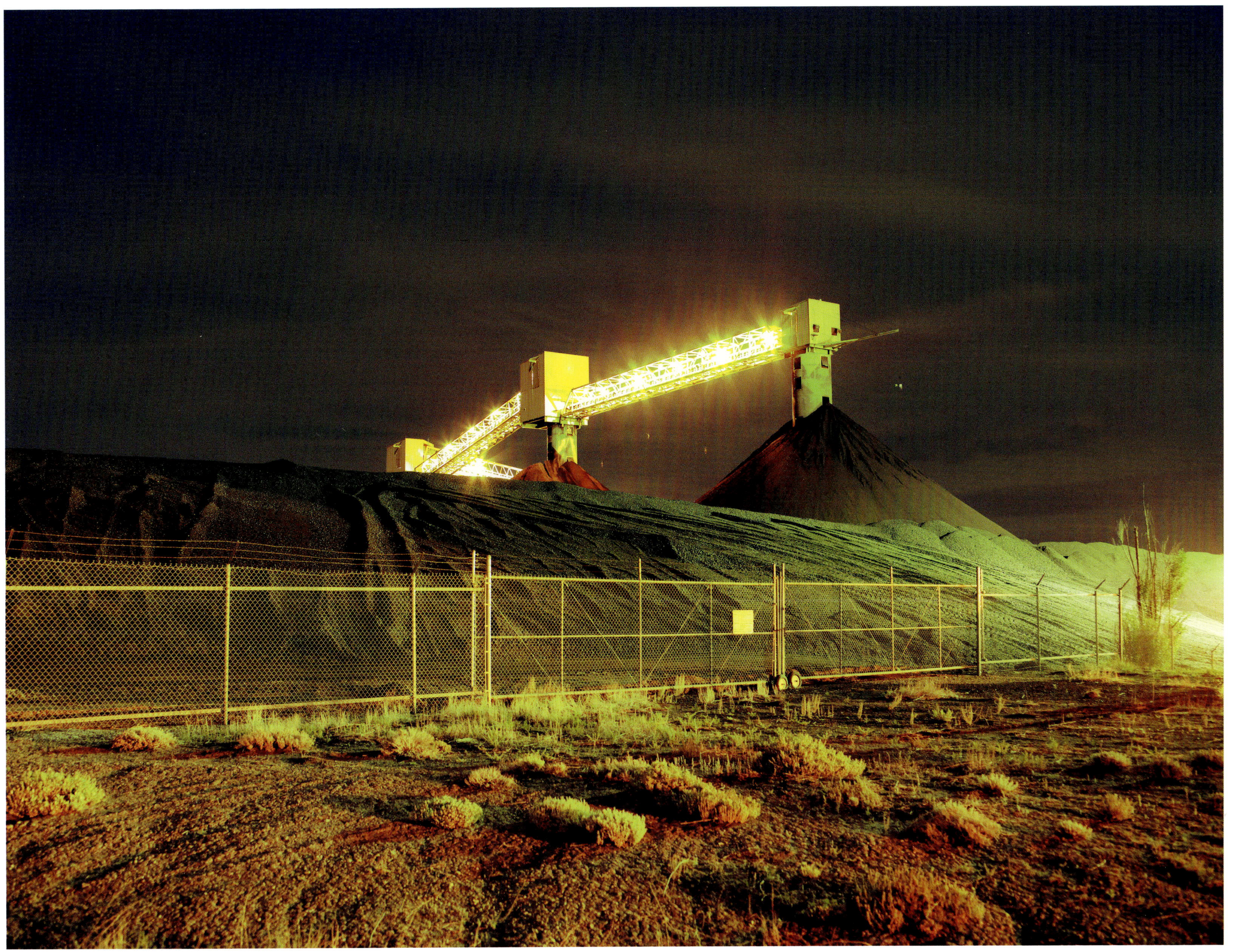

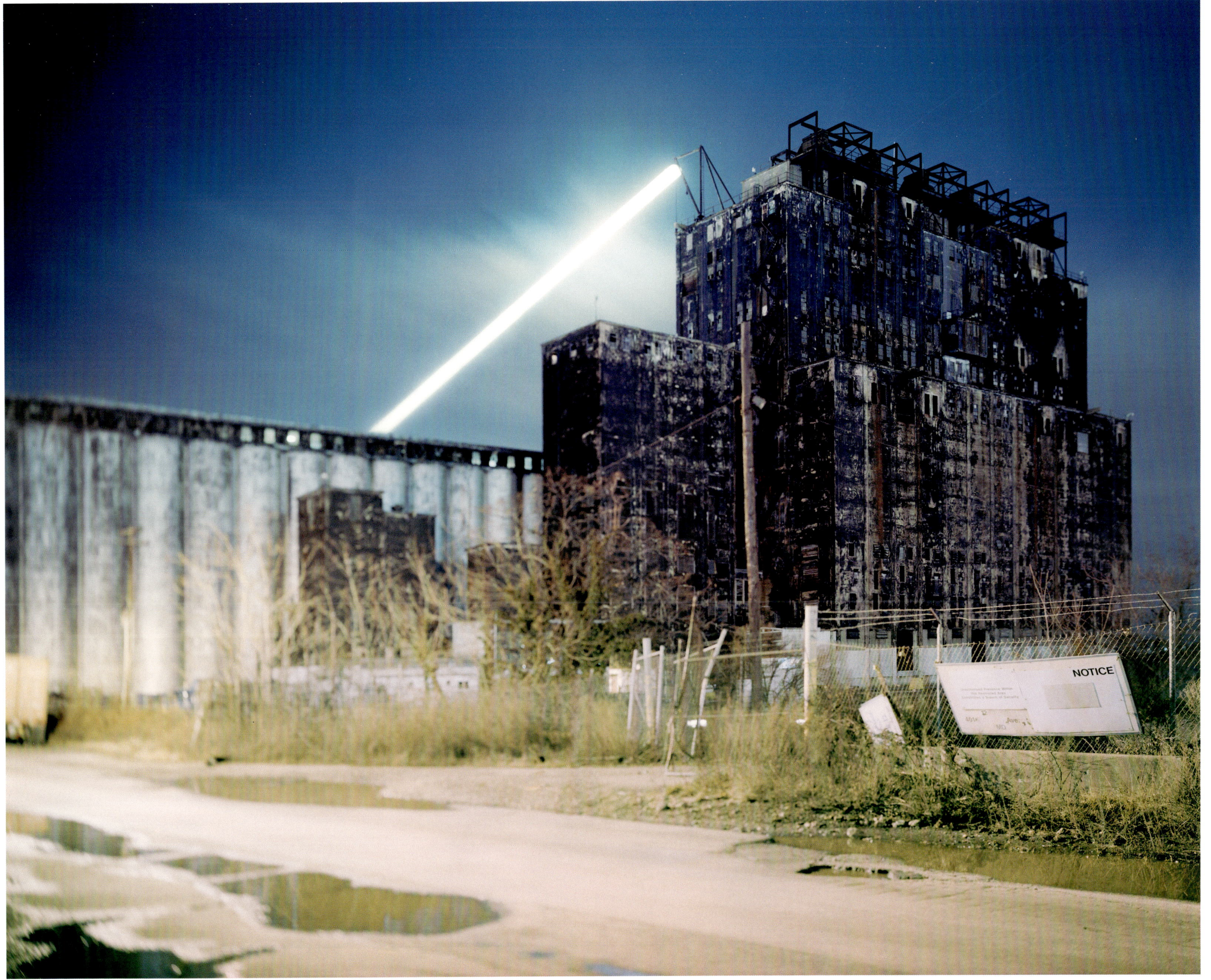
NOTICE

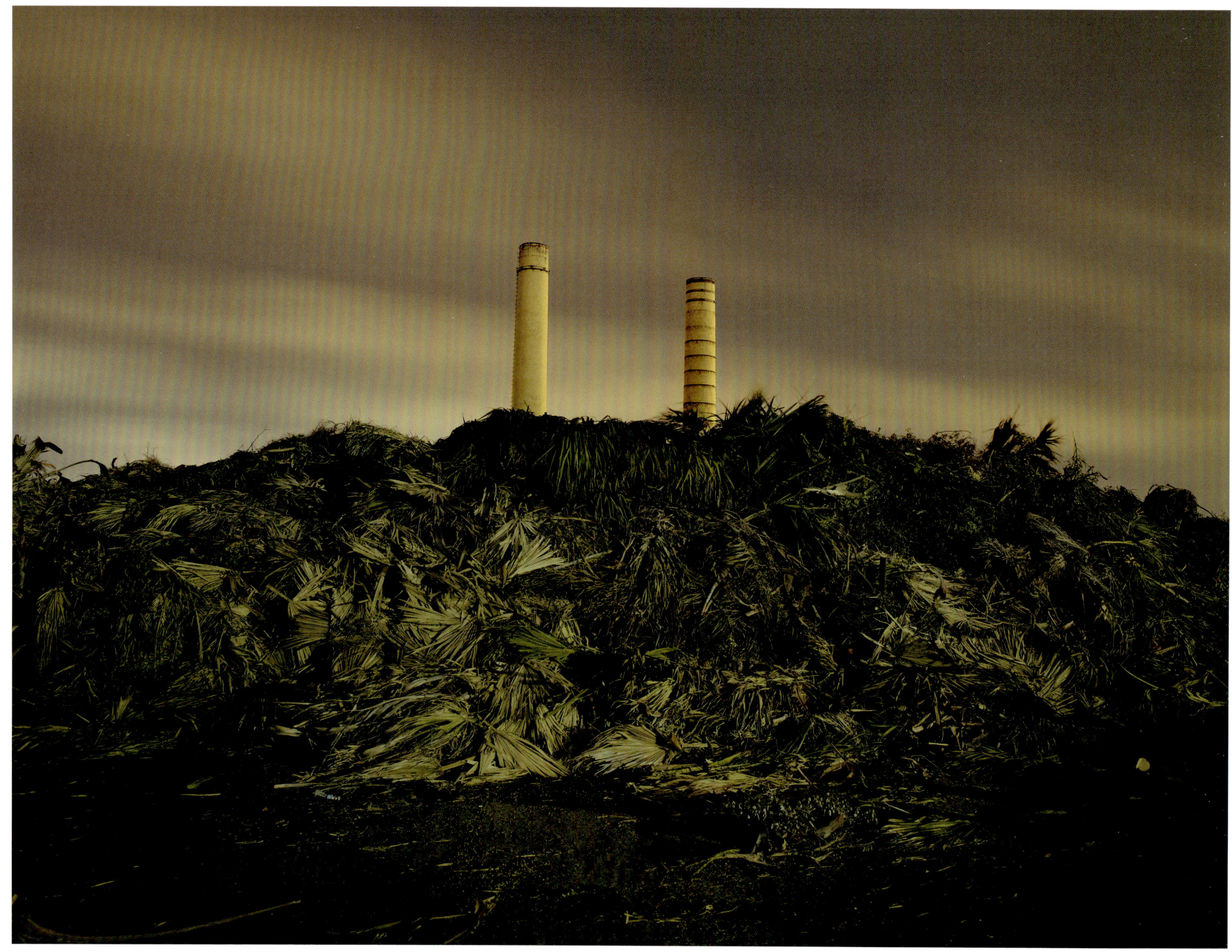

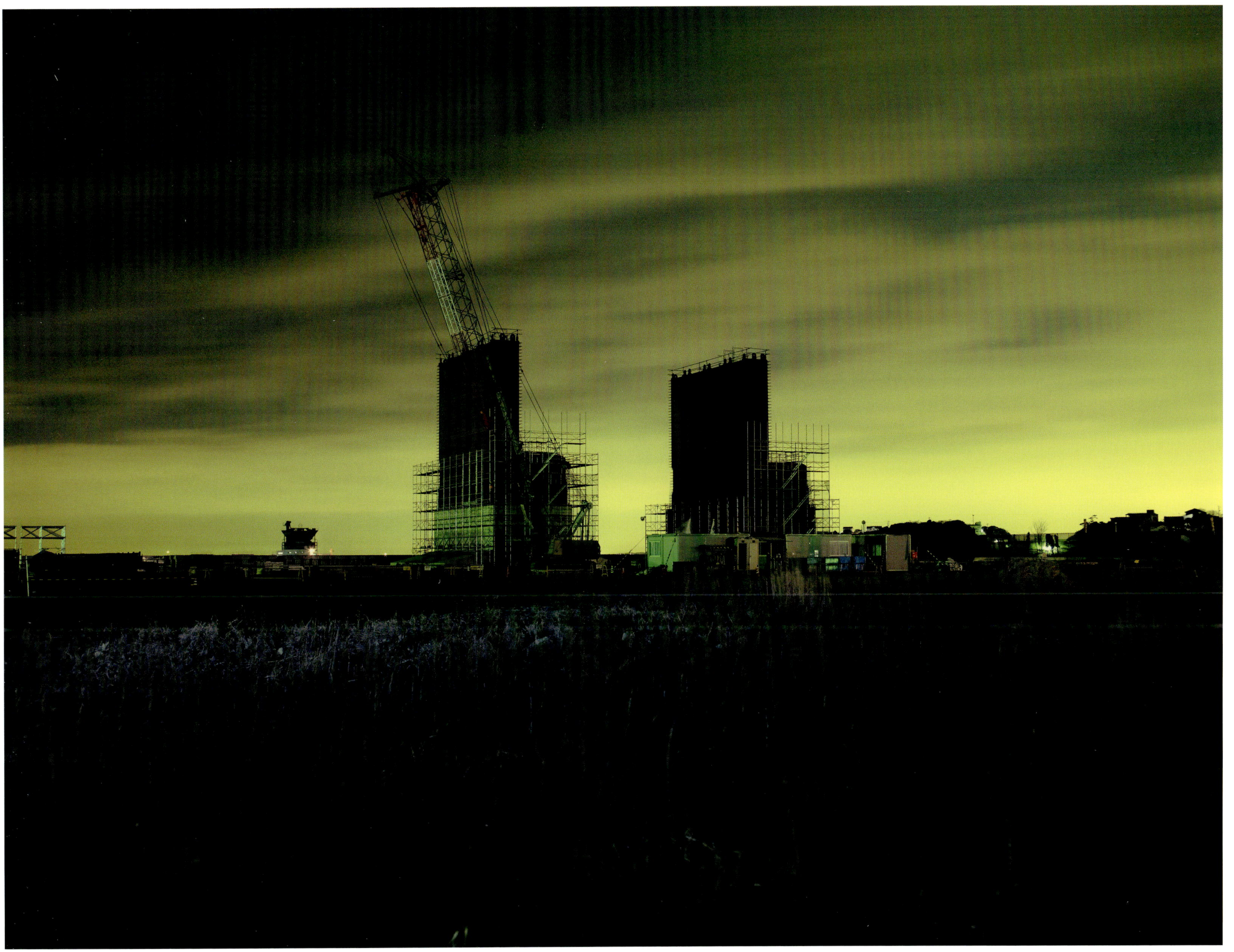

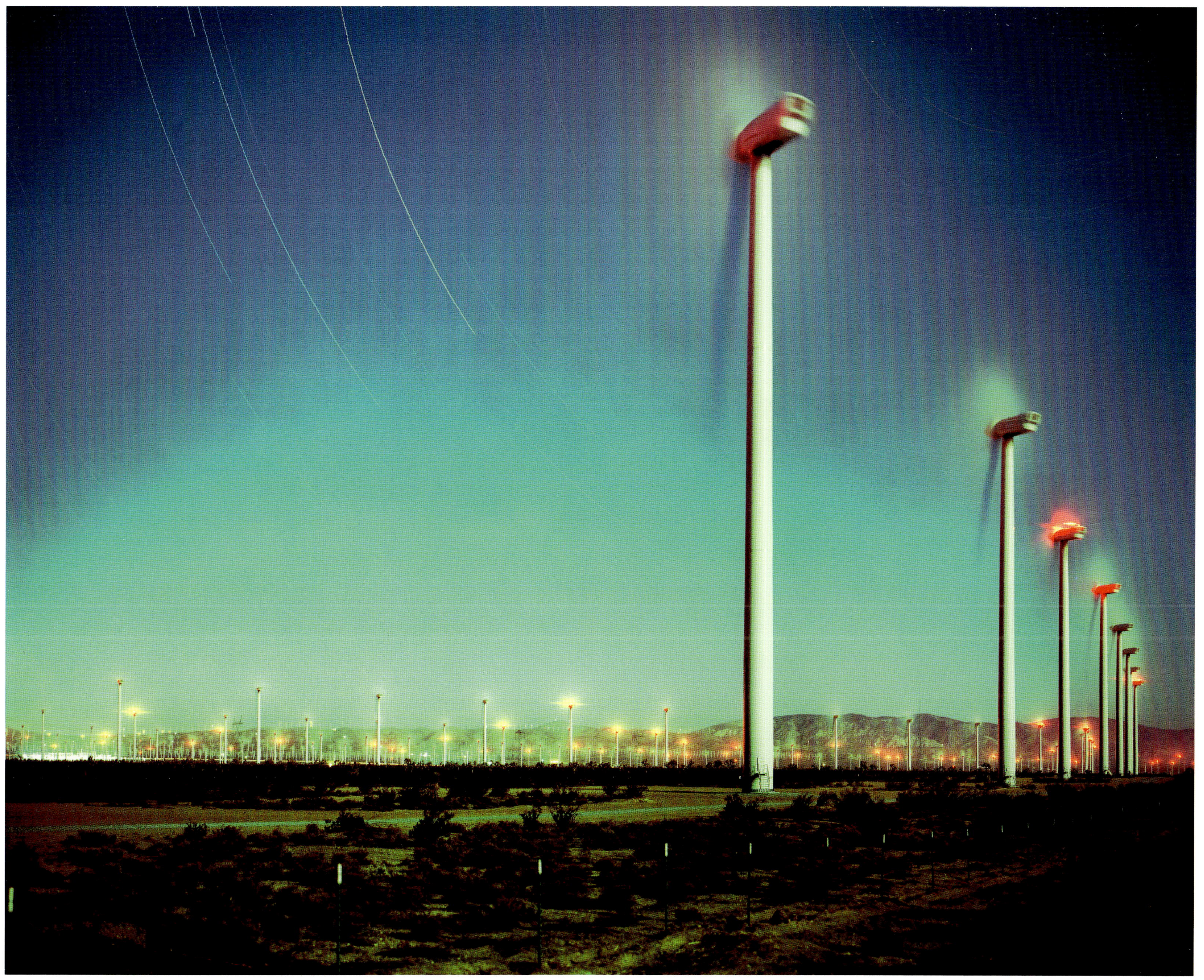

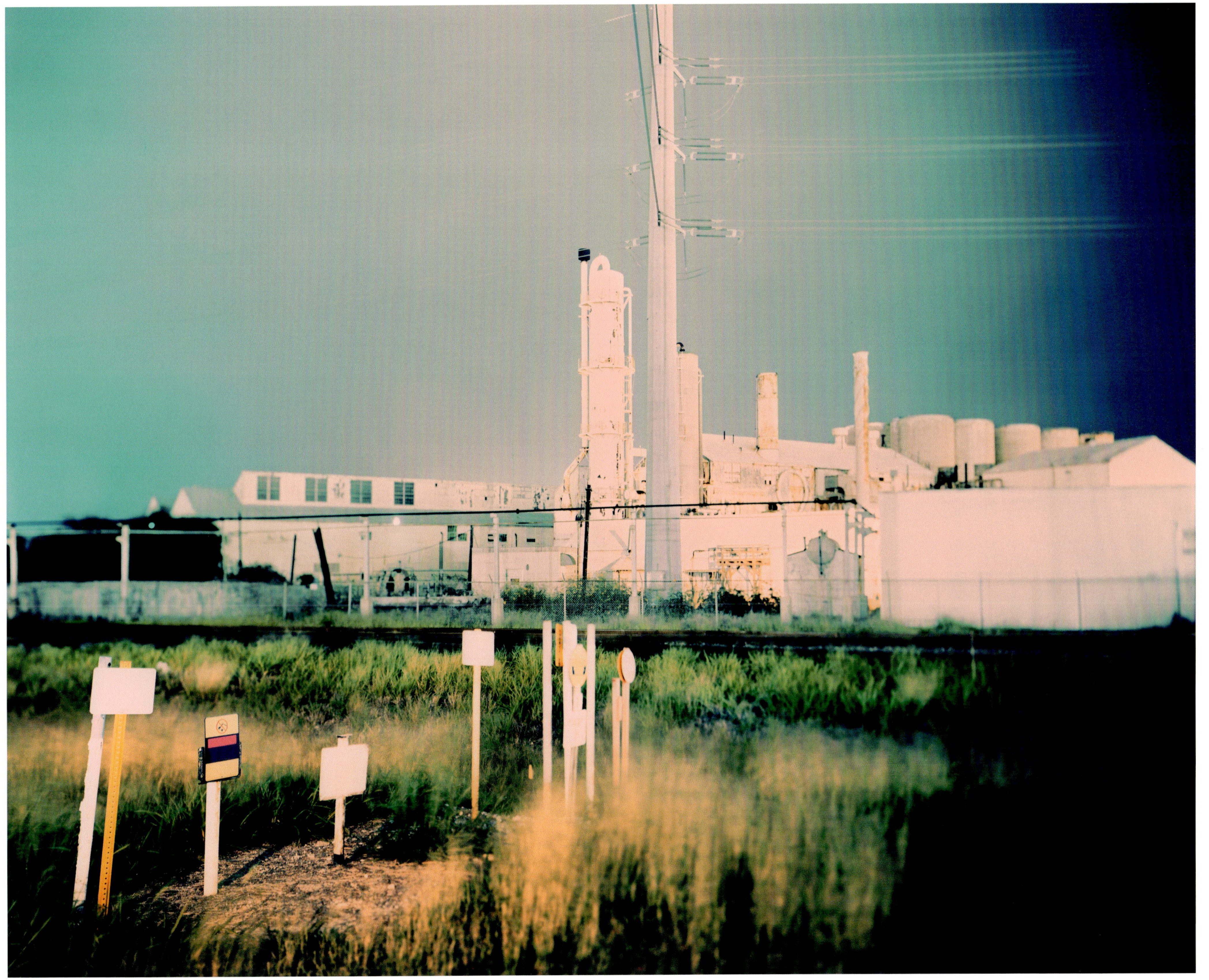

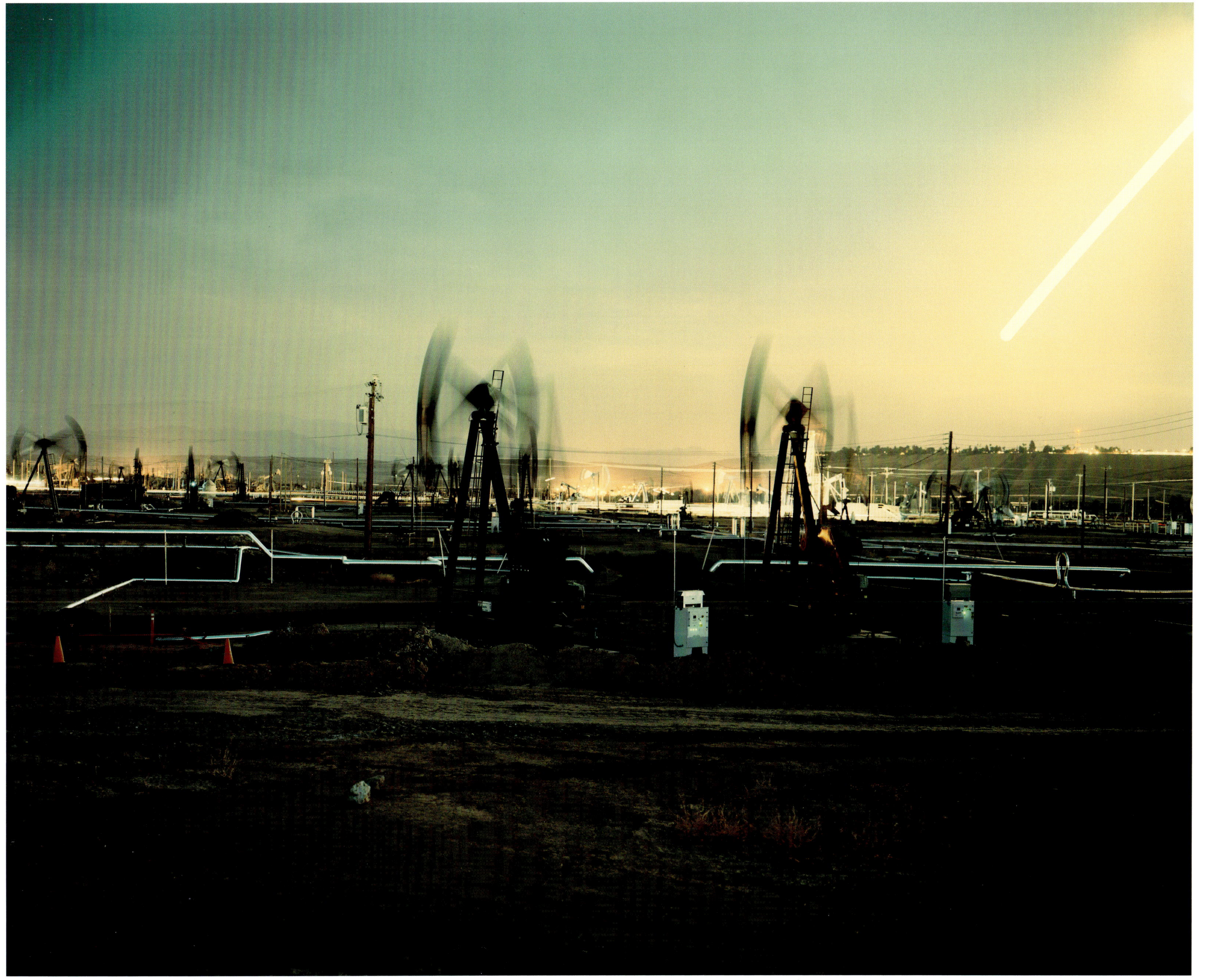

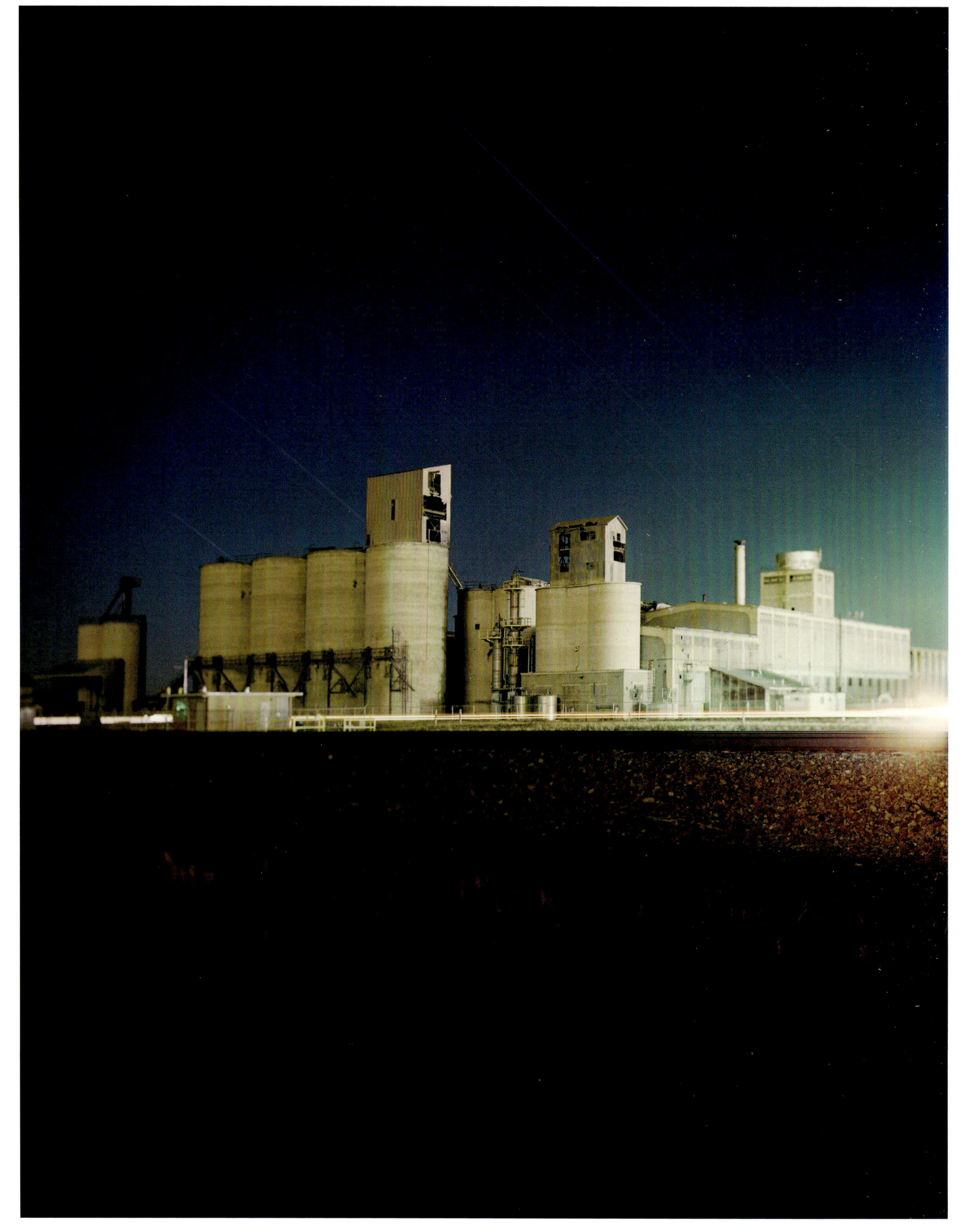

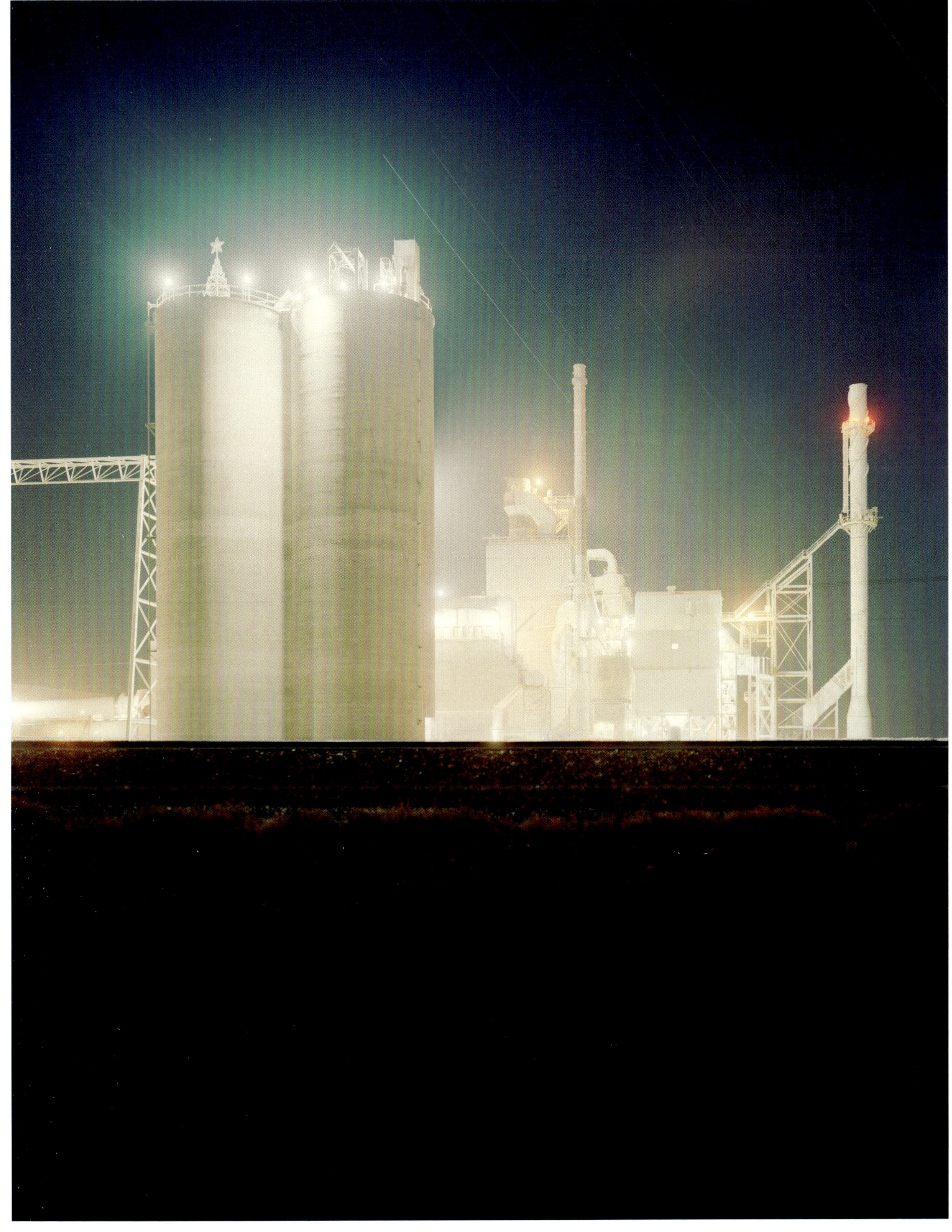

LYLE REXER

After Night Falls

"Night unnerves us and surprises us with its strangeness;
it frees powers within us which were controlled by reason during the day . . ."
BRASSAÏ

Now we must write the history of the dark photograph.

So much of what is happening in the world takes place at the border of vision, at the edge of night (so to speak), at the limit of visibility. Although the challenge of making a photograph in darkness was implicit in photography from the beginning (How much light is enough? How much time is enough?), Brassaï identified this as a quintessentially modern ambition. No longer utter darkness, a naturally descending darkness, and this was his point. With the lighting of city streets, first by gas and then by electricity, darkness surrendered its totality, became the negative, the reverse, of the light that bracketed it. It became also a space, a territory to be navigated and colonized. The artificial illumination of cities released human activity from the tether of a diurnal rhythm and fostered—demanded—nightlife, that latency that Brassaï visually explicated. He is justly famous for his photographs of the demimondaine and the café dwellers of Paris, who could, by then, exist at all hours, but his most complex image is that of a car traveling through the park-like Avenue de l'Observatoire, its headlights cutting the fog. The park is a forest of night, each lamp revealing emptiness and concealing menace. And the car itself is inscrutable, an uncanny signifier suggesting love or crime, either way, clandestine. Prophylactic light, the light of control and security, spurred its opposite, the proliferation of the illicit.

But the burgeoning of the new night world wasn't limited to sex for sale on street corners and second-story men planning a heist. An extensive catalogue of Brassaï's photographs detail the activity of a society devoting itself to the industrial ideal of ceaseless productivity and round-the-clock labor. Bertolt Brecht wrote of "those in the shadows you do not see." He meant an underclass, the lumpen criminals, but he also meant the truly invisible workers building a society that would run 24–7 for the benefit of those who could afford to sleep when they chose.

It took dominion everywhere, and became the glow of a global capitalism that now stains the night of the developed world, of the whole world, a background radiance that often erupts in bursts of excess energy. Some years ago, at a point of anxiety in his life, Taewon Jang had an intuition about the semisecret night of a country constructing itself, Korea, and he set out to photograph it under its own power (so to speak), using no flash and letting his film record the ambient light through long exposure. He titled that early series "Collusion," suggesting not only a relation among light, time, and the medium, but also among the powers-that-be responsible for massive construction projects, high-rise apartment complexes, ominously colored skies—the ziggurats of a new Nineveh. Since then, he has traveled around the world (and extensively across the United States) to record a global society slowly but surely banishing its night. Taken together, this remarkable archive, with its many references to the history of travel photography, testifies to the fact that darkness is now a theme, a problem, and its explication a demystifying act of literal and metaphoric importance. As Jang has said, "For me there must be darkness to reveal the light." And as chemical photographers know, all things latent are revealed to those with the patience to wait in the dark.

The photographs indicate that Jang's choice of locations was not haphazard. Based on his early work in Japan and Korea, he developed the following procedure: He researched—on the Internet—places where the landscape, natural or urban, was in the process of transformation, especially where industry and energy production were involved. And then he went there, found the precise spot he wanted—in some sense a formal, rather than a political decision—set up his camera and went to work, usually until he aroused the suspicion of security patrols, in which case he would withdraw, only to return again. The night paid him back spectacularly. The photographs do not allow us the luxury of comfortable condemnation, for they embody a new and problematic beauty, a beauty that hovers between the fabricated and the natural, a visual, political, and semantic relation in which these opposites are necessary to each other, suspended and irresolvable.

For example, the most dramatic presentation in the book involves a vast energy project that has, certainly, a positive side—a wind farm in southern California near the Mojave Desert. This monument to technical ingenuity exerts a hypnotic fascination and inspires a formal celebration that far exceeds the "joy before the object" of the Neue Sachlichkeit photographers of the nineteen-twenties. Faced with these pictures it is impossible not to feel a kind of optimistic delirium, perhaps similar to what Goethe felt when he walked through the Palladian arcades of Vicenza, a sense that the species capable of producing such excellence cannot perish and must be divinely inspired. Goethe ate grapes, a perfect expression of his ecstasy at the perfection of imagined things. I cannot help thinking, also, of early photography's projects to document monuments of the built world, from Nelson's Column in Trafalgar Square to the pyramids, in an expression of limitless confidence and inspecting power.

Taewon Jang brings us full circle on this ambition. In its repetitive purity, more emphatic than any project of minimal art, the wind farm also provokes a kind of cold revulsion, even paranoia, that in the effort to "save the planet," we have to rely on technical systems so complex, abstract, and beyond human scale that the solution seems to have come from somewhere else, as if we had suddenly been invaded by our own technology. No wonder there is constant objection to such farms by local inhabitants, quite apart from their "aesthetic" incursion on the landscape (aesthetics in this case amounting to no more than if someone about to go before a firing squad complained that his last-minute letter of reprieve was written on the wrong color paper). Better the crude towers of a nuclear plant, familiar-like castles, or cathedrals. Perhaps the emotion these pictures arouse is simply despair at the recognition of defeat, an awareness that no matter what scale, technology cannot save us, or, rather, preserve a certain lifestyle.

The other face of the wind farm is the vast oil refinery of Galveston, to which Jang devotes even greater attention. These pictures are all shot from a distance, so the oil processing enterprise appears as a glowing vision on the horizon, literally a city of energy extraction, production, and distribution. The wind farm and Galveston are both devoted to the global frivolity of energy consumption that makes possible the so-called consumer society, with its necessities (automobiles, air conditioning, heavy weapons) and its diversions (automobiles, weapons, entertainment shopping complexes, and media devices, including the cameras that Jang carries).

And light, of course, filling the sky and time, altering human and animal sleep cycles, eliminating dichotomies everywhere, leveling experience, and banishing myths. It is impossible not to think of Galveston's true counterpart in the economy of waste and consumption, Las Vegas, a metastasizing tumor of light in the desert. Jang has not photographed Las Vegas, because this is not a sociological expose, and yet the connection is more forceful by its absence. Is this what Plato and Zoroaster had in mind? Disastrous revelation, an excess of insight, blinded by the light? As riveting as the particular images may be, it is the totality of the photographs and the linkages they suggest that make the book so valuable. I hesitate to call Jang's work disaster porn, but the end of the world—or the end of the civilizing process represented by global development—never looked so compelling or inevitable.

A key element to Jang's project is time—time the revelator and time the destroyer. Shooting at night has required that Jang use long exposures, and much of the "special effects" of the photographs are artifacts of that open eye. Energy literally accumulates in the sky, and a background glow can appear as a sudden flare. Even the atmosphere itself seems to become visible. In contrast, other moving elements disappear or leave only traces, including the surveillance helicopters that patrol industrial sites post-9/11. In conversation, Jang has made an interesting point. In Japan and Korea, where space is at a premium, buildings are usually demolished and built over, so there are no ruins. But in the United States, where there is nothing but space, new buildings and entire industries arise next to the corpses of old ones. Because of liability concerns, crumbling structures have to be patrolled along with working ones. Both the dead and the living must be surveilled. Hence the thin arcs of light that mark the helicopters' paths where they wouldn't be expected.

Jang has also remarked that when he began the project, he was interested mostly in the signs of abandonment and decay, evidence of wounds to the land inflicted by human beings. Such are the deliberately archaeological photographs shot in Blair, Nevada, formerly a gold mining town. Most of what he depicts in this sequence are foundations facing an empty desert, and the resemblance to ancient ruins such as Pompeii or the Native American cities of the Southwest is too obvious to miss. Likewise the Ozymandian irony: look on my works, ye mighty, and despair. But the moral is misplaced. The point of ancient civilizations is not that they passed away but that new ones kept arising to take their place. Jang makes a great photograph of an immense defunct power plant on the Hudson River being dismantled from the inside. The earthmovers at work seem like the mechanical equivalents of devouring beetles, creating new loam for the nourishment of what must inevitably grow there next. As time went on, Jang became more and more fascinated by this parallel process of destruction and growth, often happening in adjacent places and sometimes the same place.

Friedrich Nietzsche once made a famous remark to the effect that when you look into the abyss, the abyss looks into you. You become what you behold. This is the secret the night tells the day, that we are more than half in love with our own extinction, which we can't help but mistake for perfection. The seductiveness of the photographs confirms it. The final image in the book shows not an industrial monument or skeleton but a group of people standing in an empty field. We can't tell where they are or why they are there. In the long exposure, they appear as no more than dark shadows in the surrounding pale night. Some are sitting or hunkered down, some standing. They appear to be waiting as the sky lightens, or perhaps darkens; it's impossible to tell exactly which point in the night's trajectory Jang has caught them. What Jang has said about the monoliths in his photographs could also apply to these human subjects: "In the context of nature, they are paused, as if to rethink their purpose."

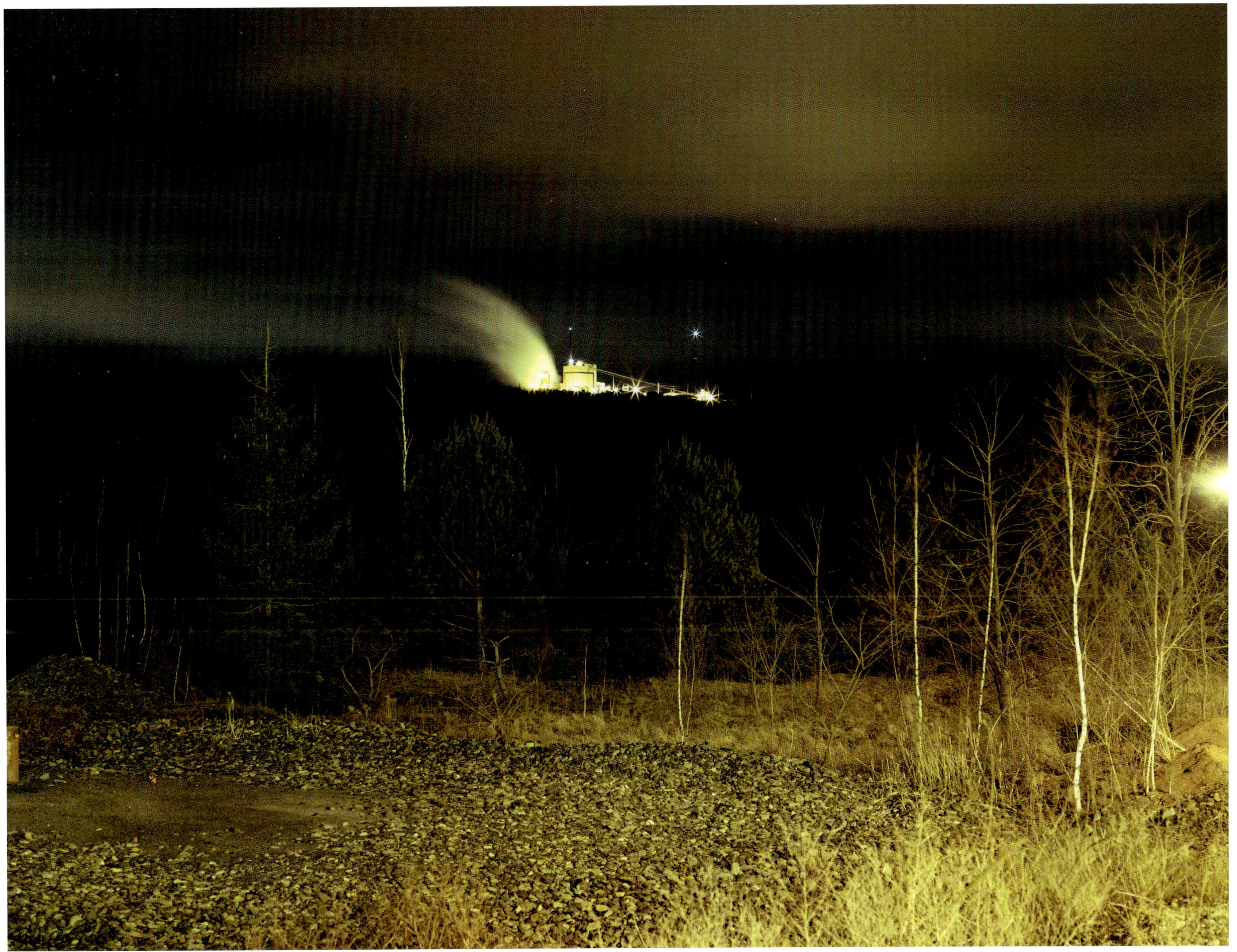

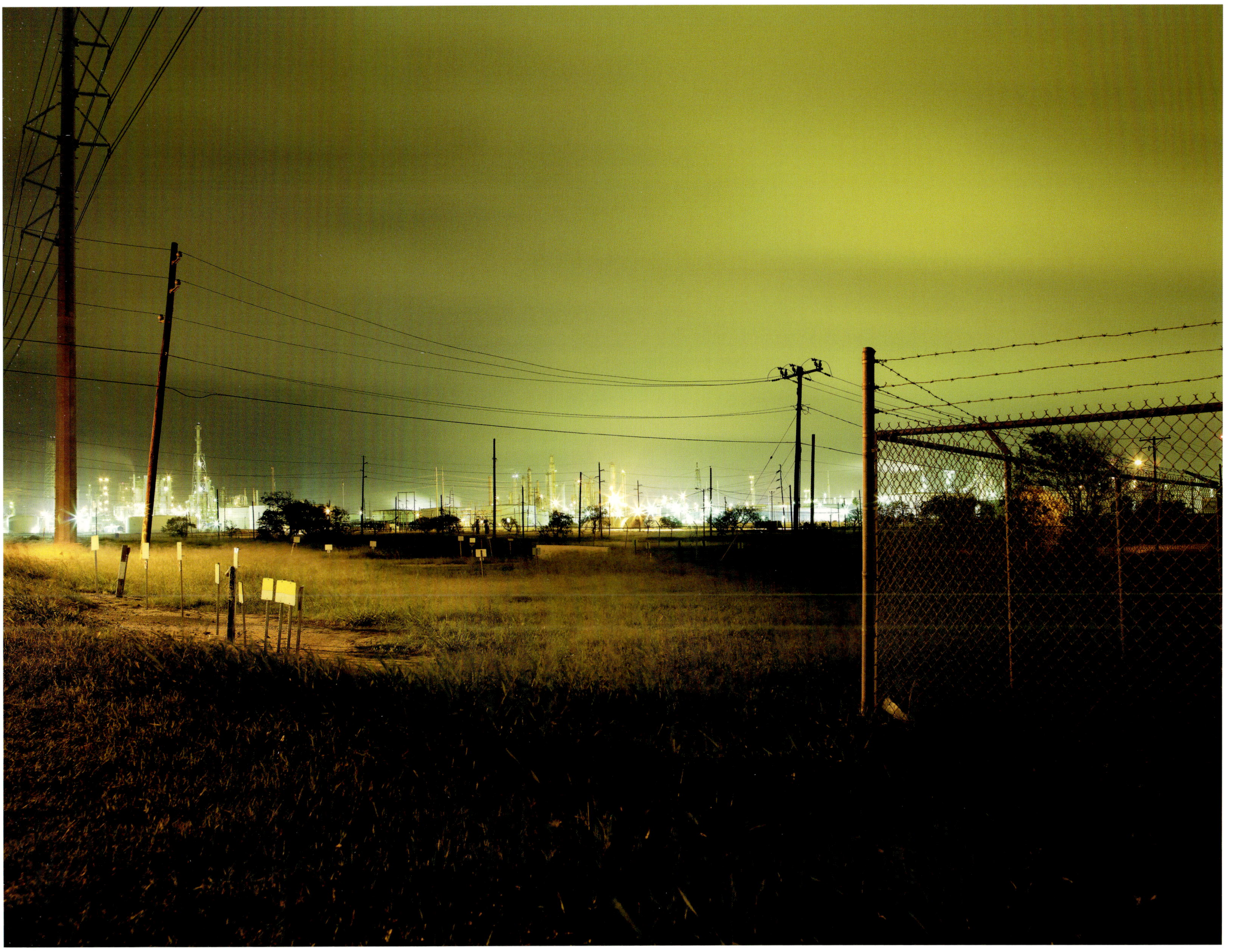

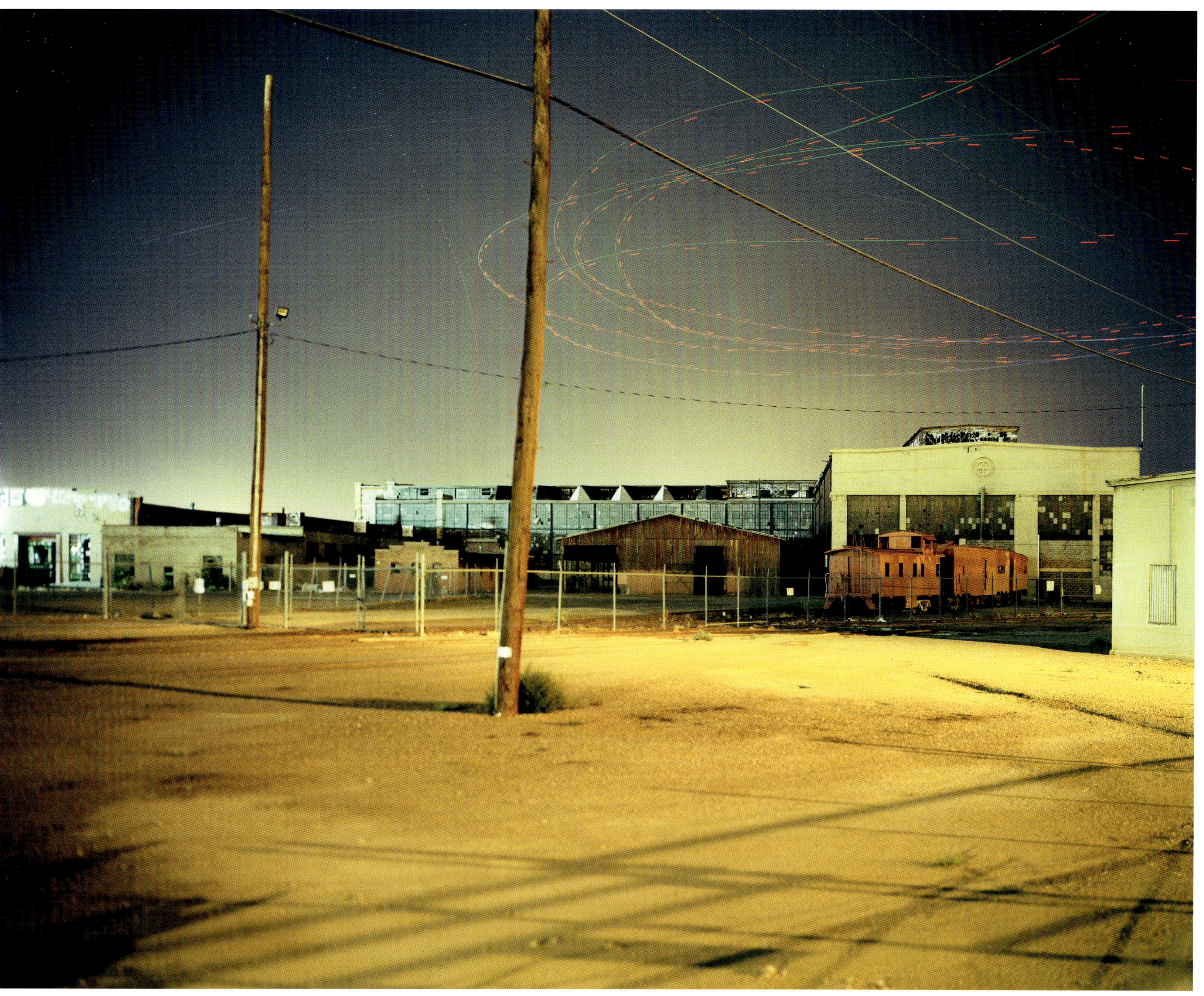

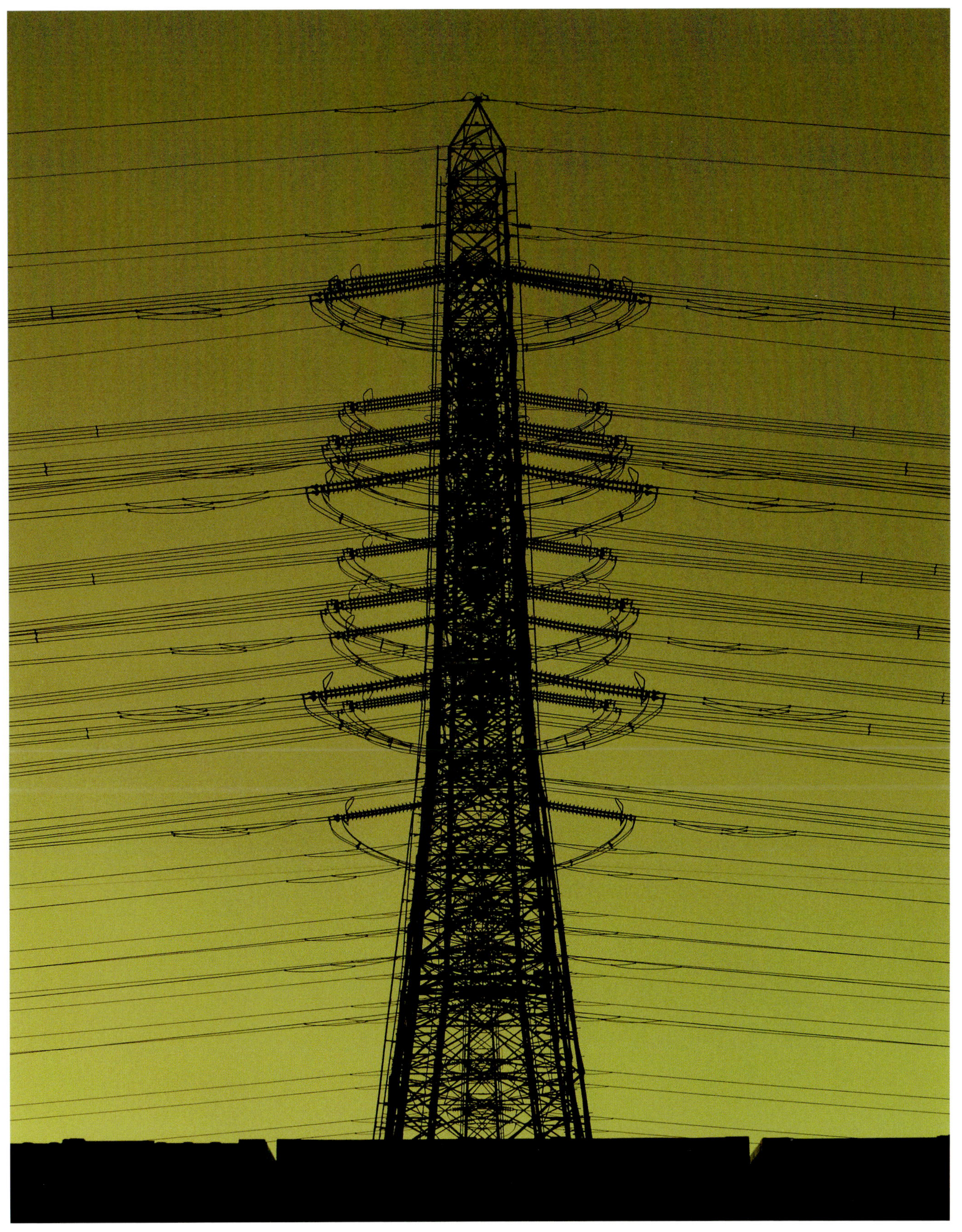

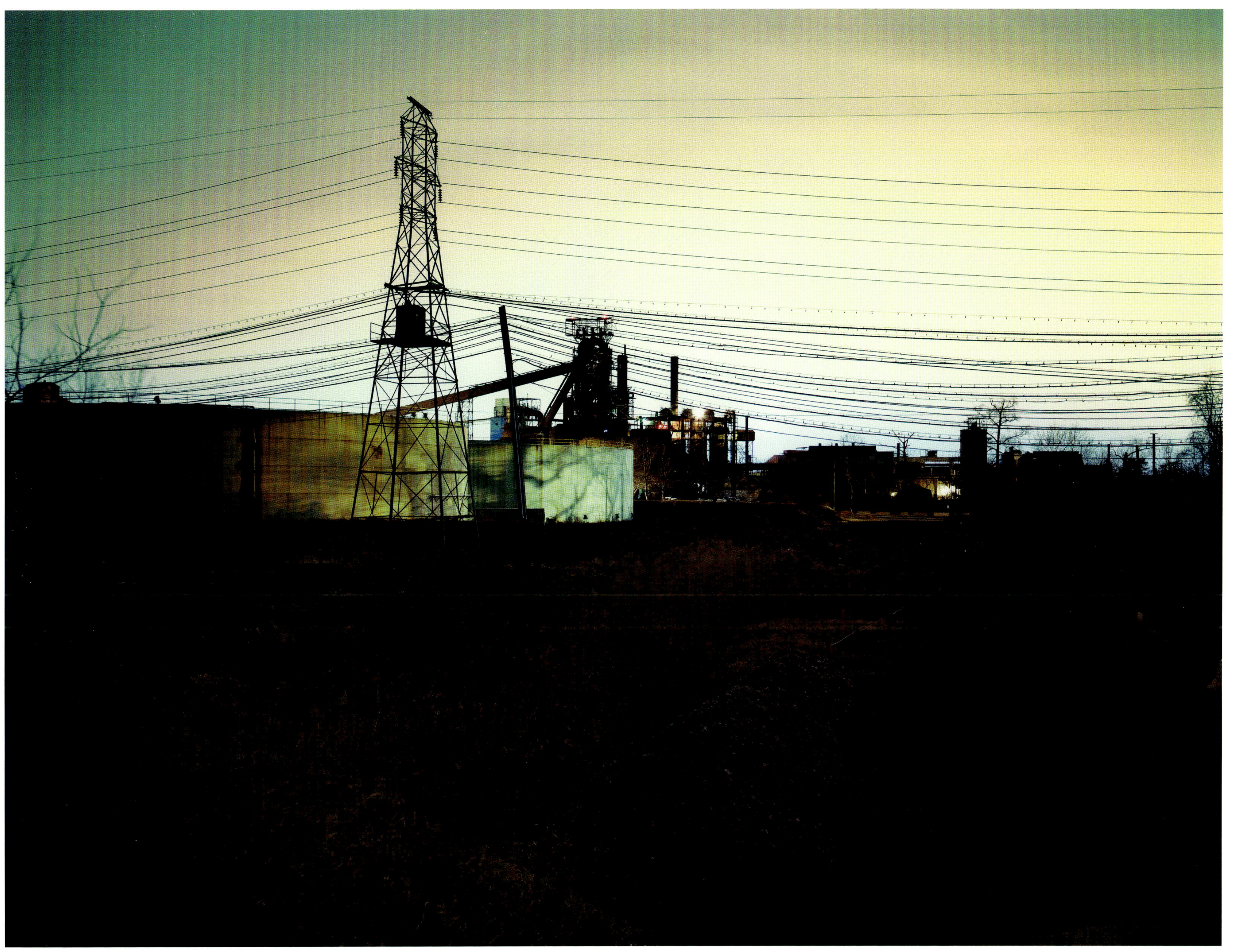

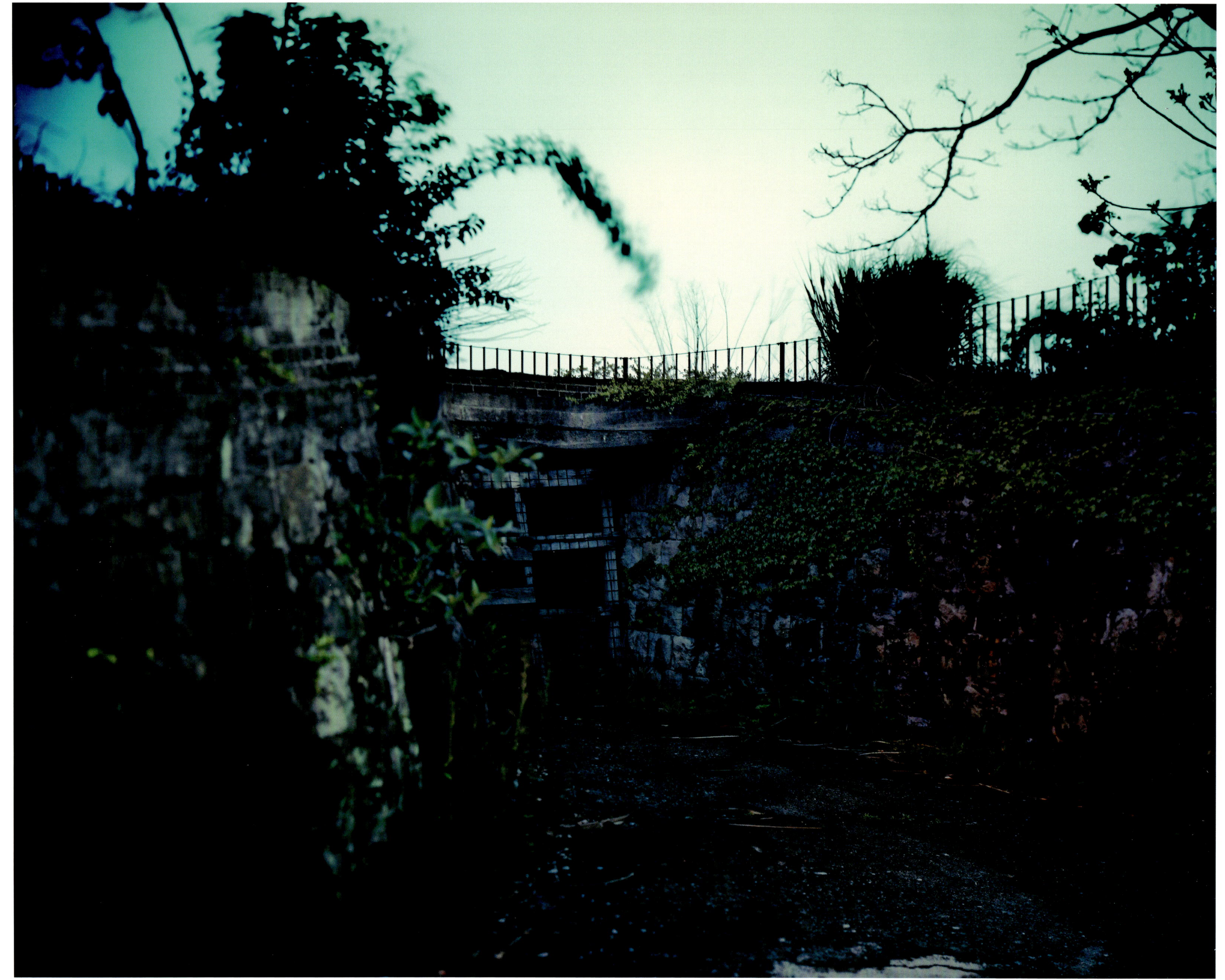

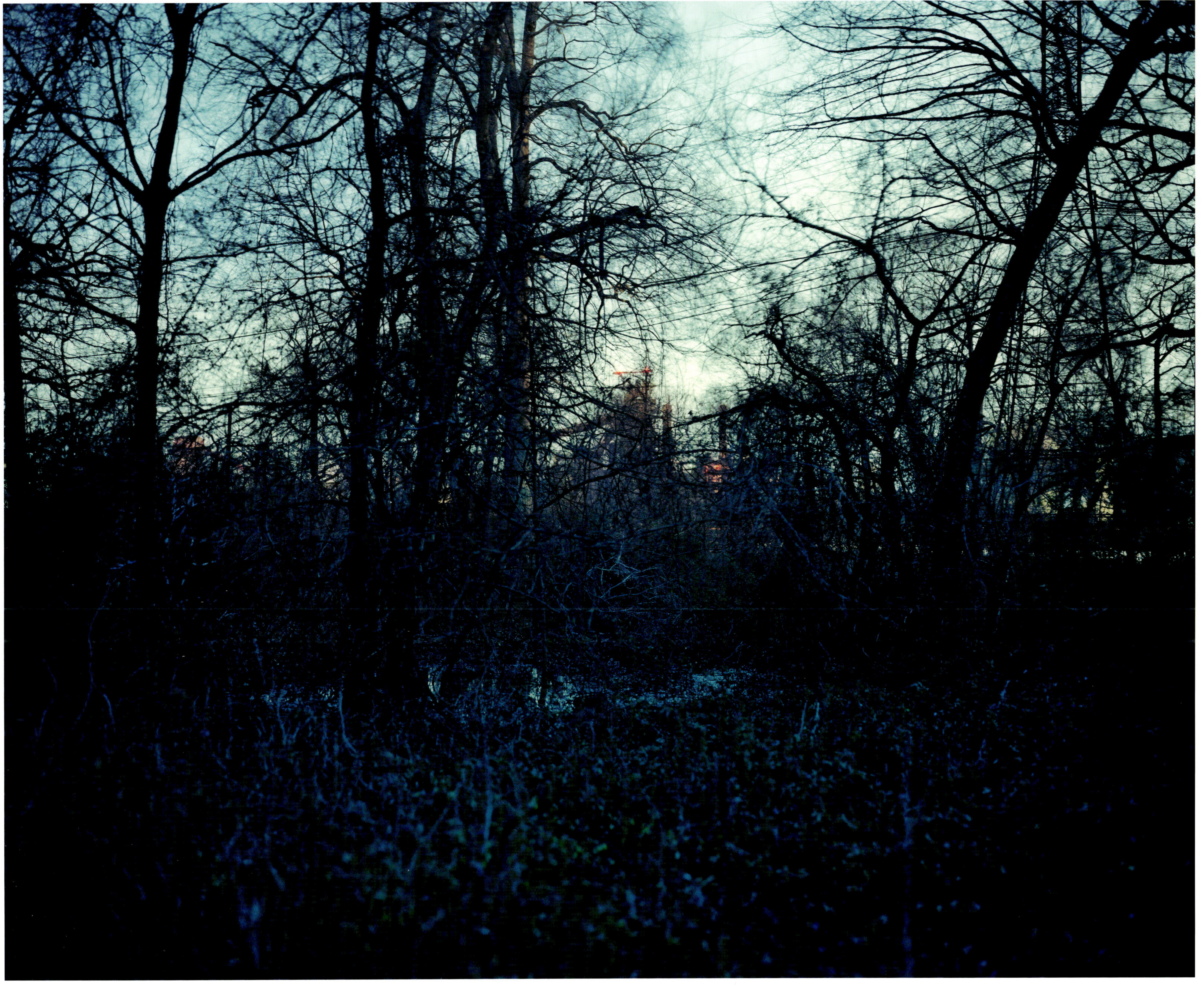

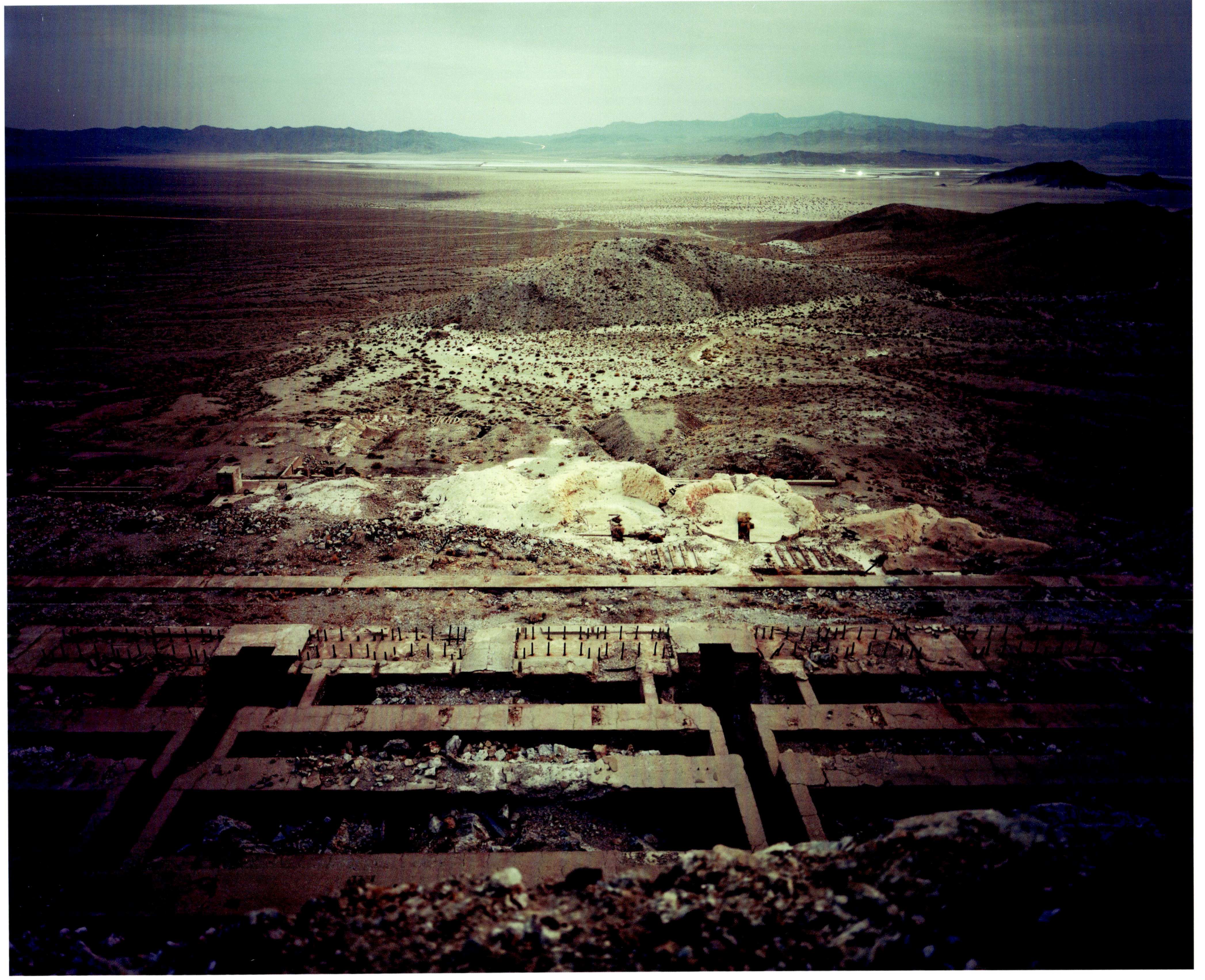

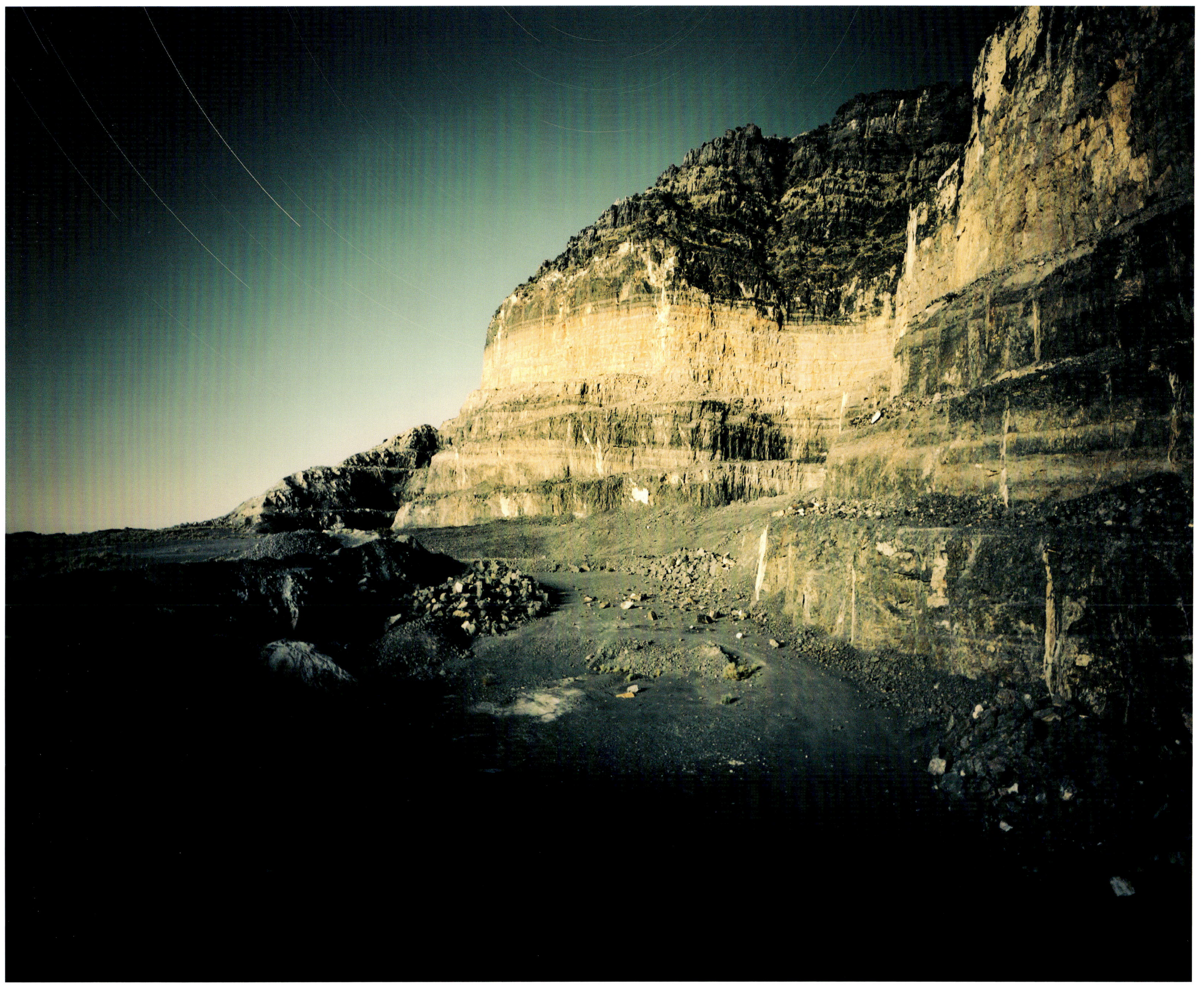

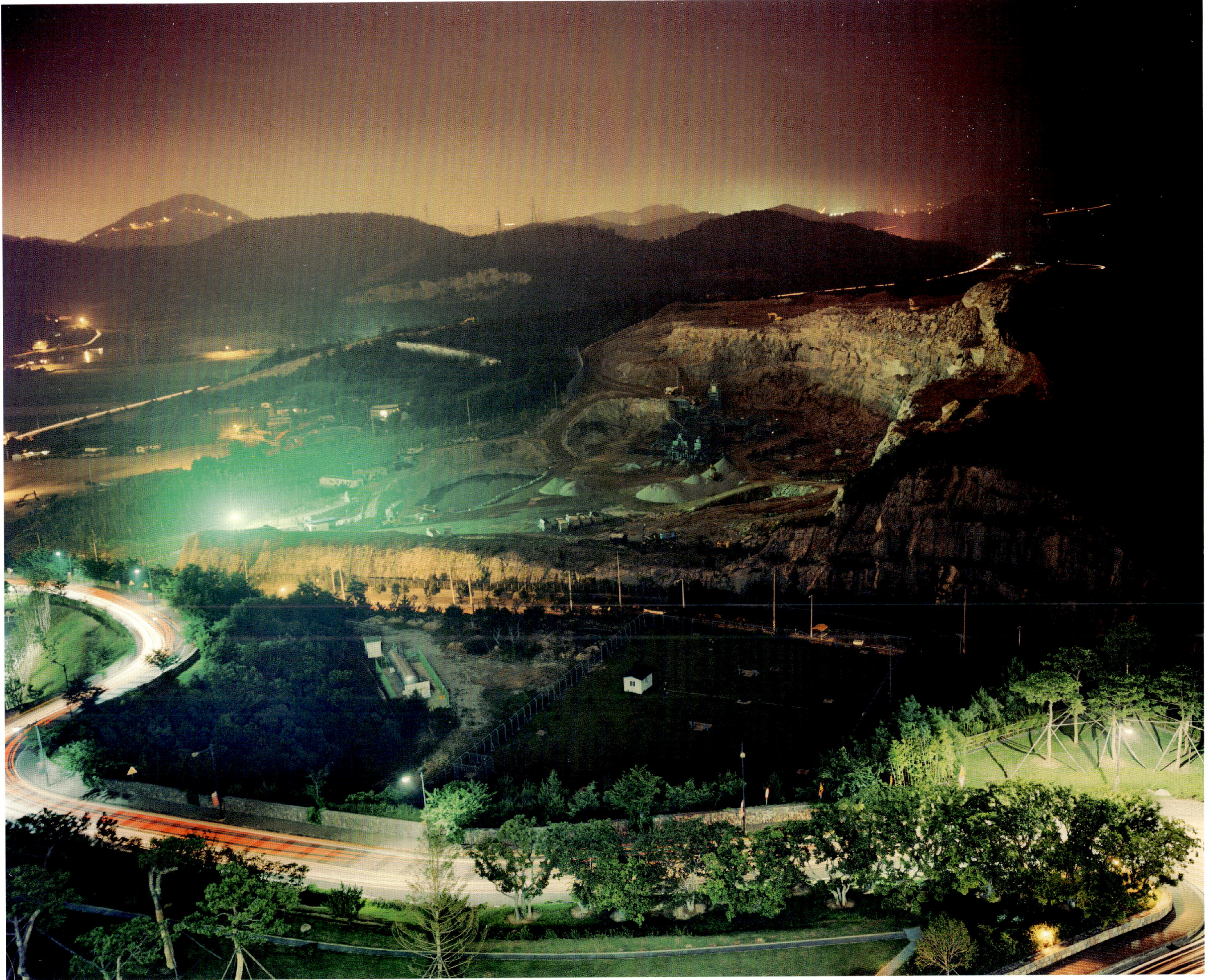

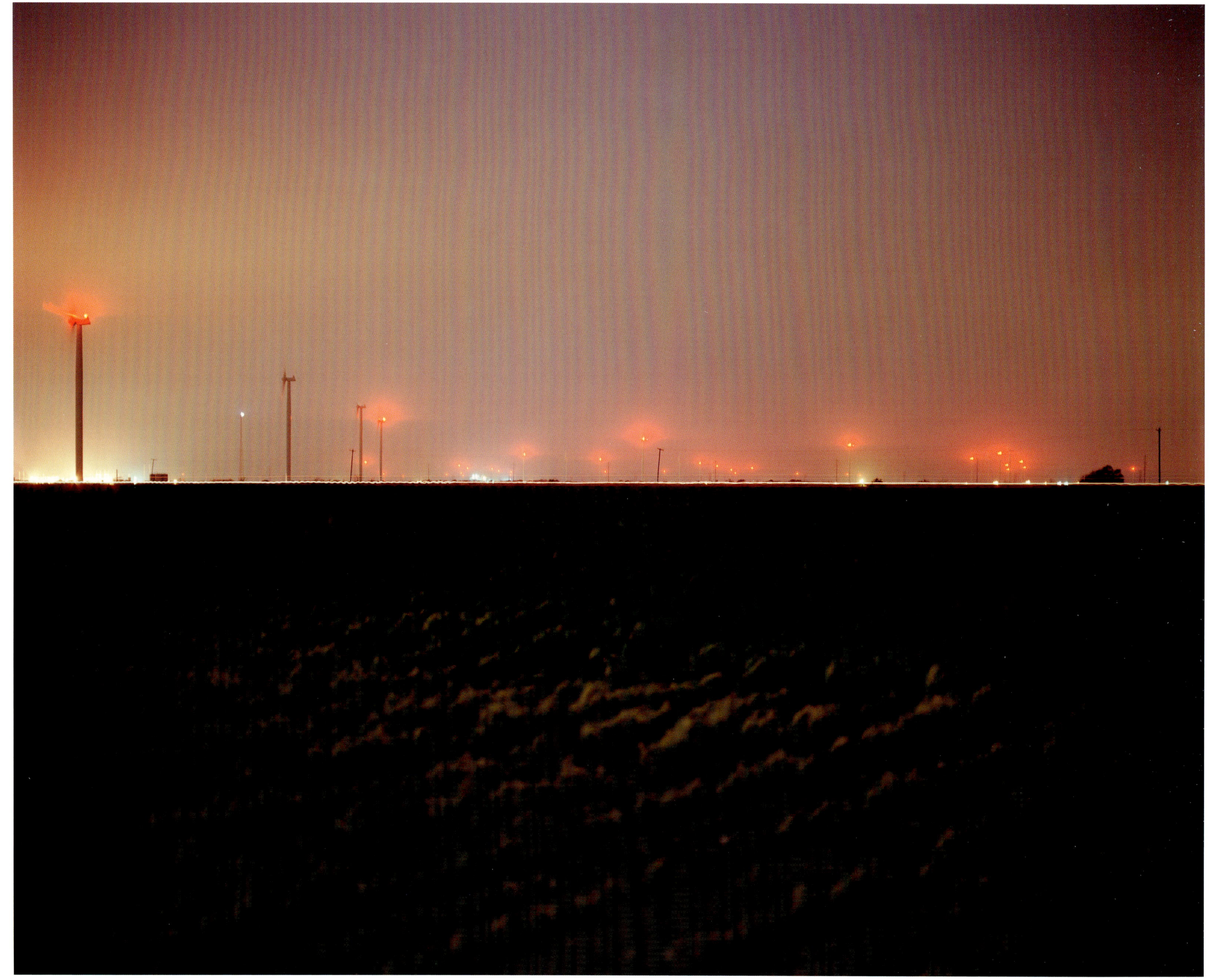

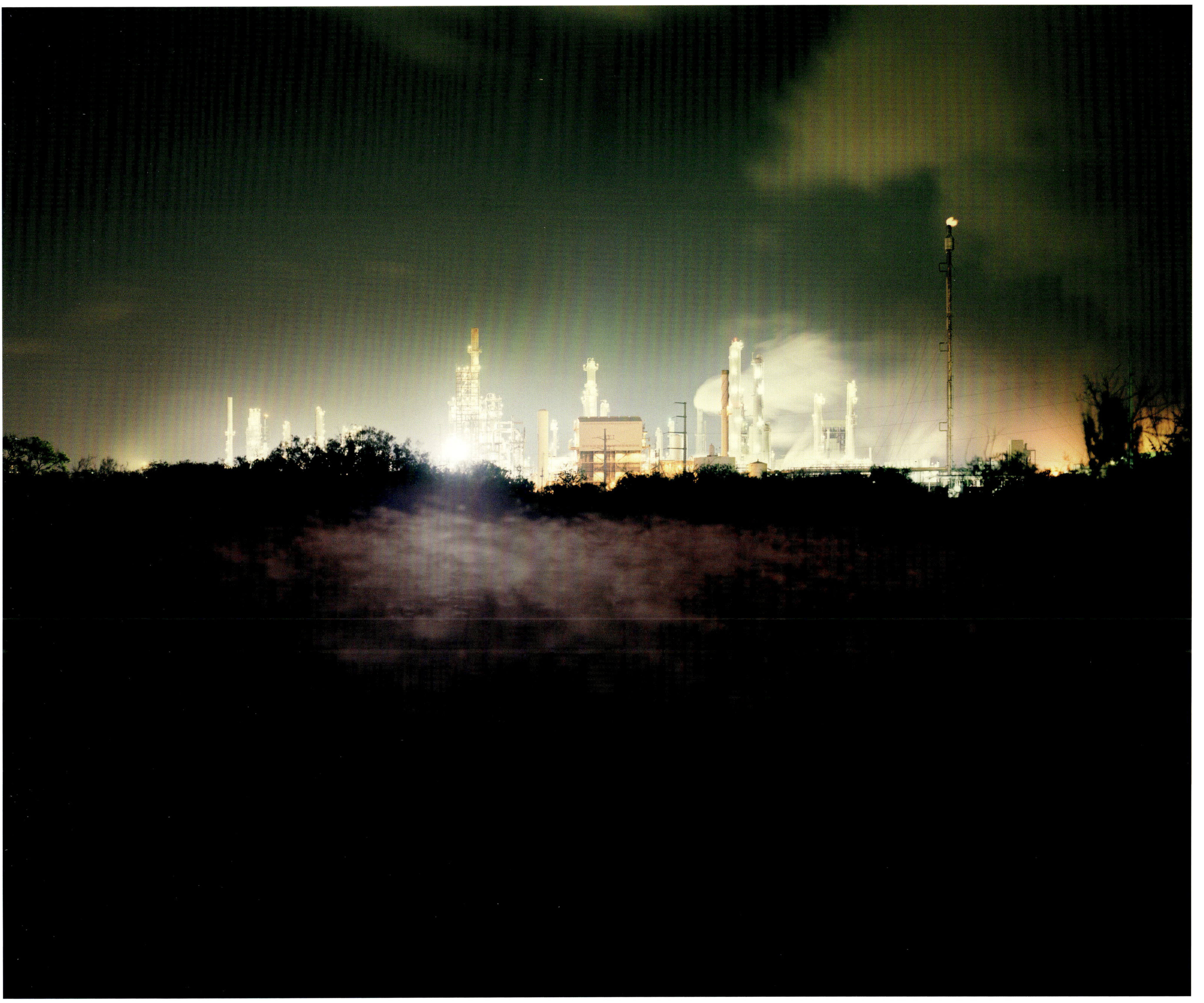

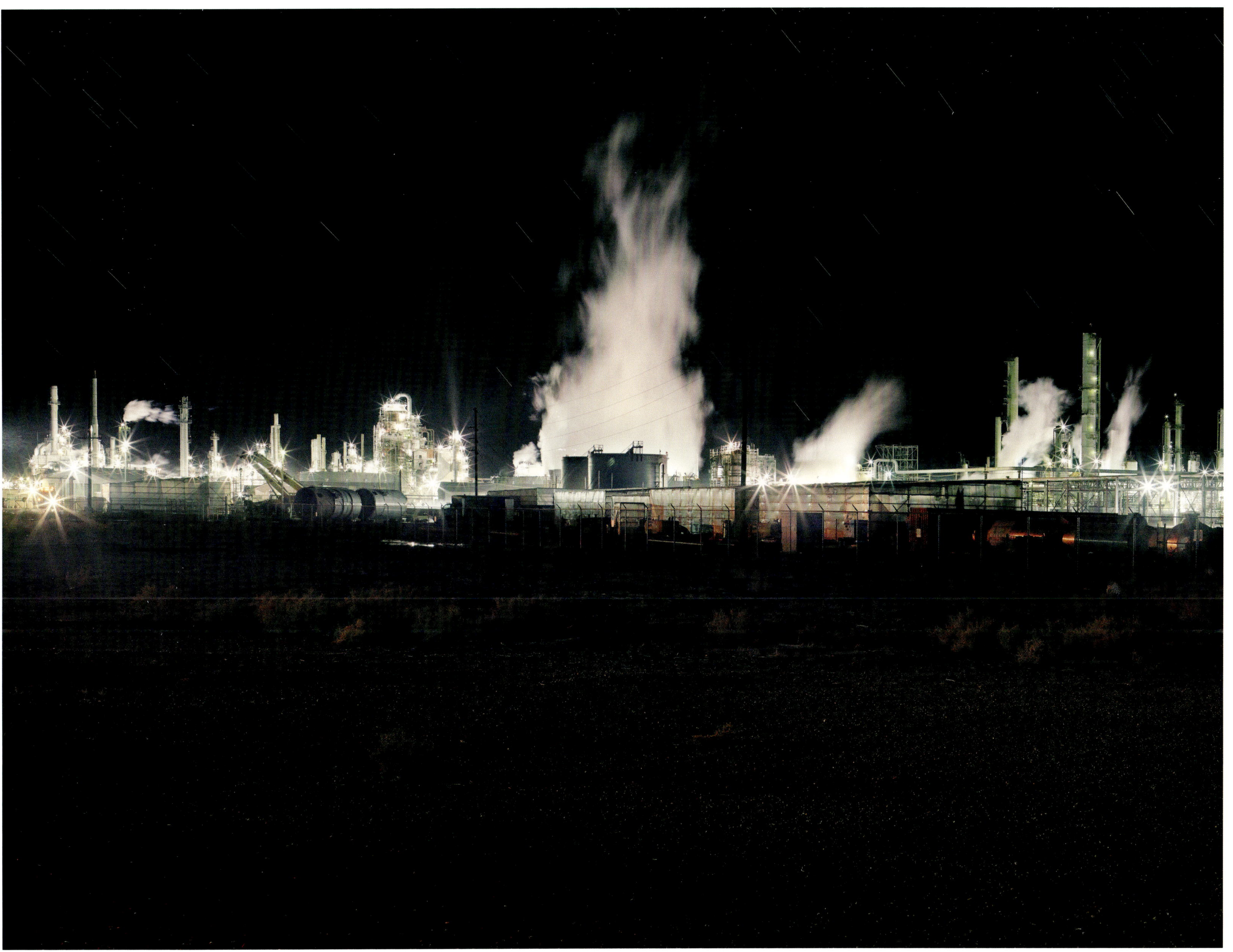

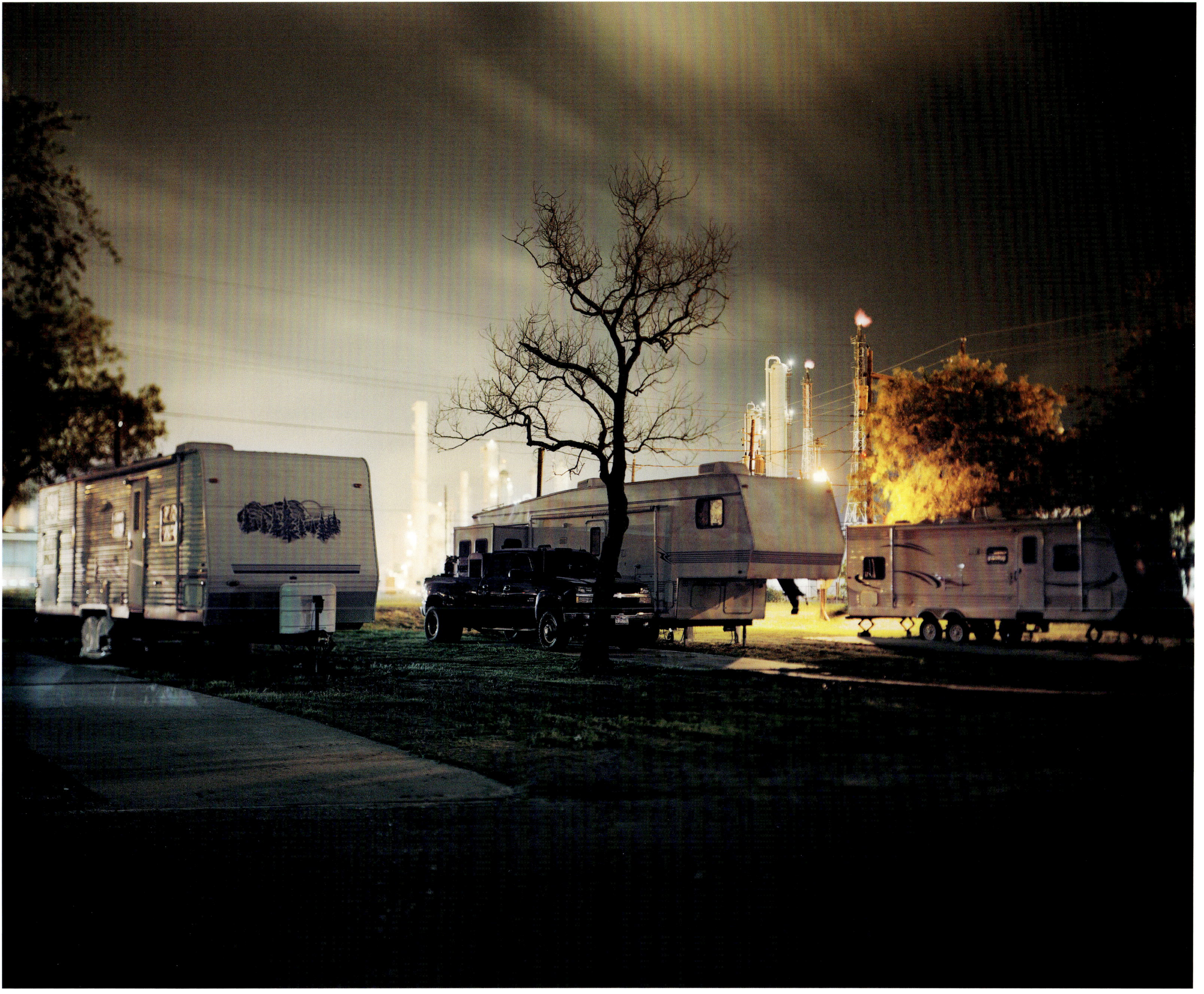

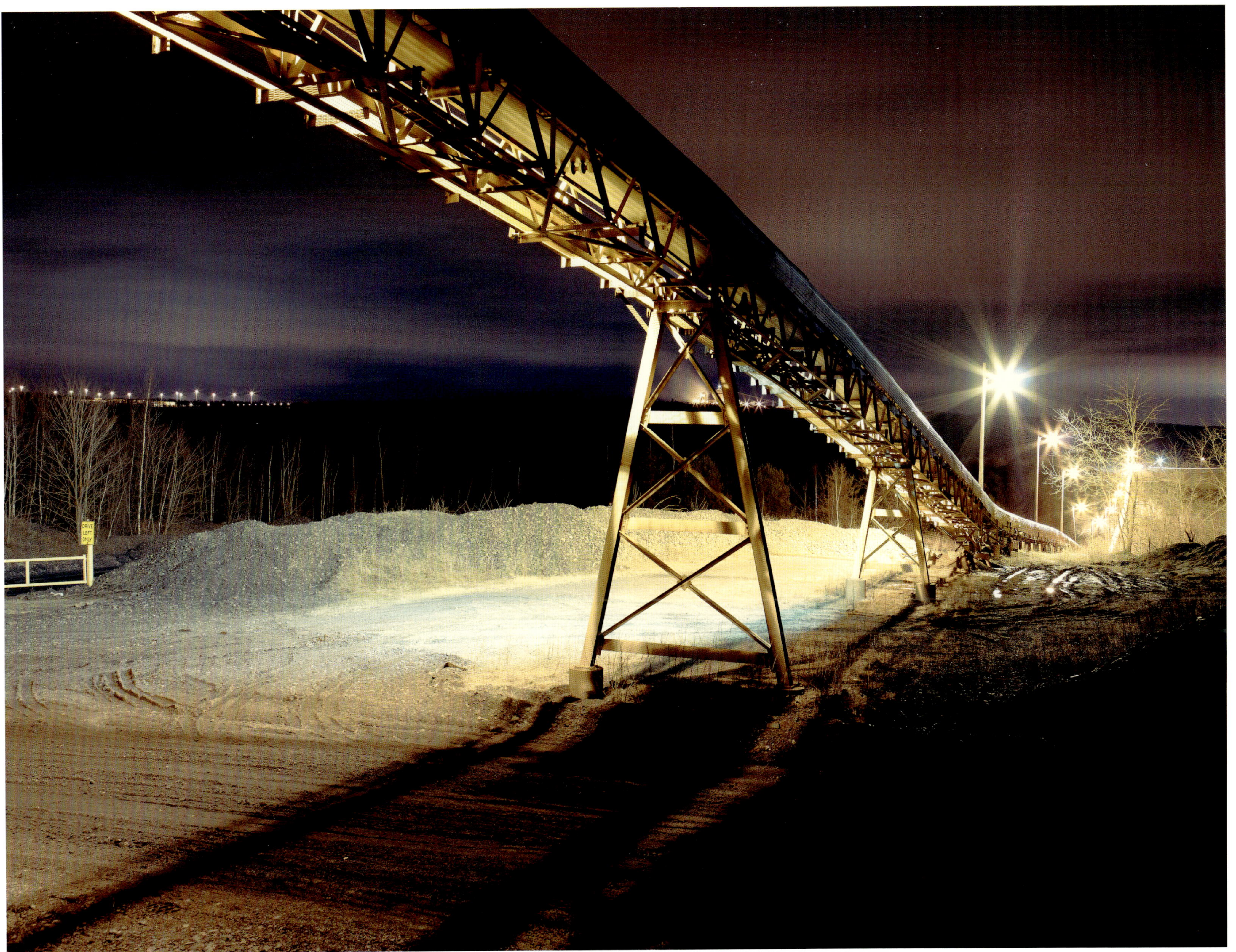
DRIVE
LEFT
ONLY

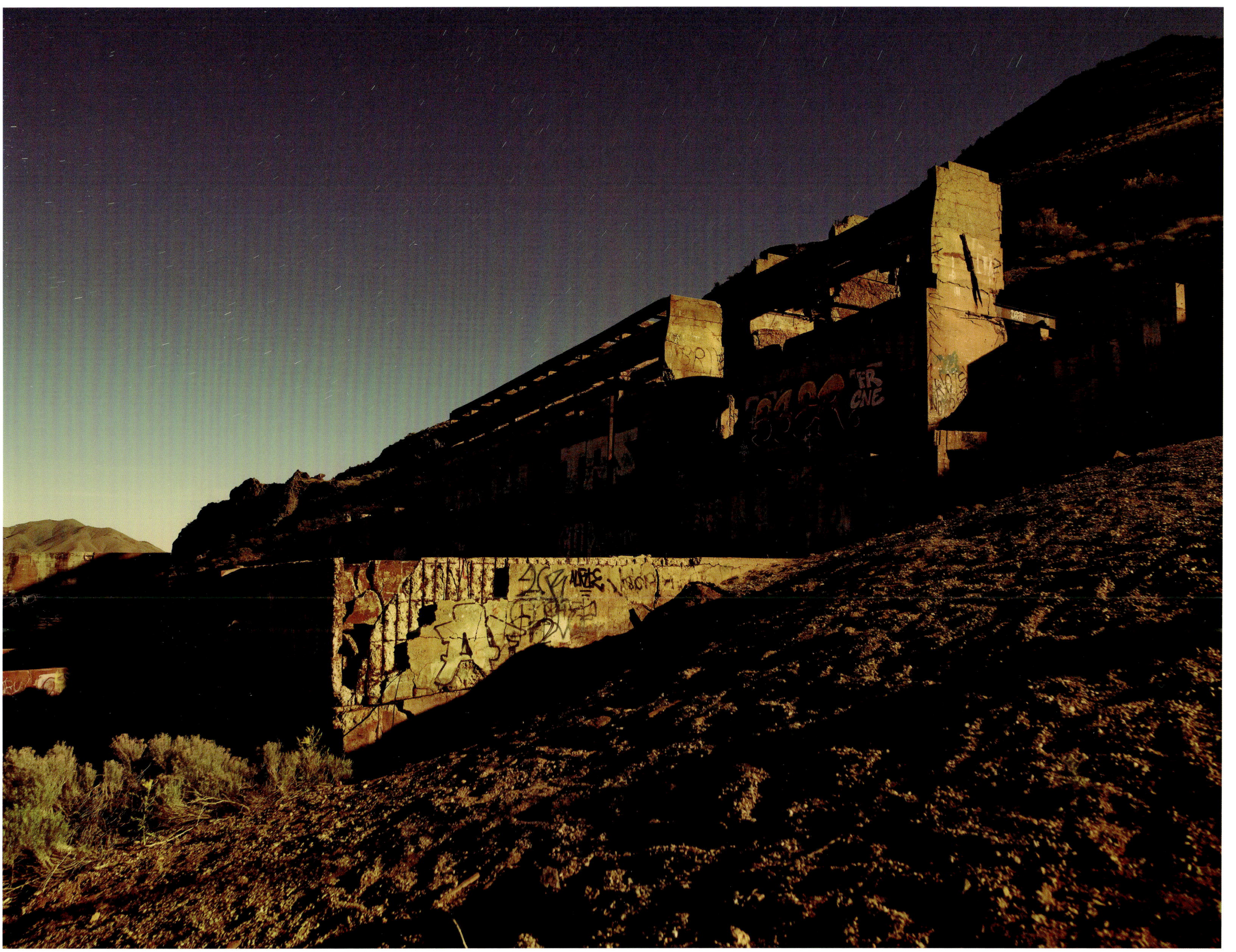

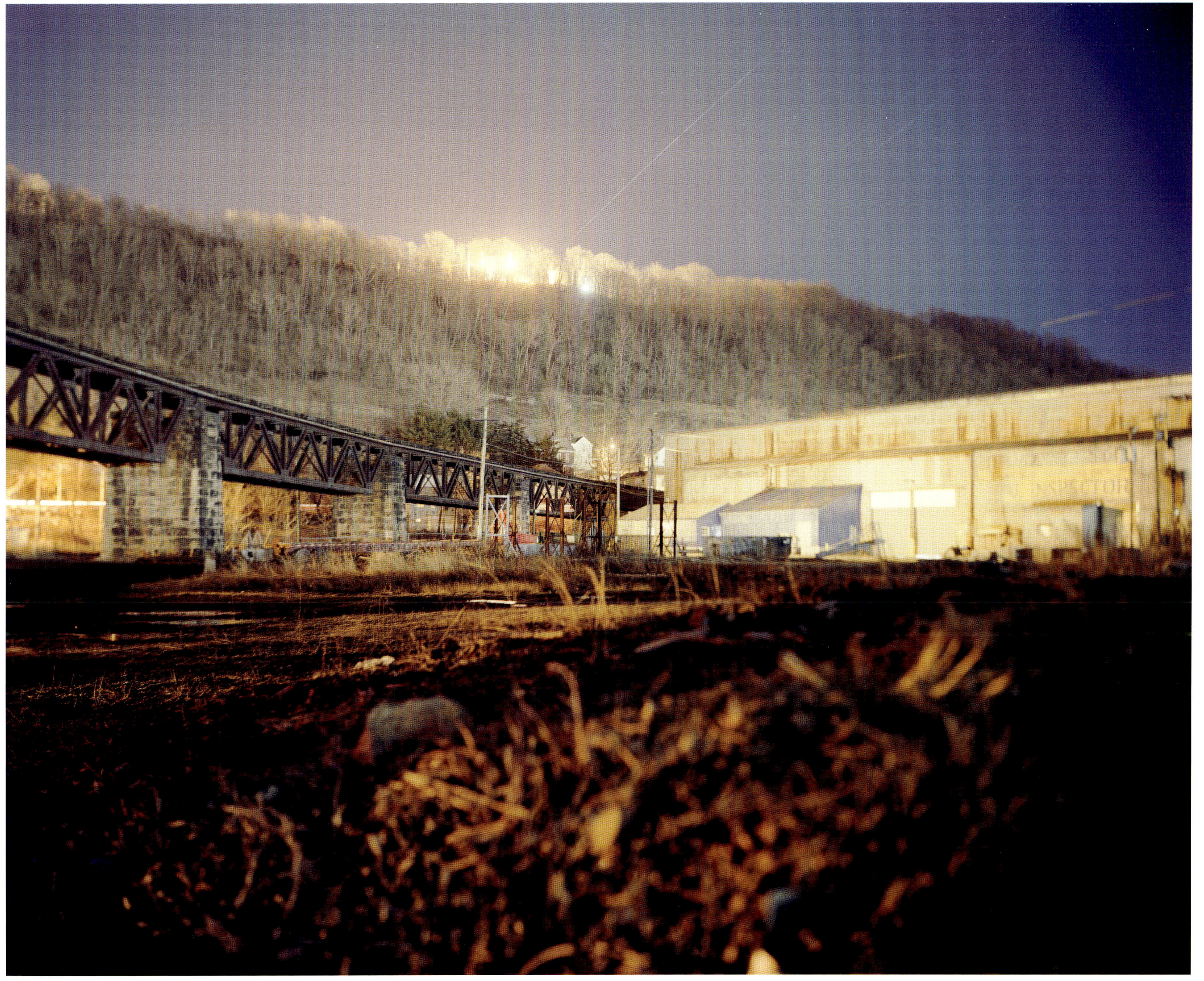
INSPECTOR

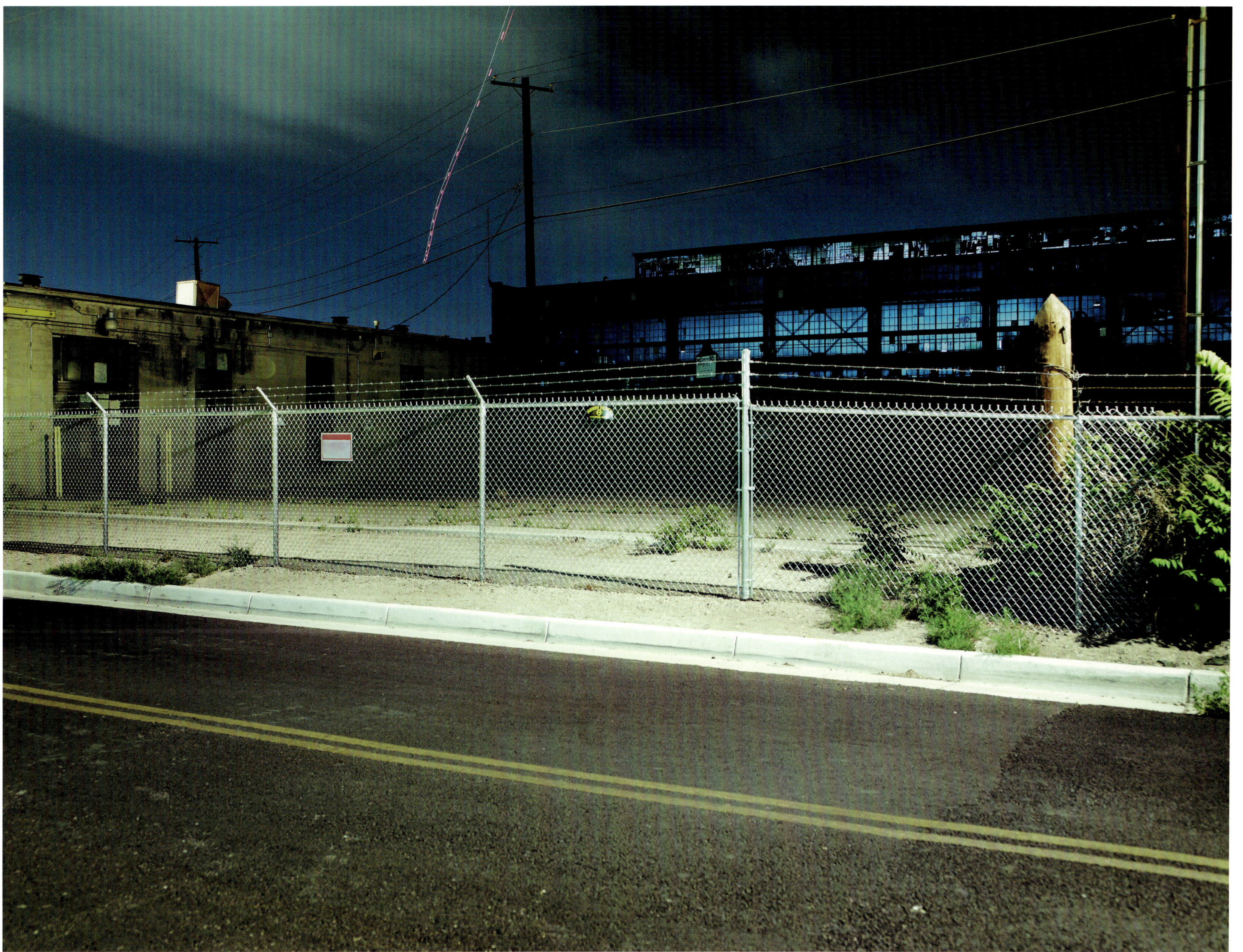

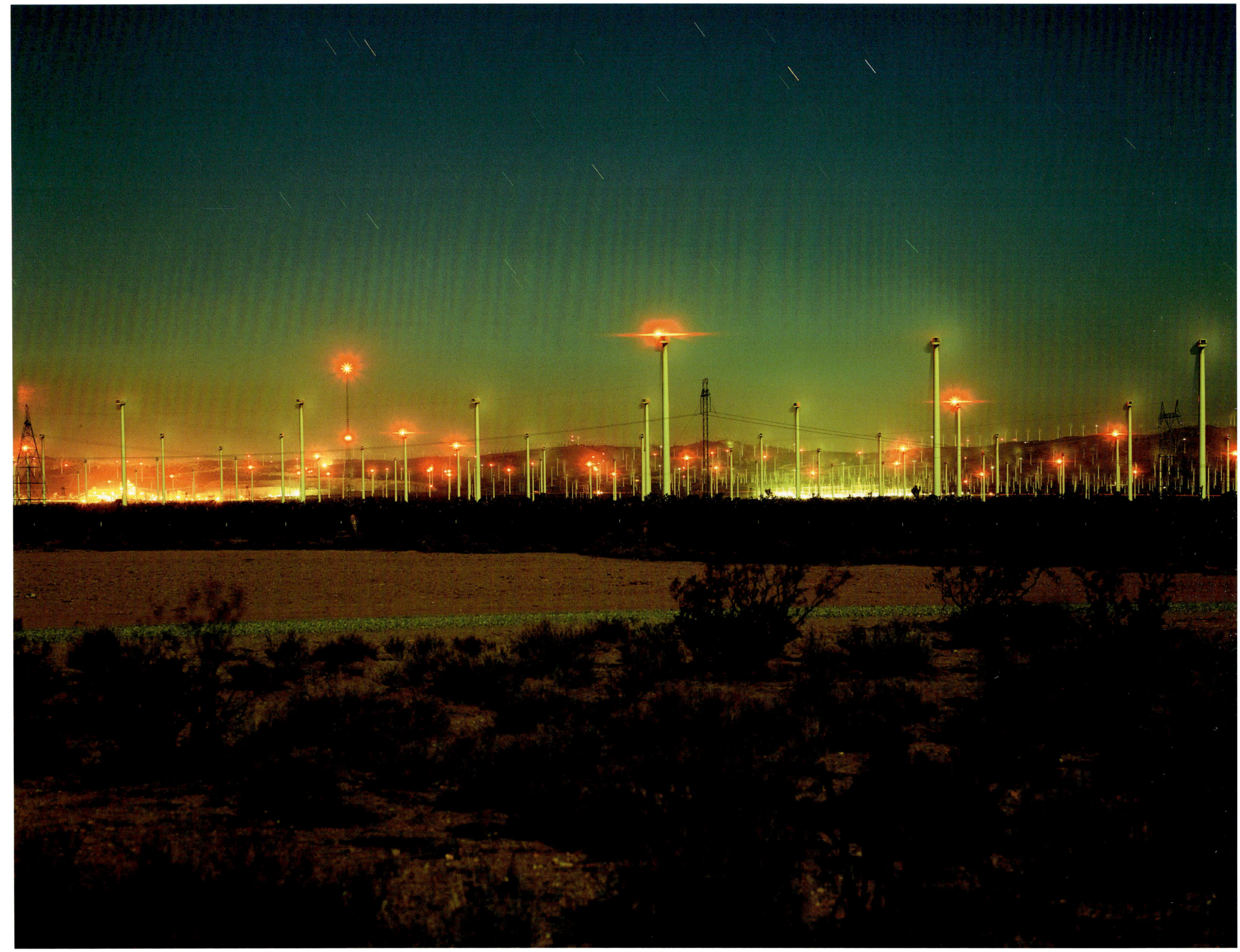

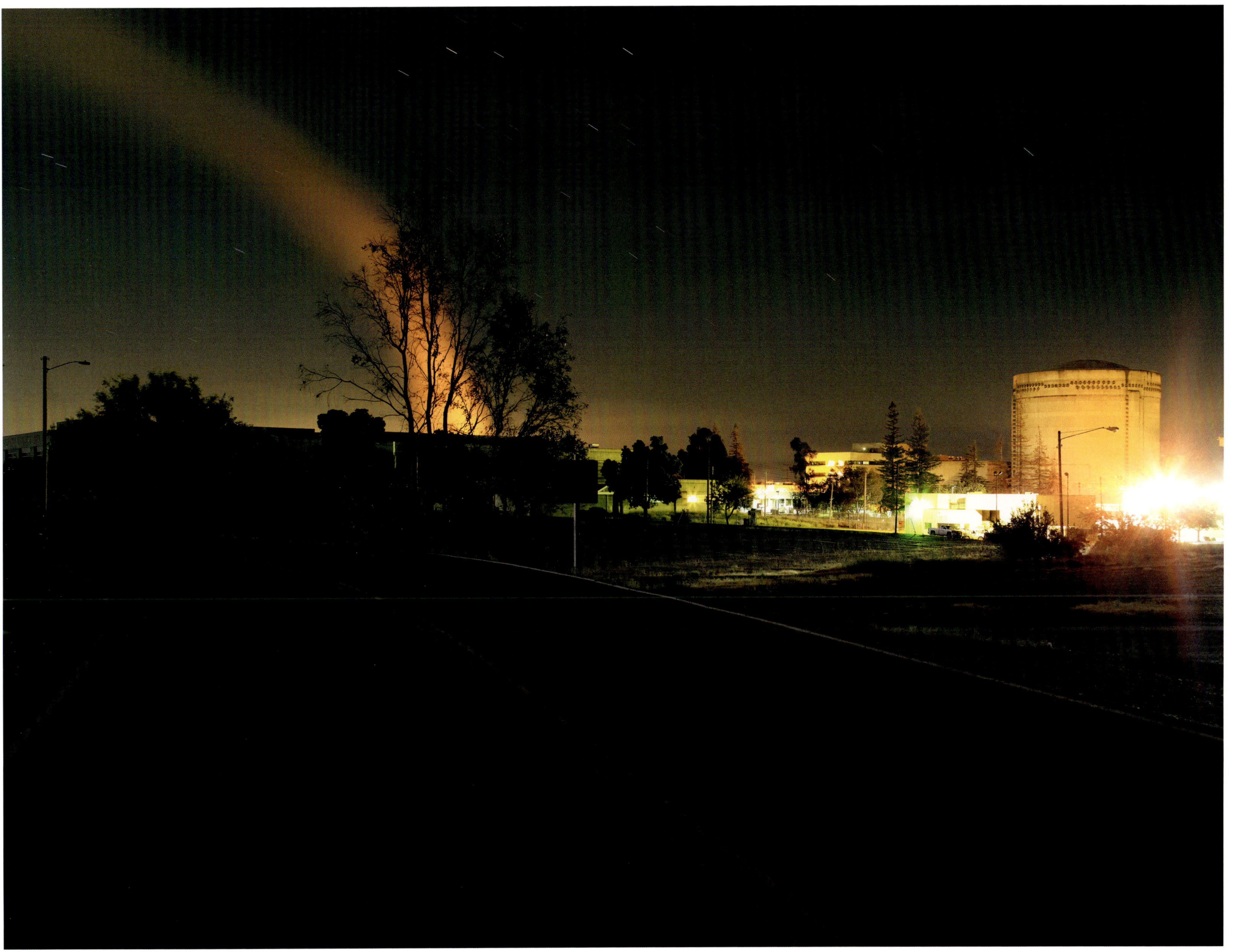

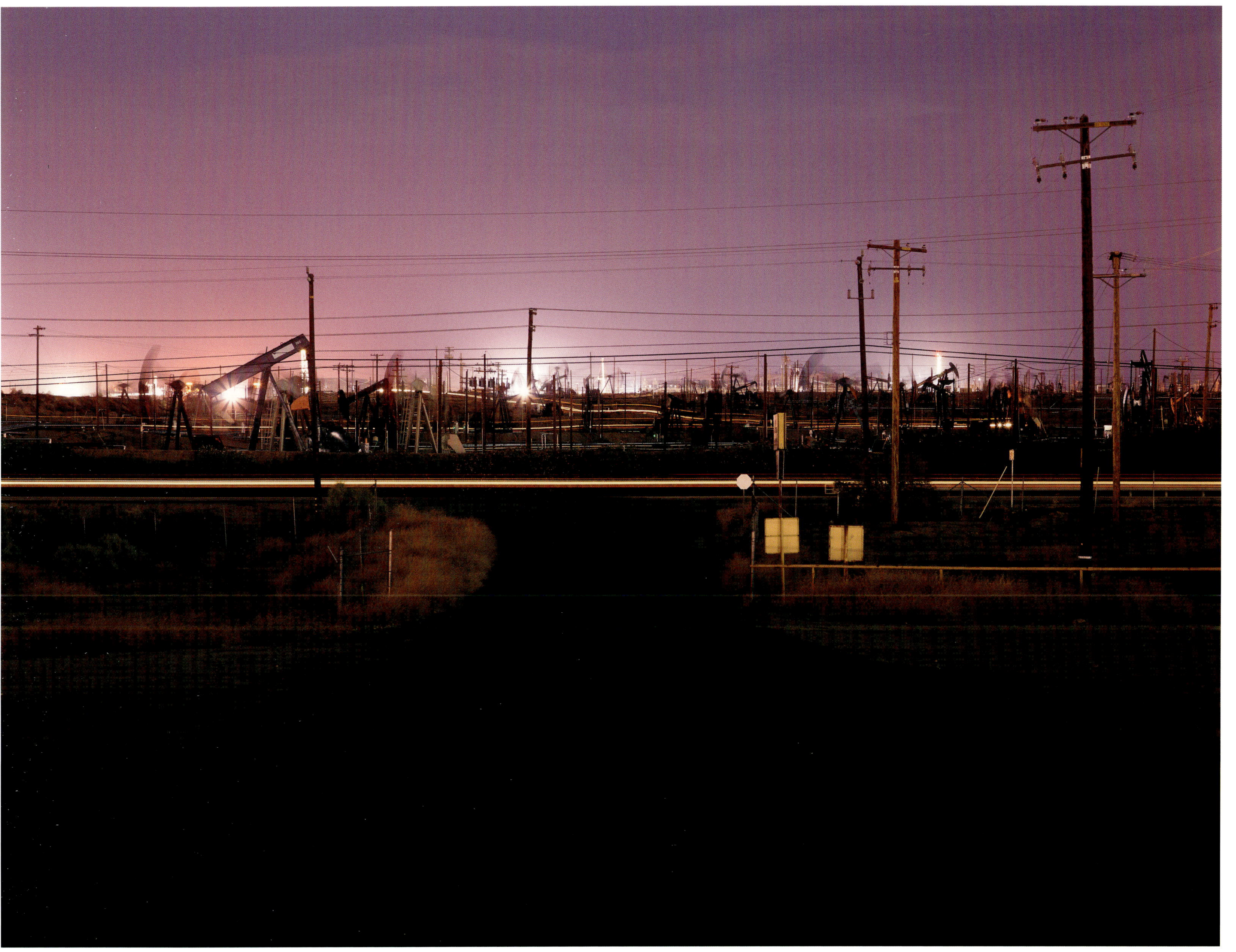

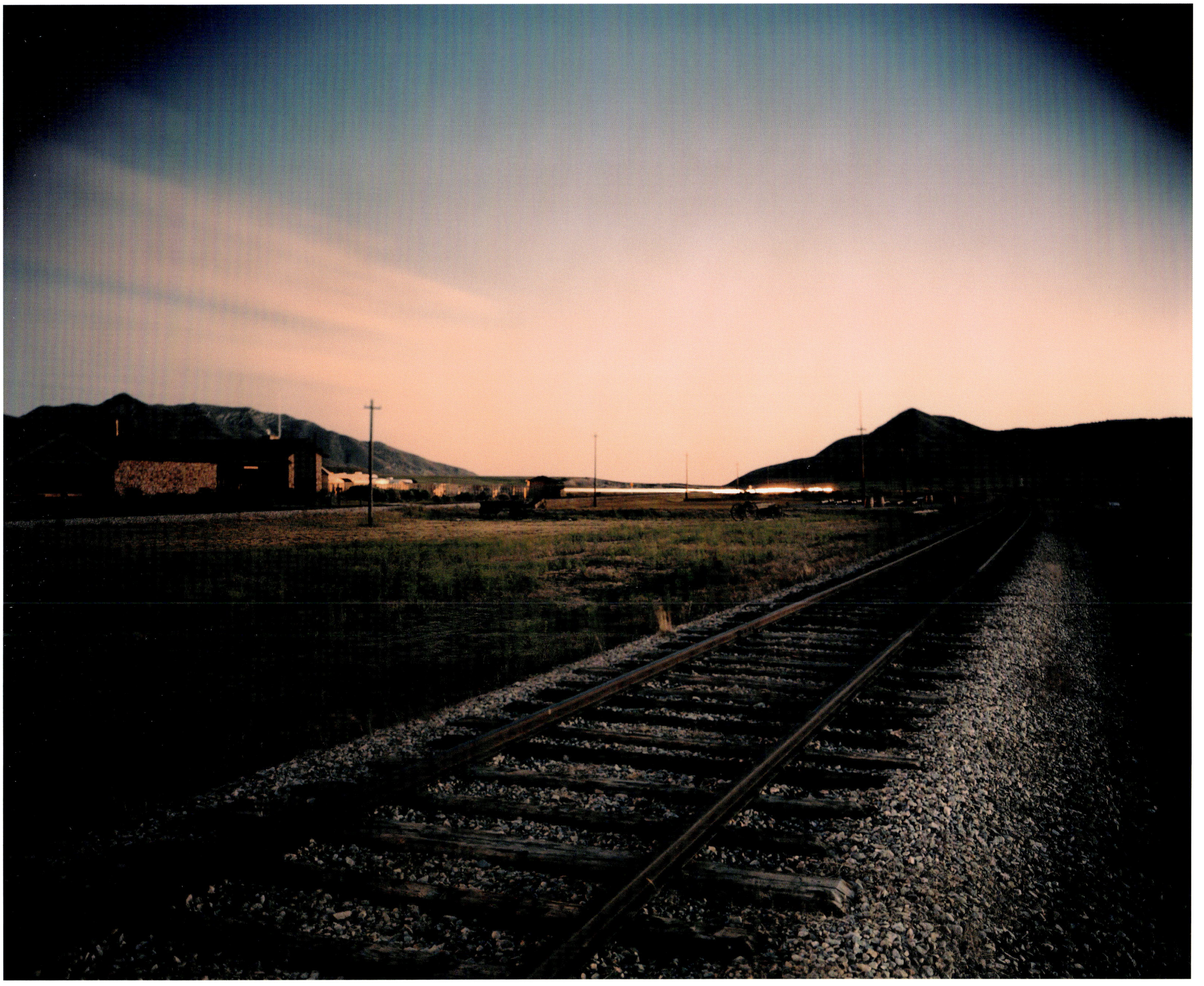

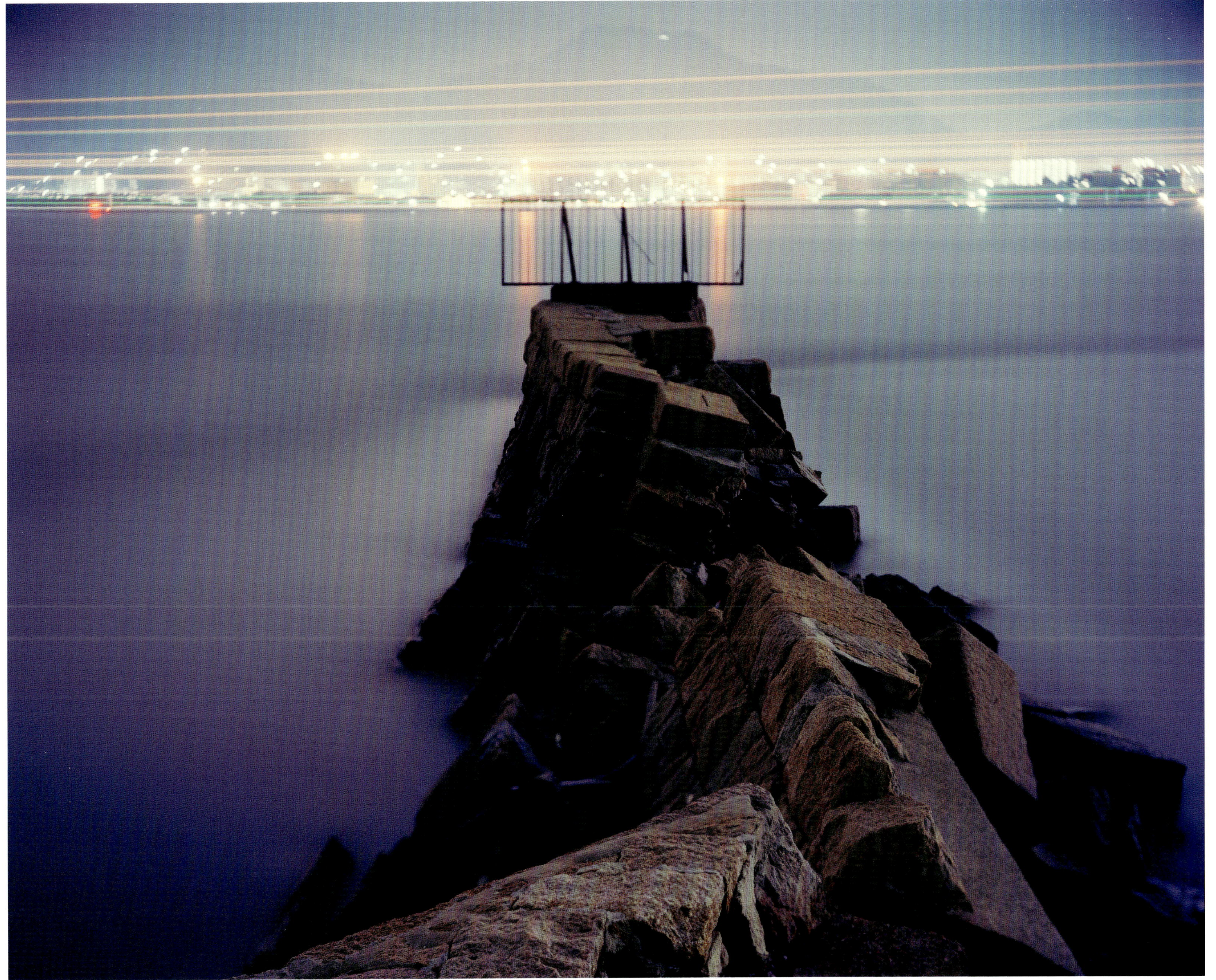

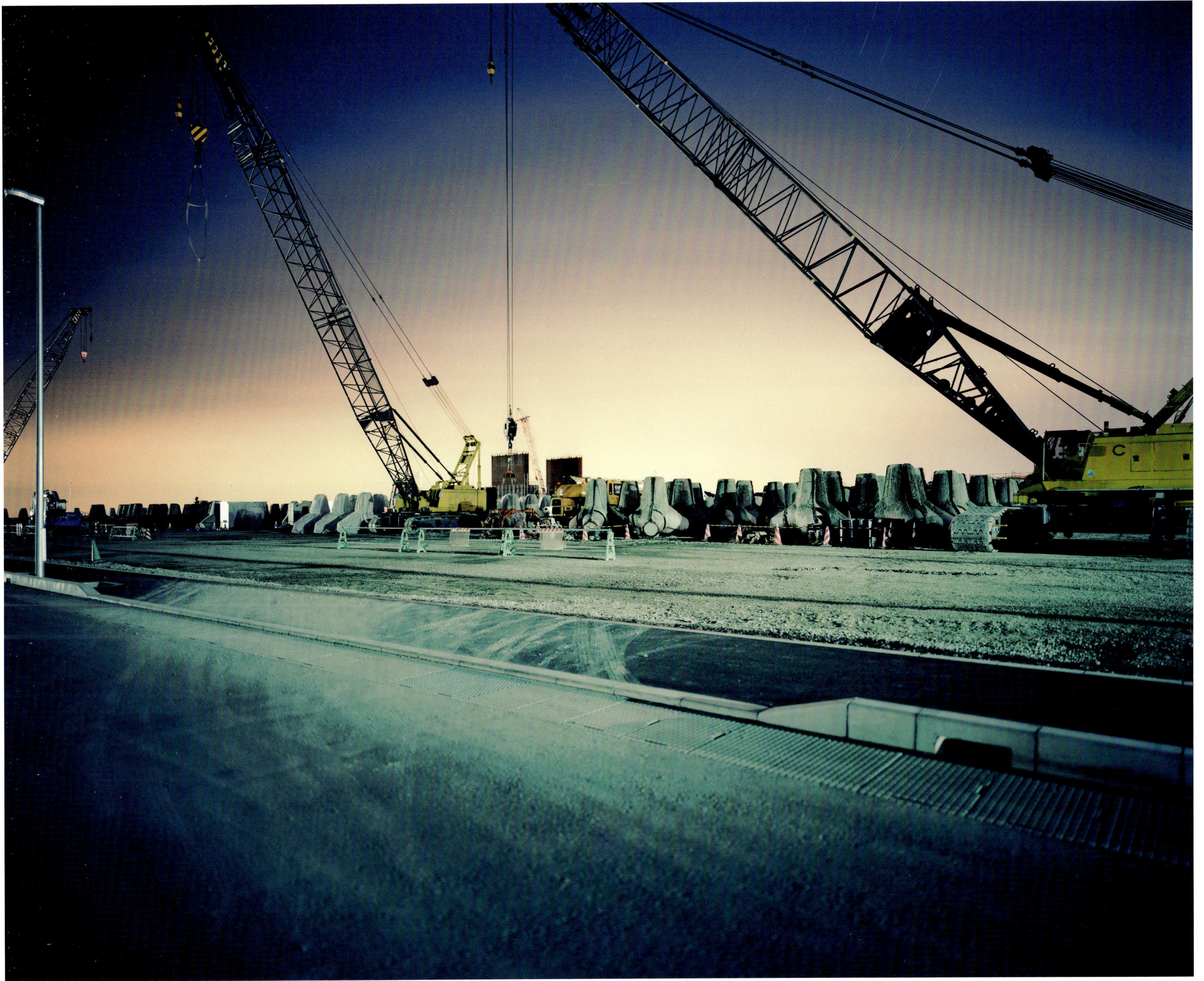

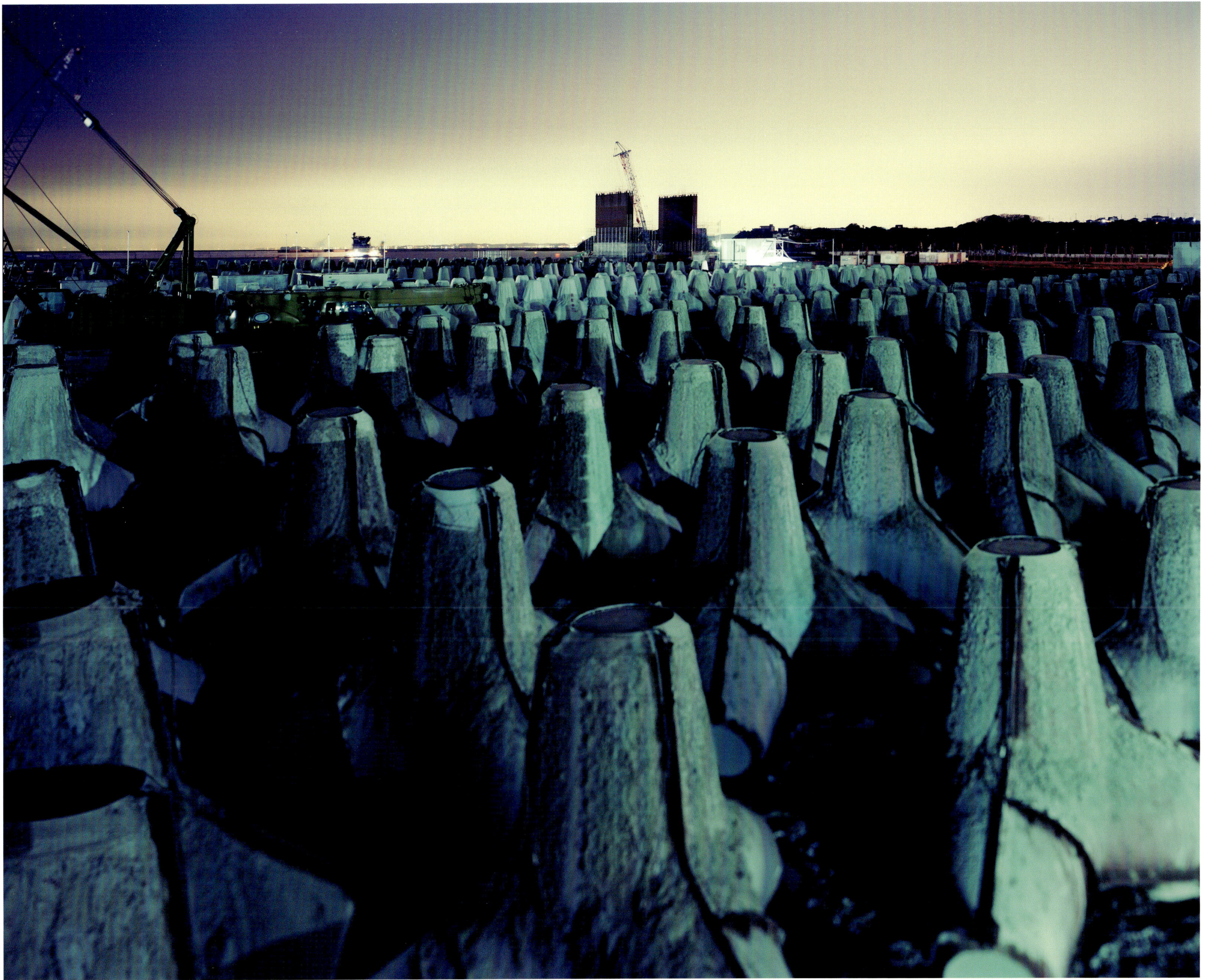

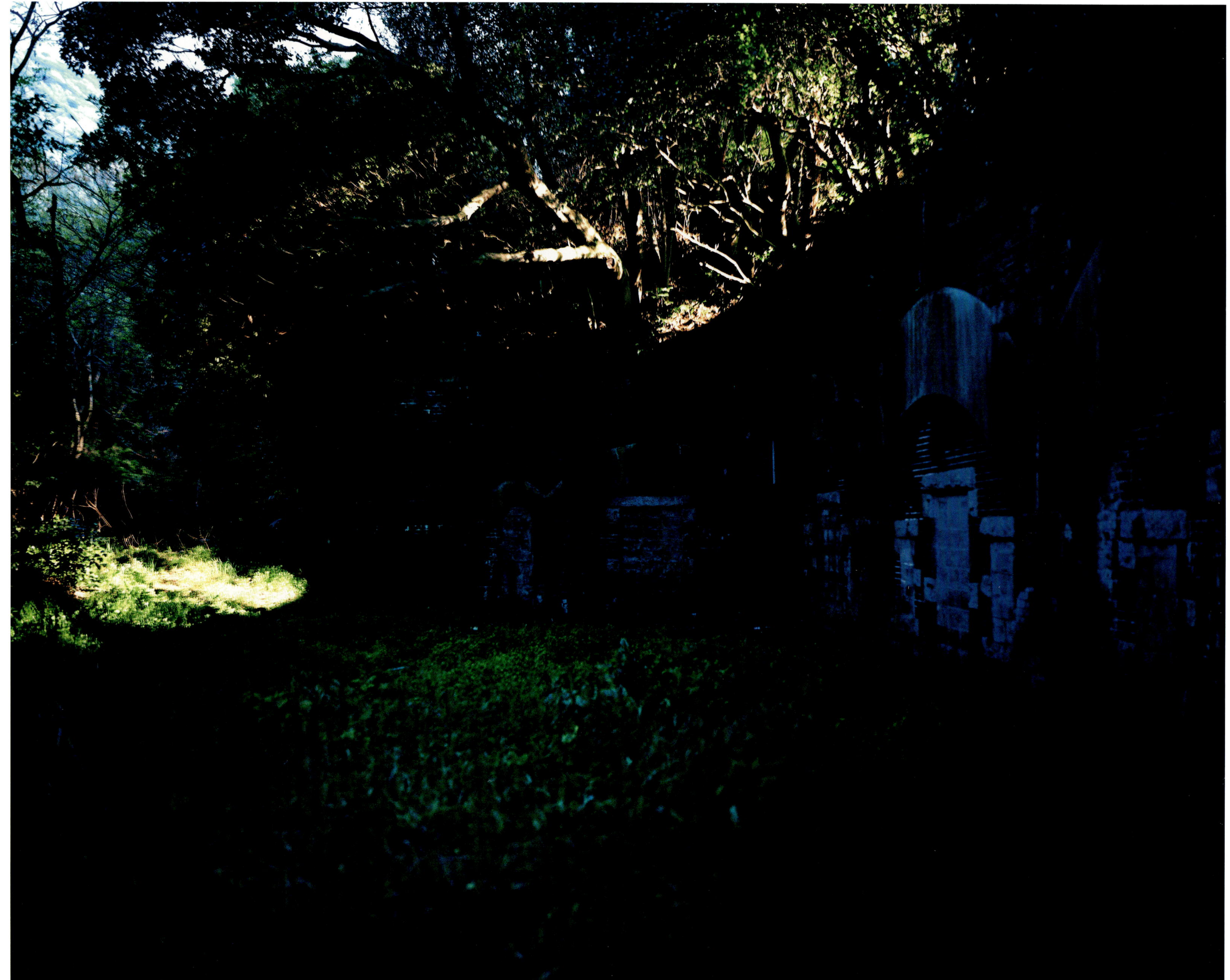

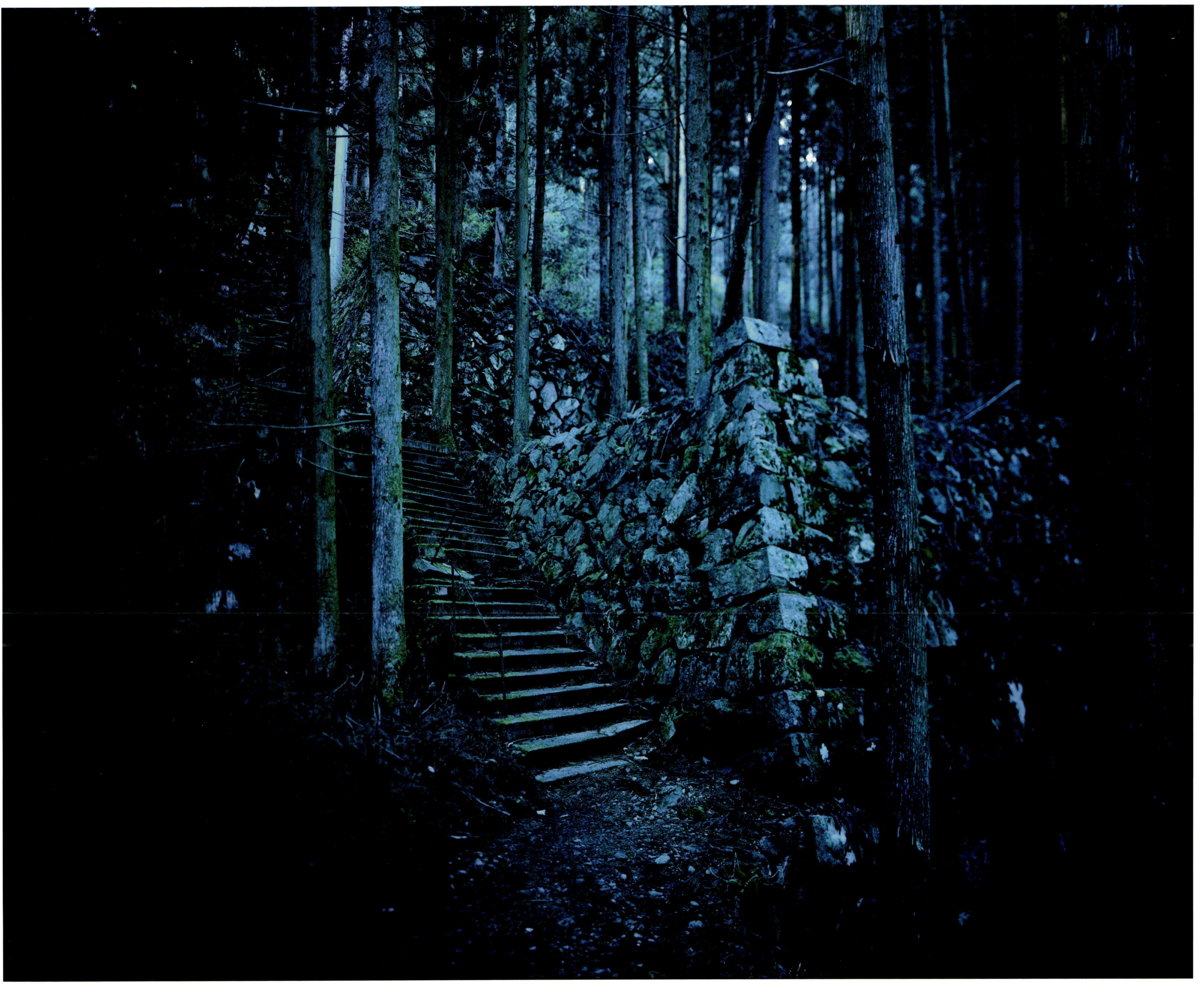

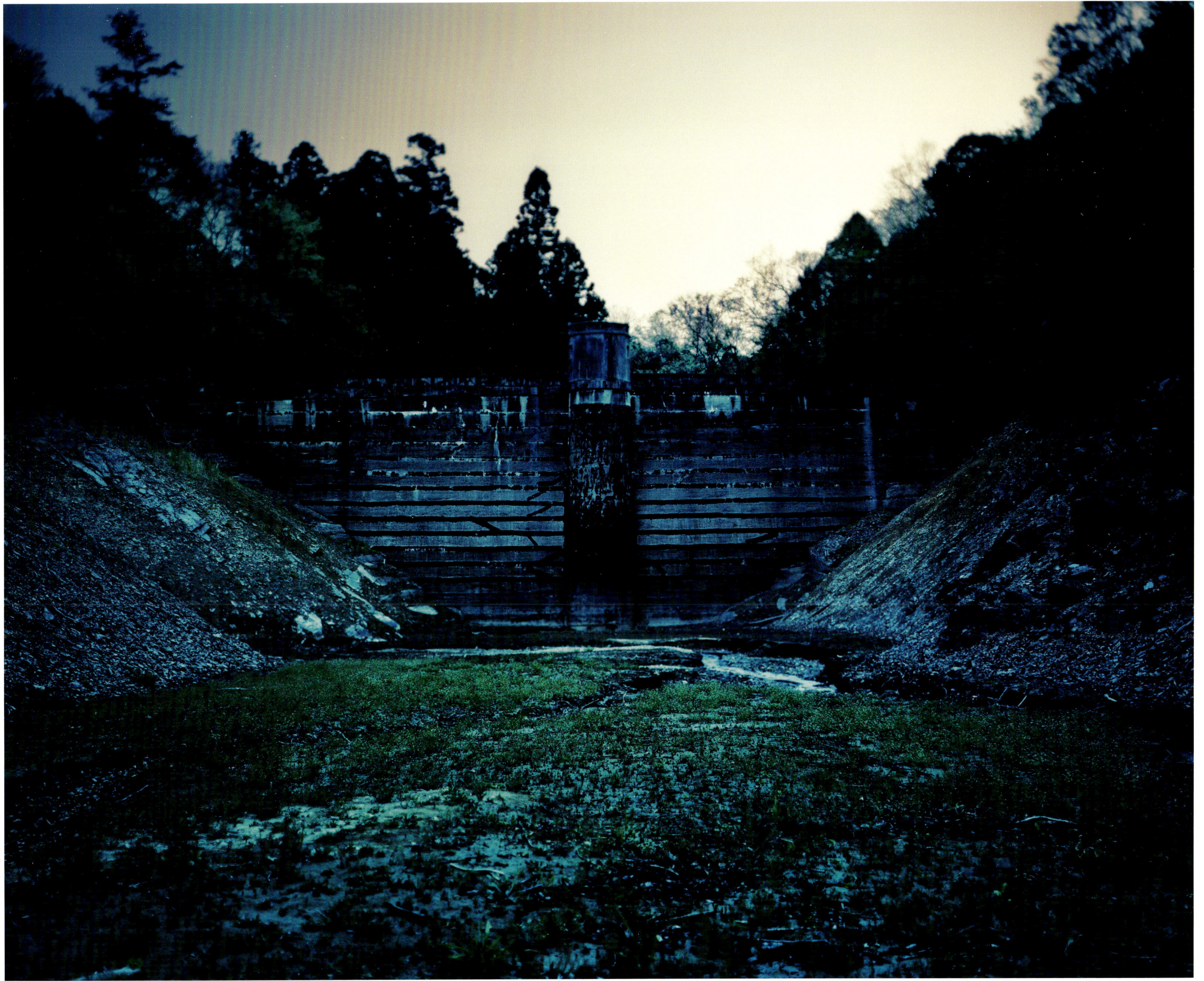

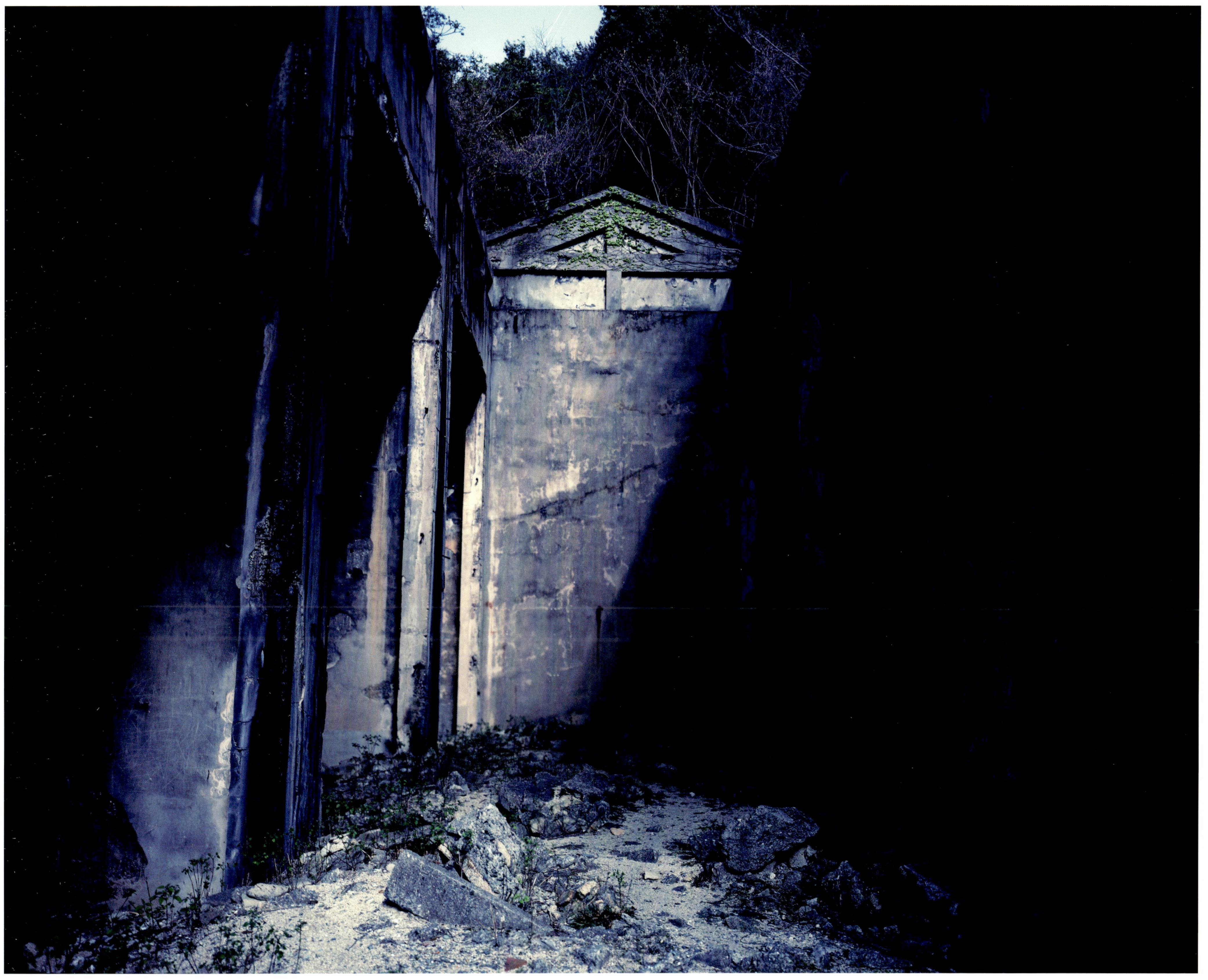

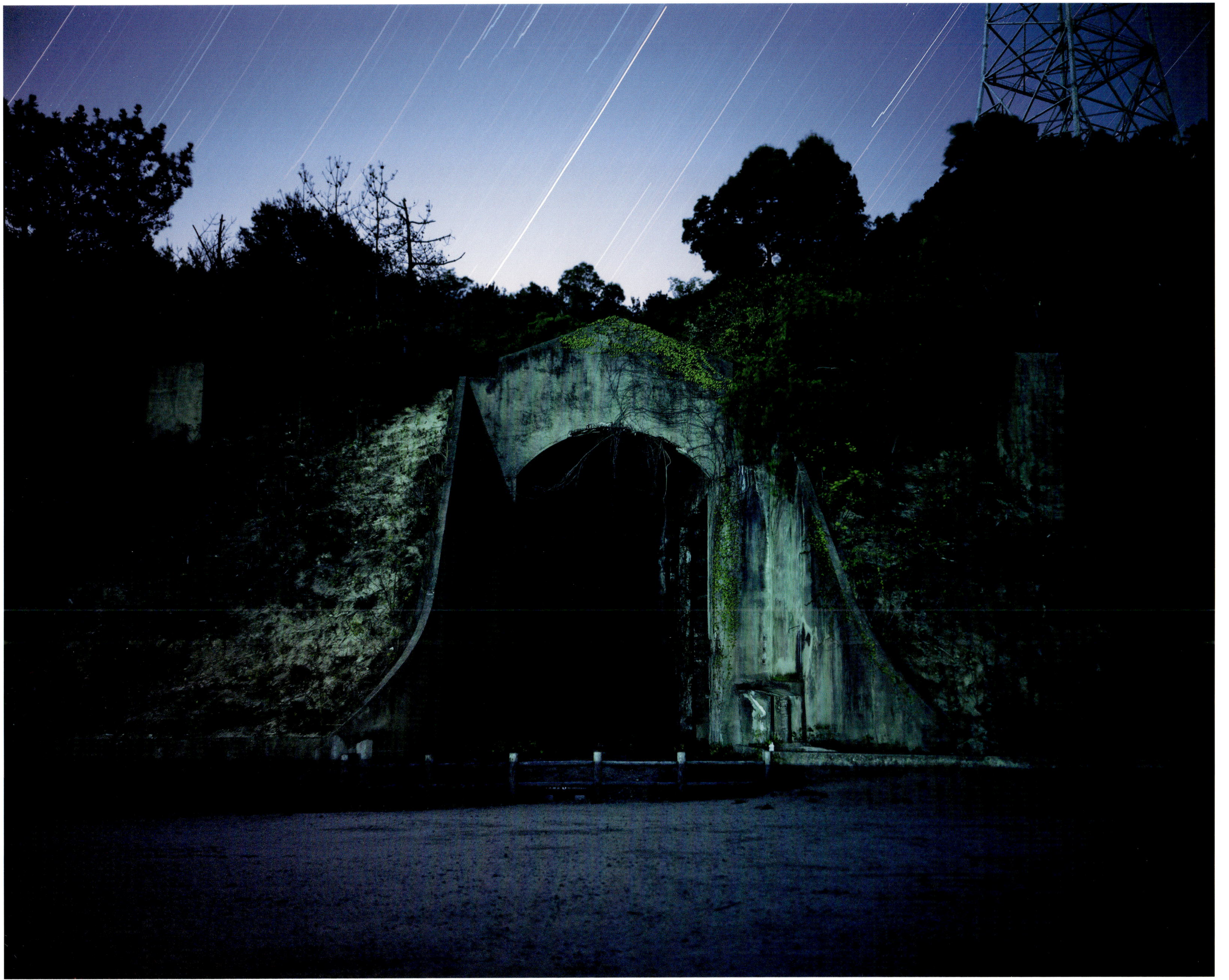

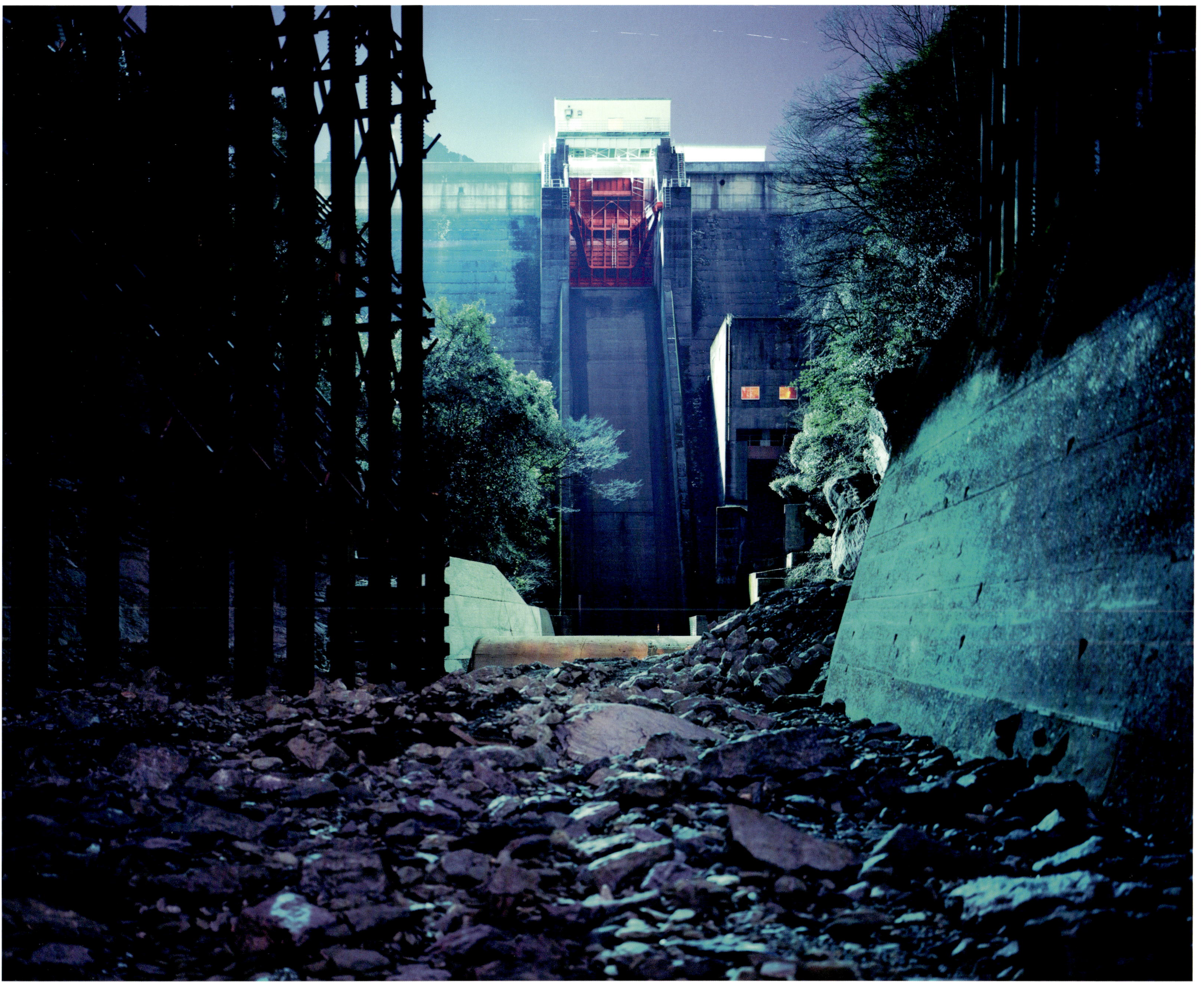

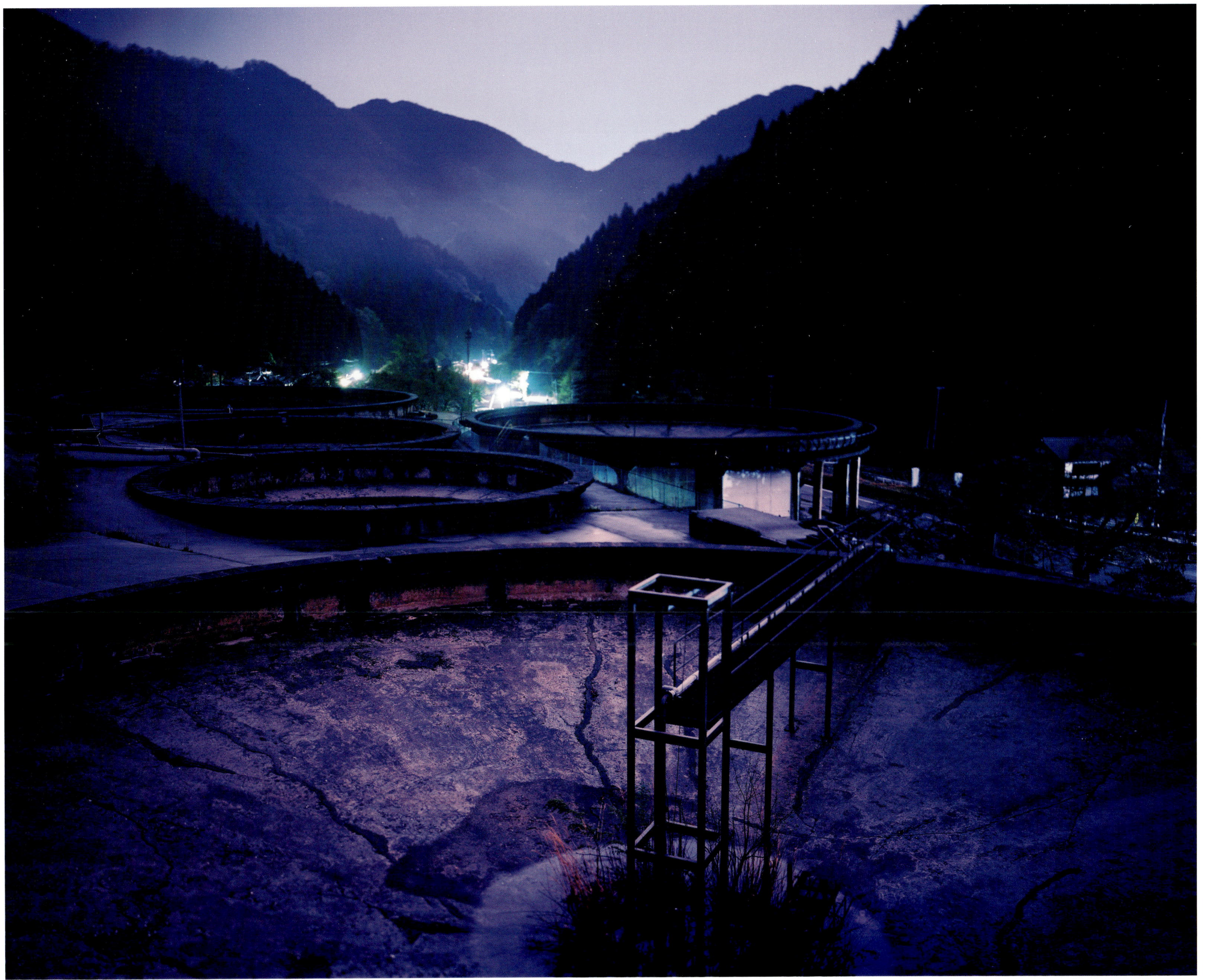

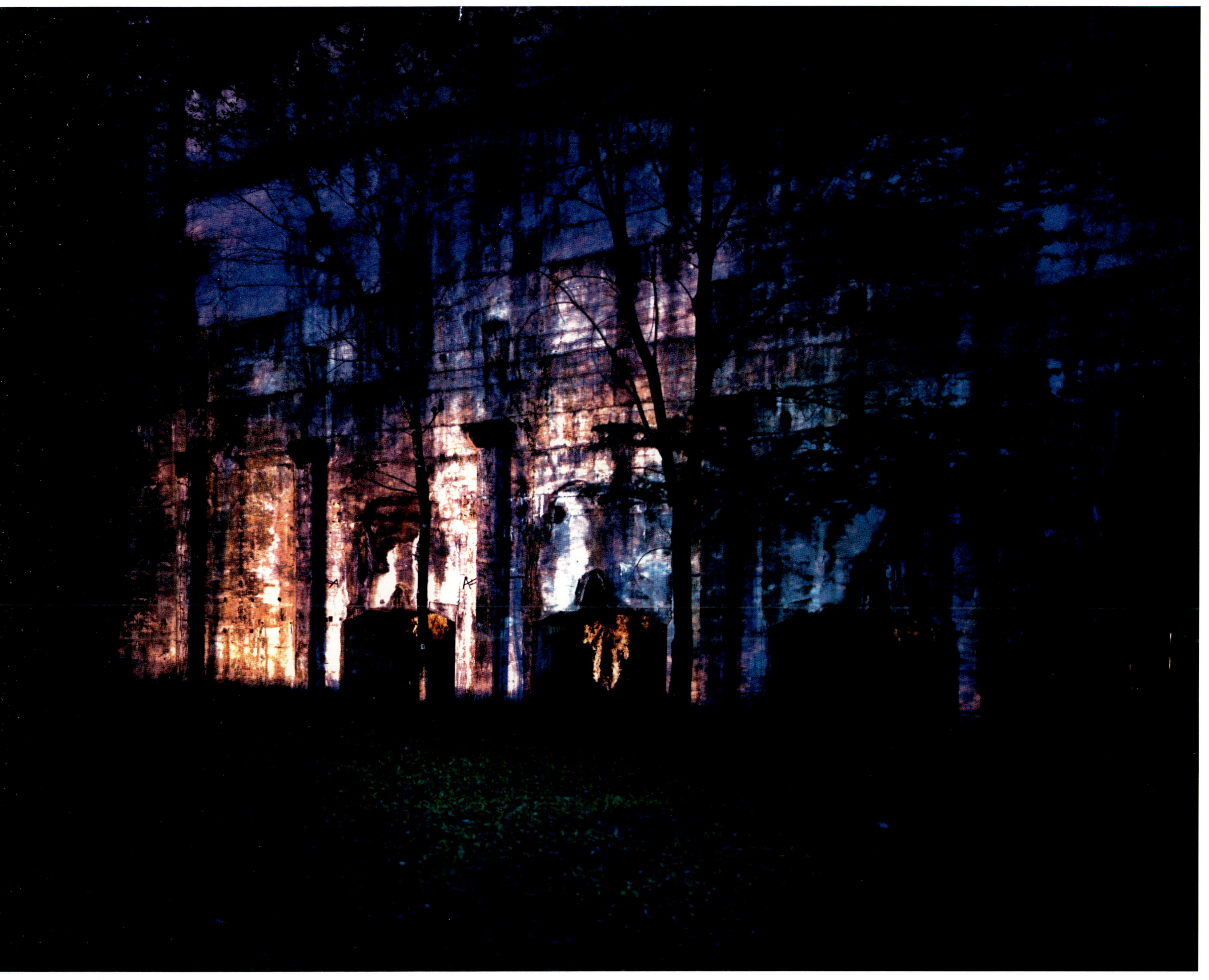

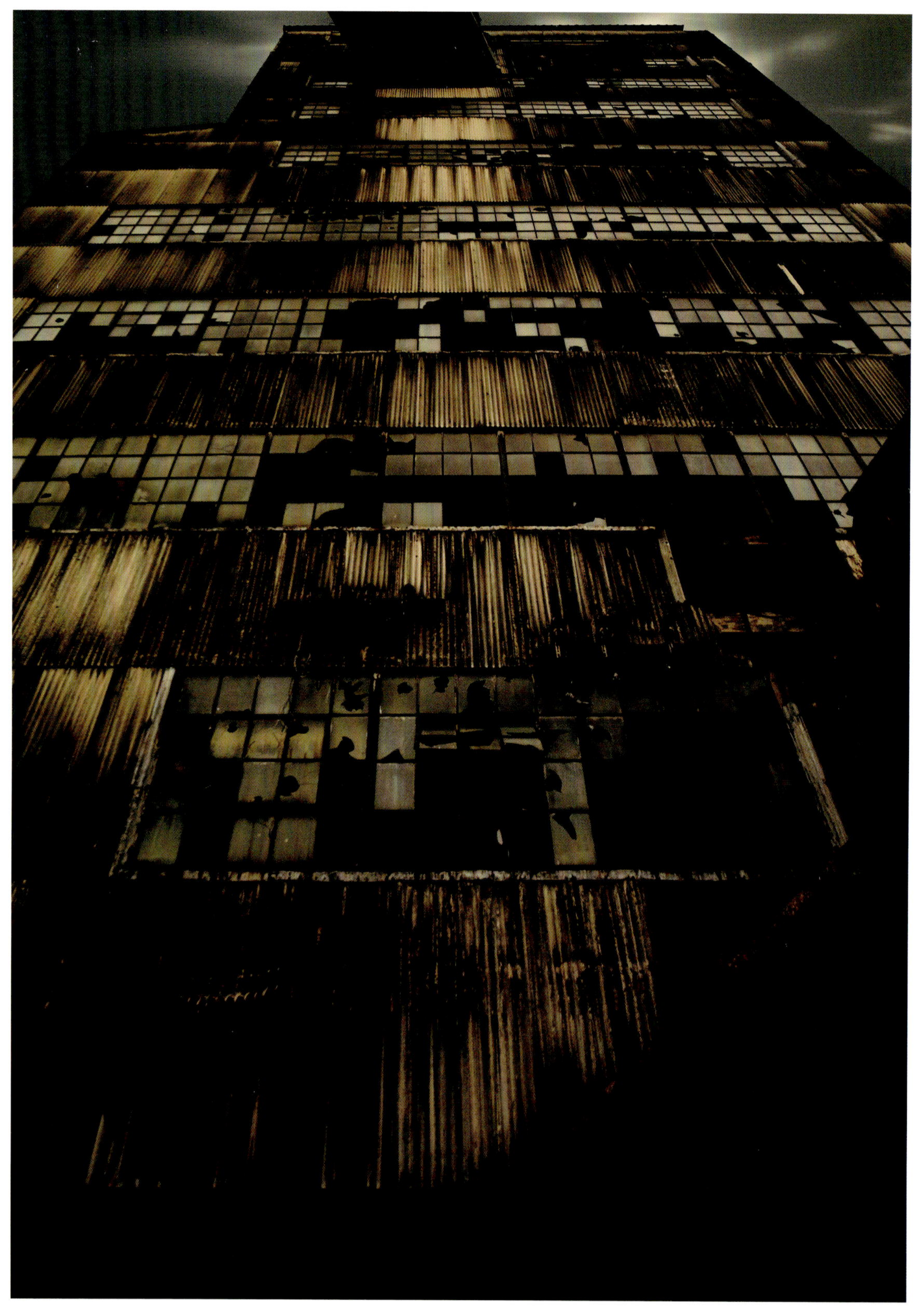

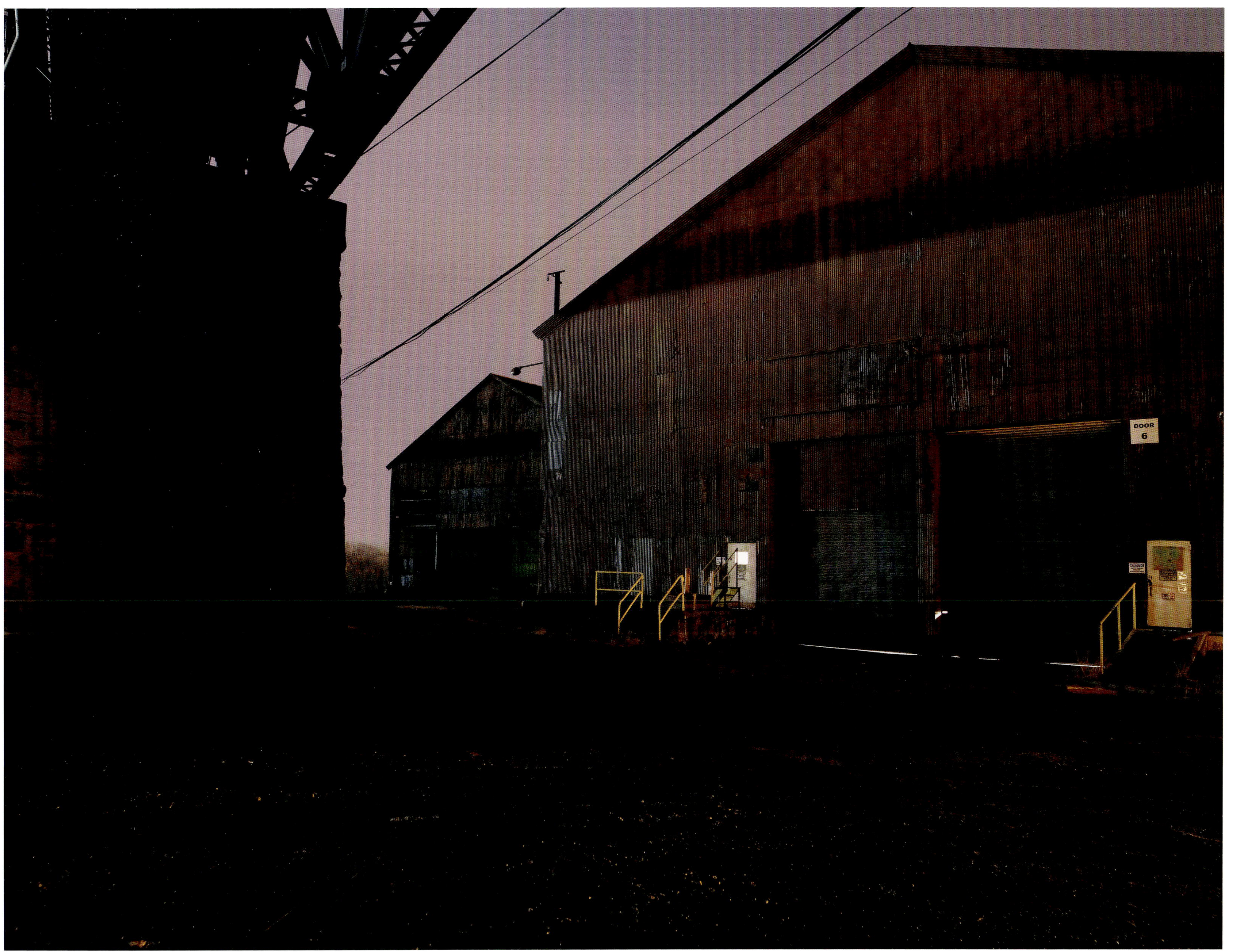
DOOR
6

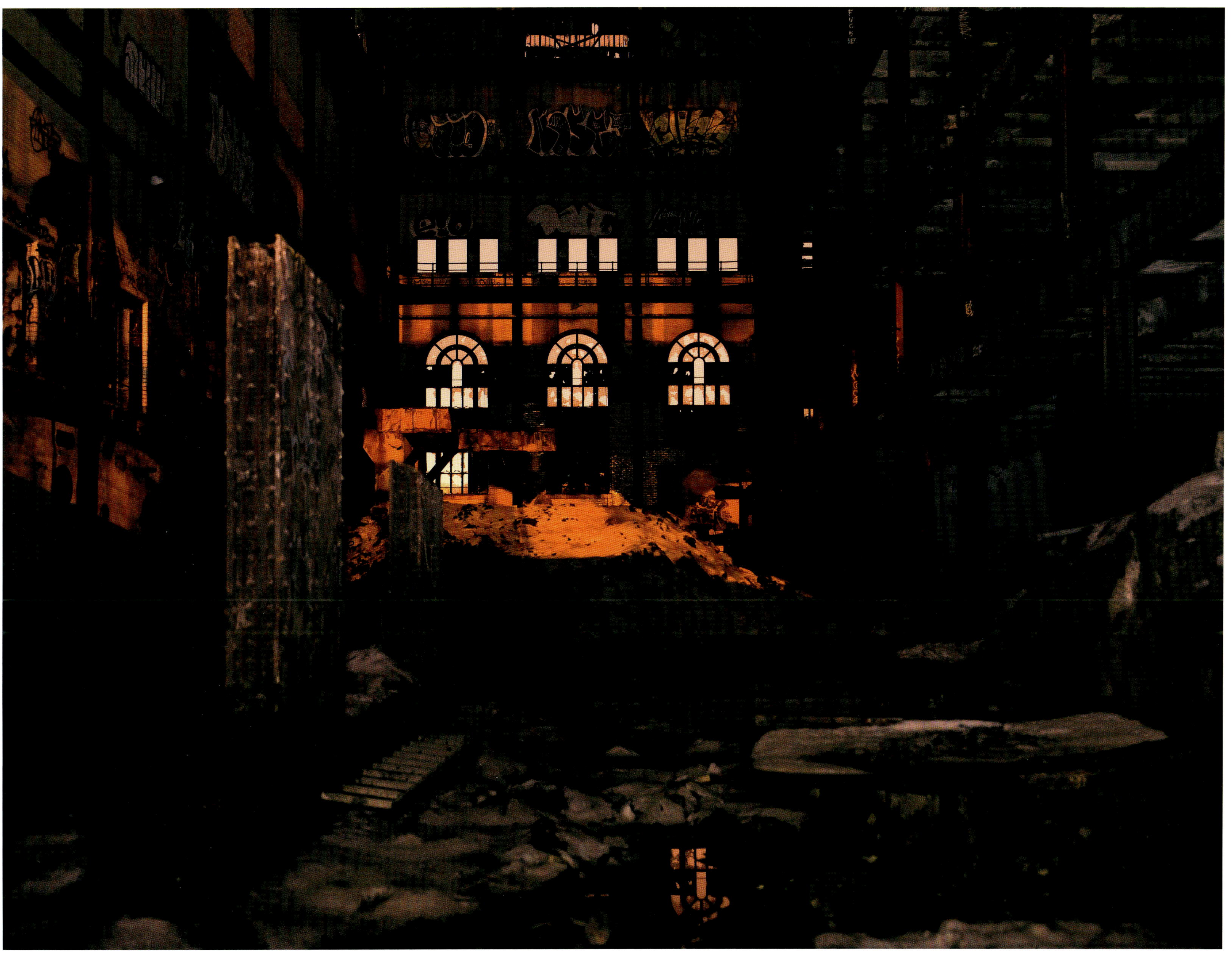

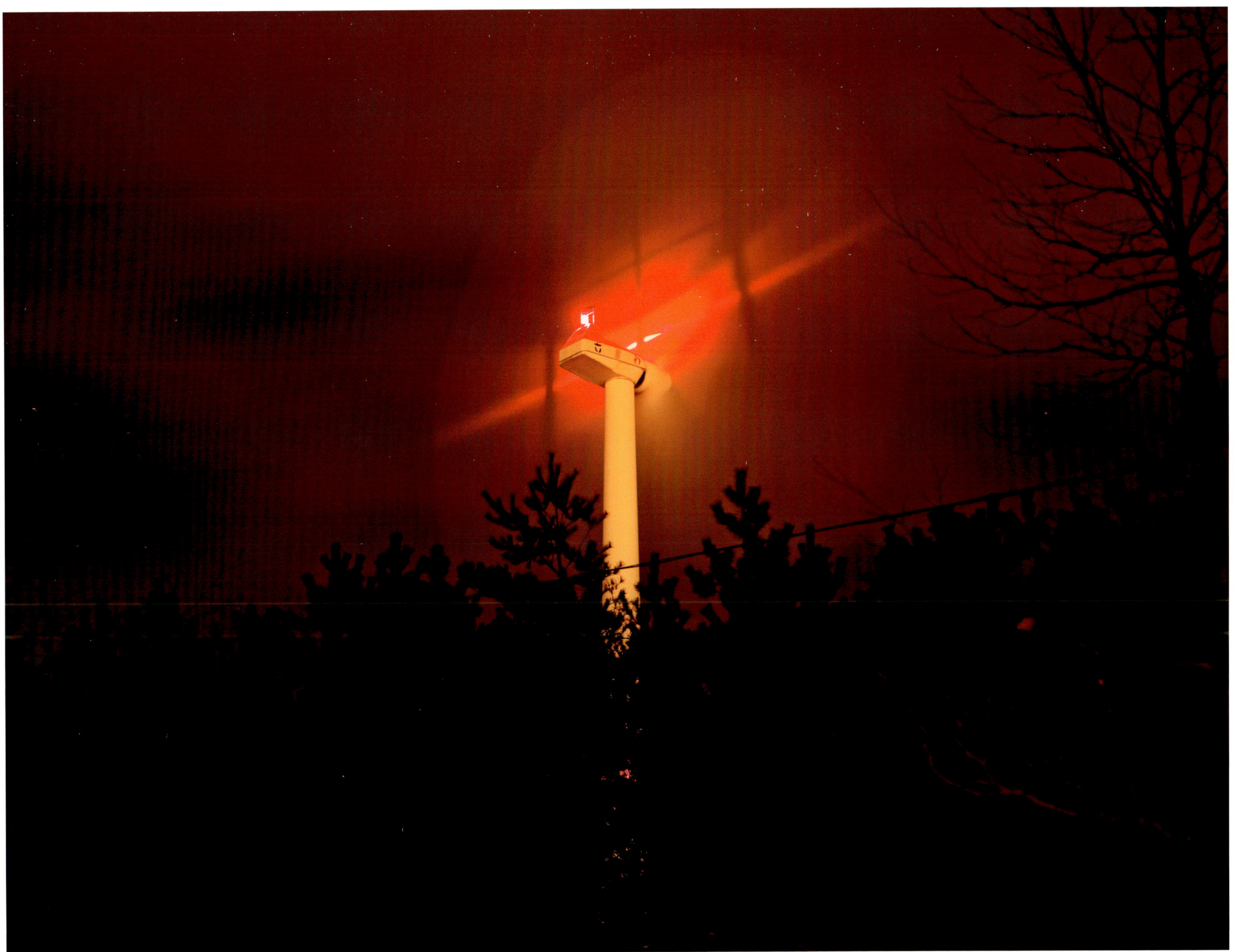

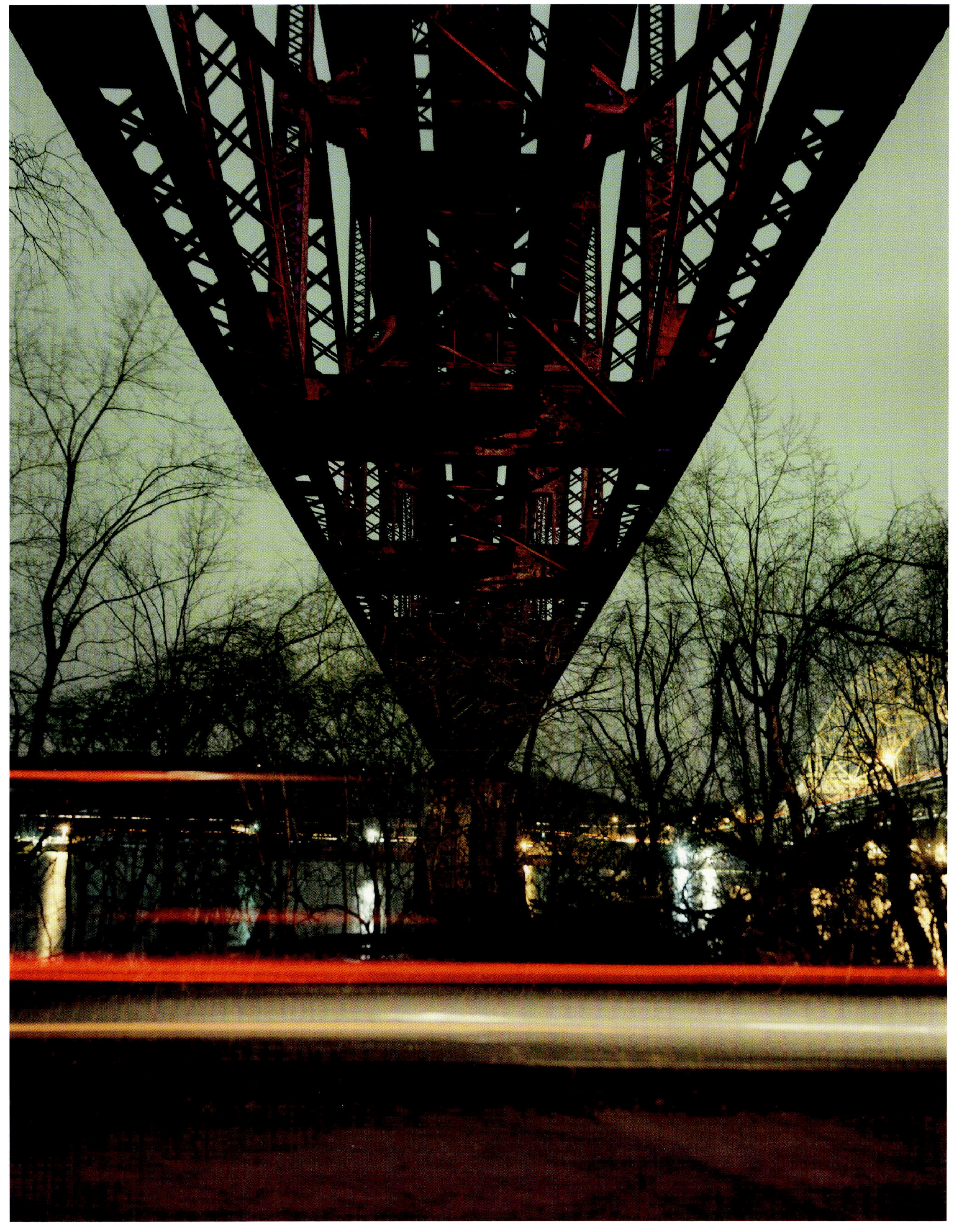

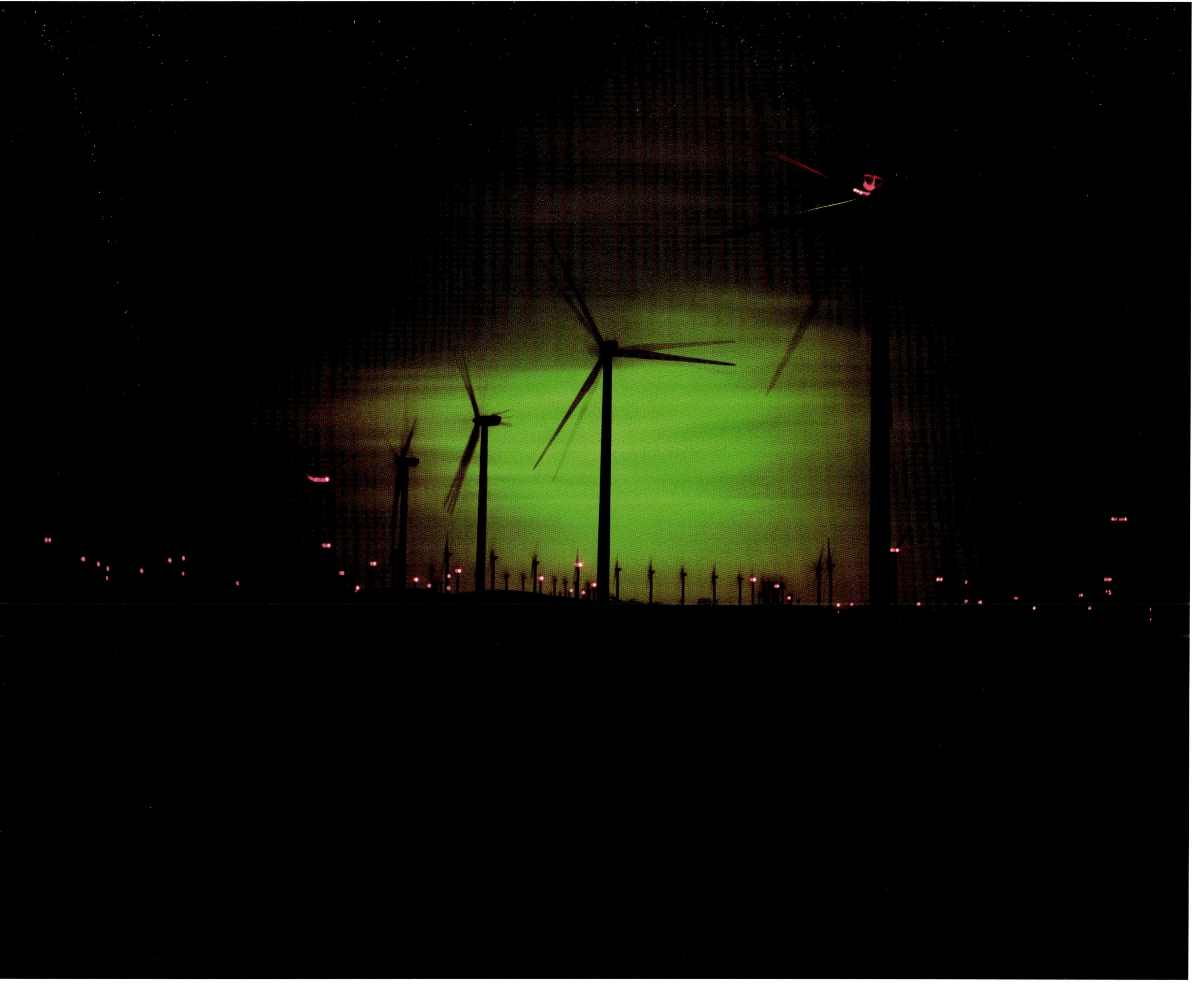

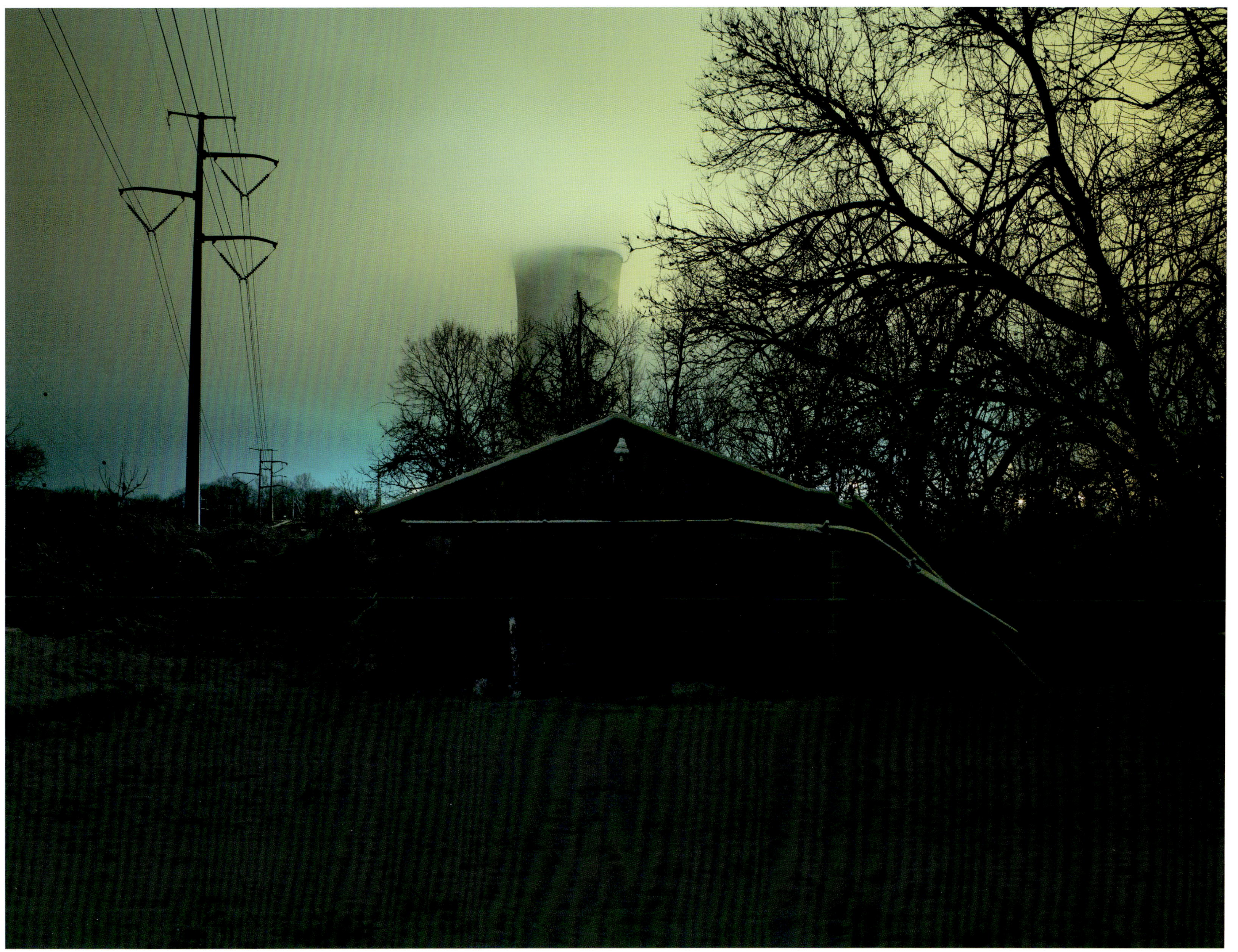

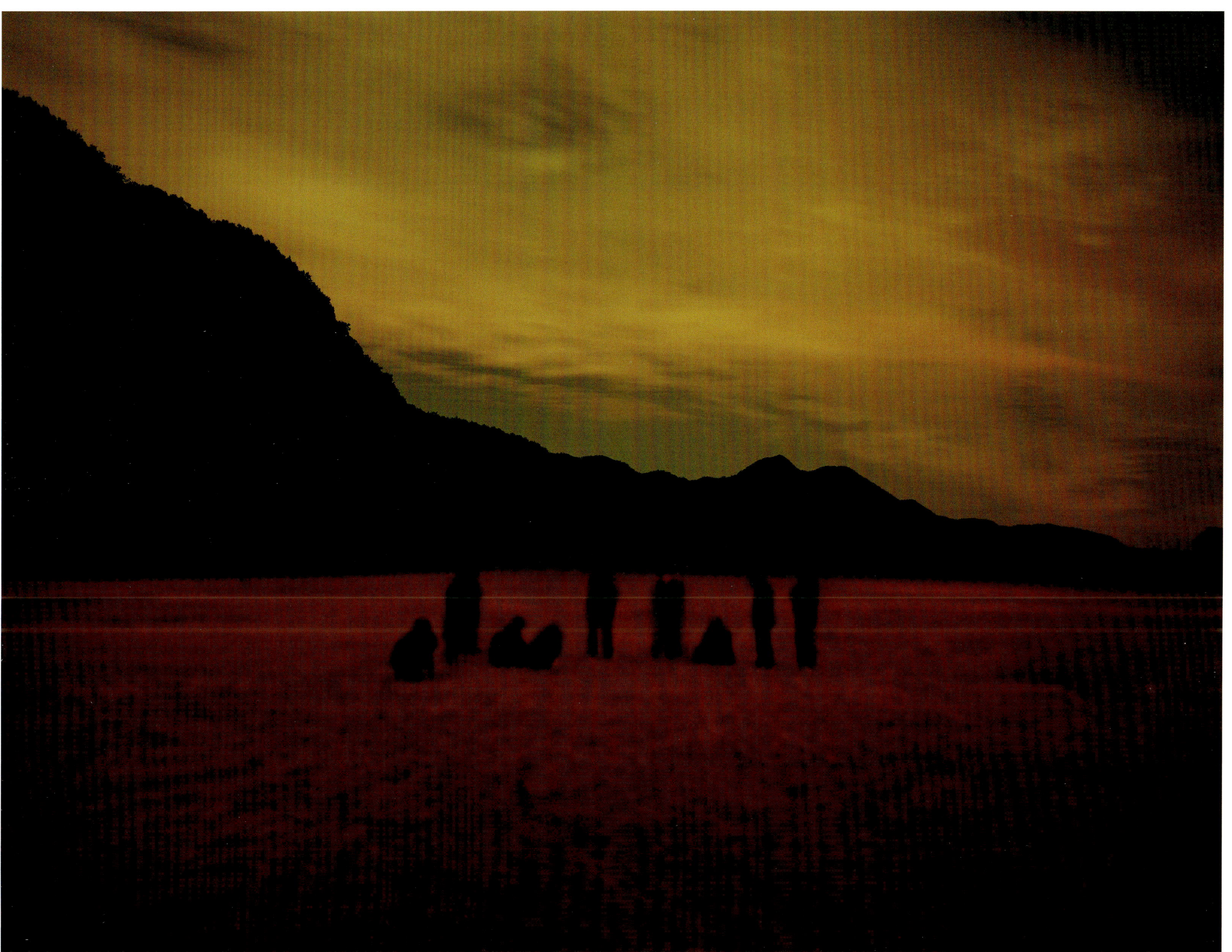

Suejin Shin

Letter to My Father: An Interview with Taewon Jang

What was your main interest for this project?

The photographs that are in this book are industrial landscapes that I started working on from 2007 until 2013. When I first began this project, I went around looking for ongoing or suspended large-scale construction sites to photograph in Korea, Japan, and the United States, but gradually expanded my area of interest to trace the process of changes that a city underwent vis-à-vis the transformation of the industrial infrastructure. I wanted to show, visually, the inherent power, which is not necessarily tangible, for example, like the economy or politics, yet one that exerts a great influence on human life.

Since the project took seven years, your photographs must express diverse viewpoints depending on when you took them. What are the changes you experienced in terms of your thought process or approach to your subject matter?

In the beginning, I concentrated on the specific topography or the architecture, or perhaps a structure, or construction equipment, thinking that these elements could reveal the strange tension I felt at the site where the construction was going on or the former construction sites that were abandoned for reasons that are unknown to me. Consequently, I found myself concentrating on the outer appearance of these complex scenes and producing many images that I had distilled visually. But then as I continued working on this project for a long time, I came to realize that what I saw was only a very small part of a larger picture. From the standpoint of an Industrial Revolution, seven years is not by any means a long period, but the places I photographed have changed beyond recognition or have even vanished from the map. As I experienced such phenomena, my interest naturally shifted to the city itself.

Do you mean you began to focus on how the industrial landscape transformed the city?

Yes. At first, I was in search of the landscape itself, but later on I began to look for cities that showed specific changes that took place as a result of industrialization. Hence, some of the photographs in this book show cities that were developed two hundred years ago and have a historical significance or places that started out as crucial industrial cities during the First Industrial Revolution but that now serve a different purpose, or some other cities that were a habitat for countless people, but have fallen into ruin in the present day. Just as urbanization took place with the advent of the Industrial Revolution, the changes taking place in the industrial structure, even at this moment, are continually transforming the characteristics of the city where we live. Thus, my photographs serve a role in recording these changes that are still ongoing.

Could you distinguish the differences in the topography and industry of the United States, Korea, and Japan?

Perhaps it is because America is such vast country, it's still common to see the birth of a "new" city with the construction of a factory and where the factory is no longer in operation, reconstruction does not take place at the same site but at a different place. In fact, some dilapidated factories are abandoned and new factories with the newest technology are built right next to them. That's why it's possible to investigate the traces of time at the same place, which is unimaginable in a small country like Korea. One can see constructions taking place wherever you go in Korea, the country where I was born. In Korea, demolition and rebuilding at the same site is such a common practice, it is quite rare that one can actually trace the past history of the place. In contrast, the Japanese have done a great job of documenting even an abandoned place, if it has historical significance, not to mention how well they have preserved and maintained the site.

A photograph has a tendency to show the present. However, your work is about probing into the history of the transformation of an industrial infrastructure. How did that become possible?

As I continued working on my project, it dawned on me that my photographs tended more toward the documentary. Although an image can be very deceptive in a digital age, it still is the most credible medium. In other words, the intrinsic capability of the medium, which can induce people to believe that it is real, is still very much intact. But even in a straightforward documentary photograph, a picture shows only a facet of reality. Even if one tried to show multiple facets of a situation with a series of pictures, an image is only an image and not the truth of reality. Hence, a photograph showing only the present time shows an interpretation of one single perspective that I captured.

I don't think that my photograph unveils only the exteriority of the present. If a place I photographed remains in ruins and one is prohibited from entering it, then that implies that this place served a very important function at some point in the past. The way I go about picking a place as a possible subject matter is similar to an approach taken for a documentary. First I come up with the list of important industries in accordance with each period, then I investigate the particular places that are relevant, devise a systematic plan, and then I embark on the shooting of the place.

Once I start taking pictures, I try my best to put aside any photographic preconception that I might have from the information or knowledge that I obtained prior to my actual shoot. In order to capture the most truthful visage of the site that I encounter in the middle of the night with my camera and without being bound by any rules, I bring my attention to a full focus. In this context, what I mean by "truthful" is of course from the perspective of my own viewpoint. At every site I photograph, there always exists something unique in the sounds and air, so to speak. It is perhaps impossible to convey this with what is seen with the eye only. One can unearth a whole range of beauty and undergo a moving experience, such as the thunderous effect of light illuminating a factory or a deadly silence of a city where no one lives anymore.

Before a vast and unfamiliar industrial landscape I always took my time, scrutinizing it in order to capture the most fantastic image. There are always numerous photographic options. Just as one would try his best to reveal a different kind of beauty of a model depending on the look or the aura of the person, I, too, explore many aspects of the scene to make the place stand out. And when I move on and shoot another place, I leave behind all my previous choices. Except for the fact that I shoot at night, I concentrate on what I am going to photograph without any preconceived ideas. Therefore, strictly speaking, my project is portraiture of the buildings or the scenes that are the result of industrialization. As I continued to work in that vein, different pictures of mine were shot according to each circumstance, and took on a look of human portraiture, faithfully revealing the traces of their lives.

Hence, you ended up presenting work that is different from a traditional documentary, which sets out to provide diverse viewpoints, or the likes of Bernd and Hilla Becher, whose work was about industrial landscape.

The works of the other photographers were not on my mind, thus, I did not harbor any intention of distancing myself from their works. I simply pursued my own interests. I did not predetermine the size of my subject matter or the angle from which I was going to photograph it. Of course, my photographs reveal the plasticity derived from the architectural function, like in the works of Bernd and Hilla Becher. I don't repeat a process just to demonstrate an objective point of view. Furthermore, I don't like to present a specific city or architecture in a series, simply for the purpose of a three-dimensional view. In the photographs that are reproduced in this book, there are only a few instances where more than two pictures of the same place are shown. As I haven't set down any stipulations for myself as to how I should perceive an object, I knew that my approach to a project would be formed by way of a long and arduous journey. The only rule I might have had was that I would photograph at night.

It was, in conclusion, your unique attitude and perspective that helped define the meaning of your photographs. So then, let us talk about shooting at night. Why then, nighttime?

When I first started working on this project, many people told me that my photographs looked more like paintings. The color scheme was different because I photographed at night, but also because of the fantastical look that some have noted in my photographs. This is expected. I presume it is because long exposure shifts the color scheme dramatically. Human beings are not used to the nighttime. Since electricity was invented, we have spent more active hours at night, but it is an artificial light through which we view the world. The nights that are captured in my photographs are the images that cannot be experienced by the human eye. That is due to the nature of the camera, which collects light. Therefore, even if it is a familiar sight, the camera will reproduce it in a completely new way. Half of the places I've been to are devoid of any light whatsoever. When I'm photographing I can't even see the edge of my foot. As I wait patiently for the moon to provide a scene, I can feel the kind of beautiful things that were totally invisible to the eye slowly take shape. Even if my eyes can't make them out, I can sense them.

I like the night because the objects I photograph look much more pronounced. During the day, when I go scouting for places to photograph, things look frantic and unruly and not at all appealing. Also, I don't get the same feeling from them. Everything in my purview during the day receives an almost equal amount of light. In comparison, at night there is light only in the places where it is deemed important. At night, the object of my gaze exists solely of its own accord without any disturbance. The beauty that I am in search of is produced under such circumstances. To me, this is very important.

Factories that have been shut down are shown in my photographs, but even if they have been closed for a long time, they were in full operation a century or so ago. In daylight, one can only see the decay of the place. But at night, one can feel a kind of strength not too different from a brightly lit working factory in the present day. For example, the sand factory that I shot in Wyoming was side by side with a decrepit factory. The two buildings look dramatically different when you view them on site. A factory that is well lit is actively in operation while the former factory is pitifully neglected in the dark. But I can show both of them in a same ambience in my photograph. The capacity of the camera to process light makes such a vision possible. All the landscapes in this book are like that. If one were to visit the place during the day or to view it with a naked eye at night, one would glean the meaning and the value only of the present time. One would get just a glimpse of how the place functions. But such a difference vanishes in my photograph.

One can physically capture the moonlight much longer in a photograph. I can relate to how such a process allows you to focus not only on the present, but also to visualize the transformation in time.

I find your photographs quite startling in that they show unfamiliar sights that are essentially very beautiful. From this dialogue, I am discovering that that was made possible from the outlook you had toward your subject matter.

These landscapes look very ordinary during the day. Even if a structure is of an impressive scale, though, if it's seen from a far distance where one can have an overall view of the city, it's going to lack a dramatic light effect and thus will appear dull. Conversely, it is possible to have a selective view at night. One can zoom in from one's personal vantage point, be it a place where someone has decided to light it up, because it is still of value or a place that is in the dark, having been deprived of its functionality. As I was moving from one place to another for my shoot, I could make out how the light at present could one day be extinguished and be shifted to a new place to serve a different purpose. Somewhere a new light will be switched on, then off, then on again; this transformation is taking place at this very moment and I find that very moving.

In other words, you thought the technique of long exposure was appropriate for showing the colossal current of light being turned on and off in specific buildings then on again, somewhere else. But how is it possible to work with an 8 × 10 large-format camera at night when you can't predict the result?

It is virtually impossible to foretell the results. Yet, it would be the same even if the place had light. I work in places where I can't make out the details; I therefore rely on the silhouette. I consider factors like the size of the moon, the whereabouts of the clouds and how high up they are, and the proximity of the city light to determine the exposure time. Color, in particular, is absolutely impossible to gauge. Notwithstanding these factors, there is a reason why I insist on a large-format camera.

An 8 × 10 large-format camera allows me to slow down quite a bit. No matter how much I've checked out the place, and made sketches during the day, I still have to walk around the surroundings, double-check the area, feel it out, so to speak, and to decide on the spot where to place the camera when I am photographing at night.

Whereas it's possible during the day to tell the colors apart or the subtle difference in the degree of light, at night, it isn't so; therefore, it takes a long time for me to set the focus or adjust the sharpness by searching for the boundary of the sky and the silhouette. I actually enjoy this meticulous process.

But that doesn't mean that I shoot only with film. If I use a digital camera, it cuts down on my shooting time from four hours to four minutes. Too many failures while working with film have made me appreciate digital technology. Besides, it is becoming more and more difficult to get ahold of large-format film. As I worked on this project, using both a large-format and a digital camera, I felt the experience was perhaps similar to the unlit city I am photographing and a brightly illuminated city.

One can view your photographs as praise for the achievements of modern industry that has provided the basic tenets for contemporary life, rather than an ode to specific industrial structures of a certain time period.

It was very important to me in this project that I overcame the handicap of looking at the object solely from the present-day viewpoint. In the beginning, I often felt overwhelmed by some completely unfathomable force that was inherent in these enormous structures, but gradually I was able to acquire an eye that allowed me to see them in a different light. I began to view both the extravagant grandiosity and the decrepit desolateness as something beautiful that make up who we are in the present day.

Modernization, which was triggered by the First and Second Industrial Revolutions, provided humanity with astounding affluence through tangible industries like steel, oil, and textiles. As an artist, who has not undergone the aforementioned processes, in what ways do you think these past industries have affected our lives?

As I was working on this project, from time to time, I was reminded of my father who worked for the same company all his life. After graduating from college in the nineteen-sixties, he worked non-stop for forty years and now he's retired. In the beginning his company was a small Korean company, but like many other corporations in Korea, it grew into a large global conglomerate during the time he worked there. Like most fathers of that period, he lived a life in which work meant everything. I don't remember every having a meaningful conversation with my father or spending leisurely time with him during my adolescence. When I visited Korea to pursue this project, in order to be able to spend time with my father, I mustered up the courage to ask him to accompany me on my photography shoot and he gladly obliged. During the long ride in the car, my father, who was sitting in the passenger's seat, talked endlessly about his experiences at work as a young man. As I heard him talk about the countless challenges he encountered and how he had to work ferociously to overcome them, I felt a lump in my throat. What moved me the most was not the story he told but the sparkle in his eyes as he told them. The Industrial Revolution has brought about only partial successes. There is nothing that is perfect. Development takes places with the precept that it is the best possible thing in that given era, the evaluation of it can only vary in later times. However, without the strenuous efforts of those from that period, this affluent era that we are witness to could not have come about. My father, my father's father, or his father's father's father have all given their utmost in the manner that was asked of them during their respective eras. That is why when I see the remains of what their times have left for us, I feel deep respect for them.

A Third Post-Industrial Revolution, which is based on knowledge, is taking place in our present time. How does it differ from the industry in which machinery and architectural structures dominated?

When I am photographing at night with a large-format camera, it can take anywhere up to eight hours of exposure time to take a single picture. On average, it takes about two hours. While I am waiting with the shutter open, I have a myriad of thoughts crossing my mind. It is something that busy urbanites can't imagine doing. These days, everyone is in a rush. They are busy day and night, on the phone, checking their e-mail, searching for an incredible amount of information on the Internet. I am the same. But during the several hours I am in front of my camera, when my shoot is taking place, the things that are going on within the apps on my iPhone seem trivial. It's convenience, which I marvel at during the day, and which becomes all of a sudden unreal. The Internet and other technology that shares knowledge and information have provided us with dazzling convenience. But convenience, strictly speaking, is not a prerequisite for survival. However, what I behold before my very eyes has given us all the foundations of our lives that we now take for granted. It is that grandiose and overwhelming power that moves me to no end.

***The world is always paying more attention to something new.
But your work seems to stem from your respect for things that are not novel.***

I find myself boundlessly mesmerized by what I see before me when I am photographing at night. Of course, my assistants are wrapped up with their smartphone apps, even amidst these scenes. There is a moment when I am overcome by such beauty that it leaves me indescribably gratified. For centuries, artists and photographers have captured the industrial landscape in their art. Thus, humankind has been a witness to its own accomplishments, occasionally with astonishment, at times with terror, and sometimes with concern. I can't offer a full explanation as to why I am doing this project and will continue working on it. But I can say that my work is an homage to the beauty of an era that I was privileged to be a part of.

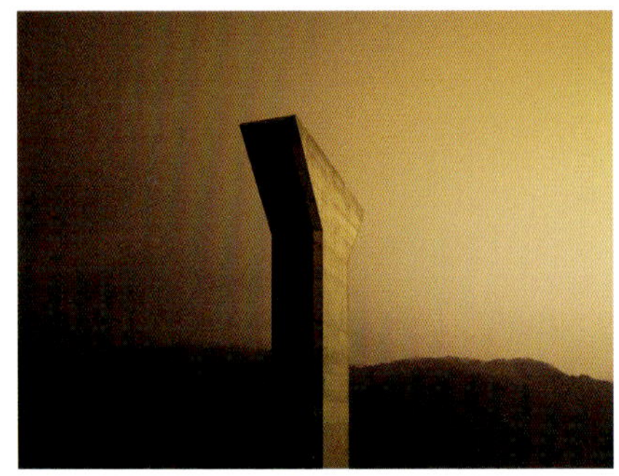

01
SG J #421, 2008
Digital c-print, 127 × 169 cm
Page 07

02
SG K #116, 2008
Digital c-print, 127 × 169 cm
Page 09

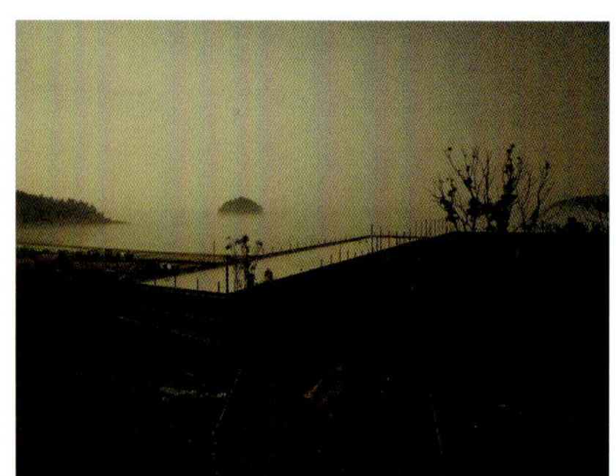

03
SG K #114, 2008
Digital c-print, 127 × 169 cm
Page 11

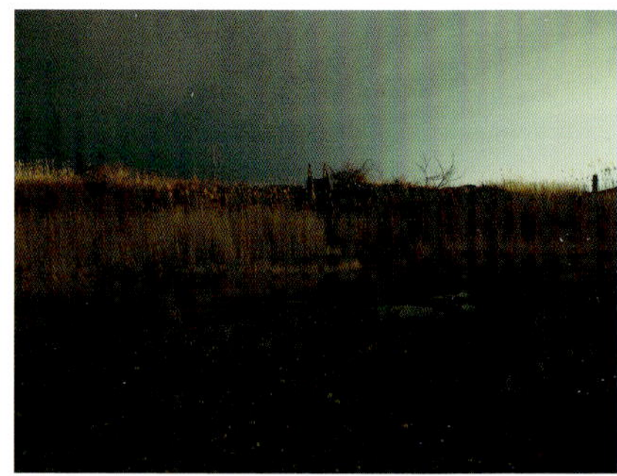

04
SG U #414, 2013
Inkjet print, 127 × 169 cm, 91.5 × 122 cm
Page 13

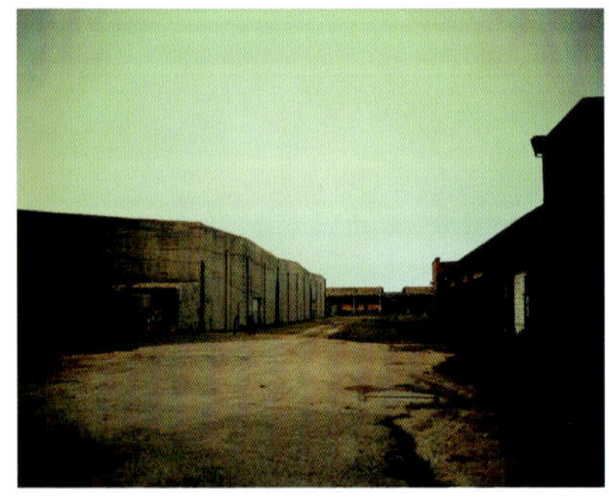

05
SG U #318, 2013
Inkjet print, 127 × 160 cm, 91.5 × 115 cm
Page 15

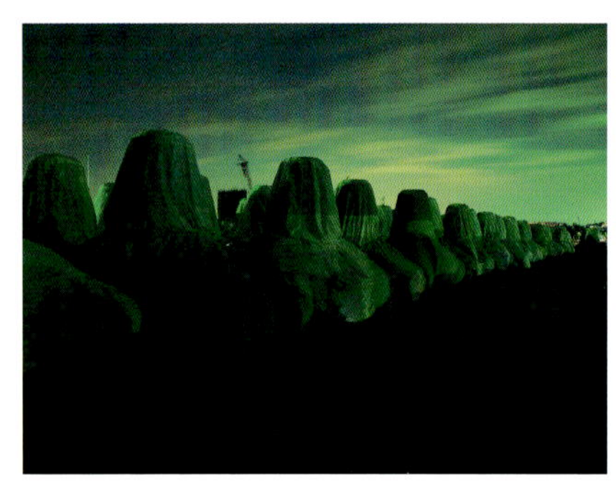

06
SG J #401, 2008
Digital c-print, 127 × 169 cm
Page 17

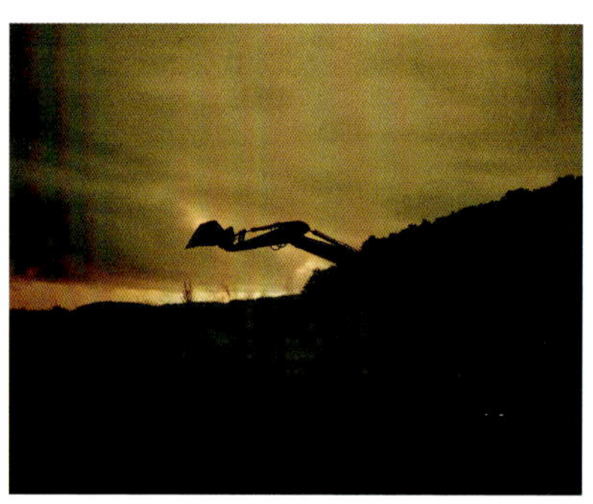

07
SG K #412, 2007
Digital c-print, 180 × 226 cm, 127 × 160 cm
Page 19

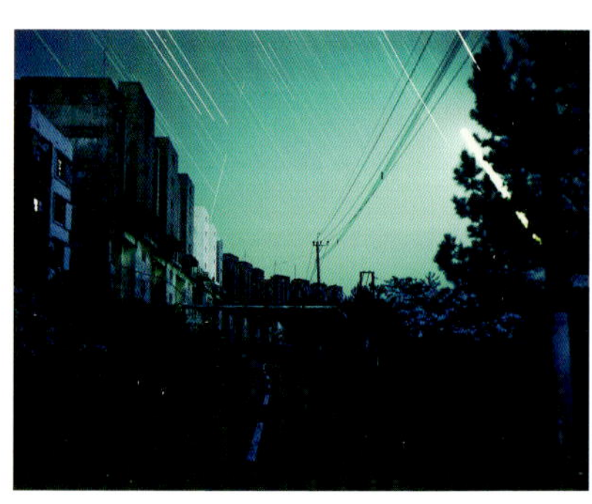

08
SG J #316, 2013
Inkjet print, 127 × 160 cm, 91.5 × 115 cm
Page 20

09
SG J #419, 2013
Inkjet print, 127 × 161 cm, 91.5 × 116 cm
Page 21

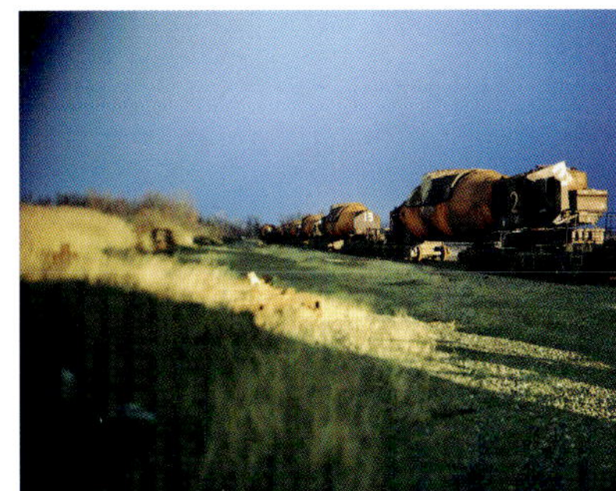

10
SG U #411, 2013
Inkjet print, 180 × 226 cm, 127 × 160 cm
Page 23

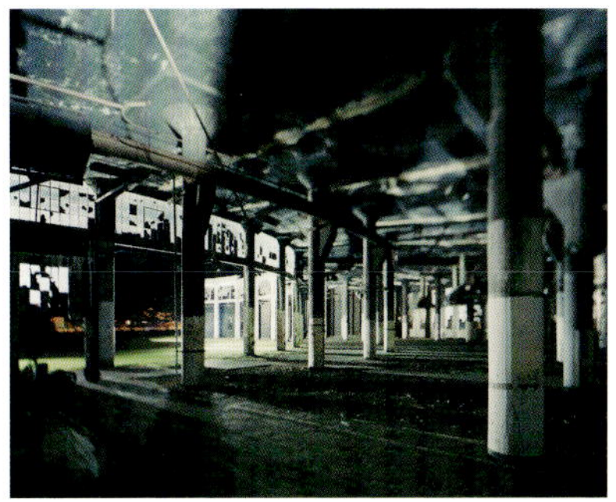

11
SG J #410, 2013
Inkjet print, 180 × 226 cm, 127 × 160 cm
Page 25

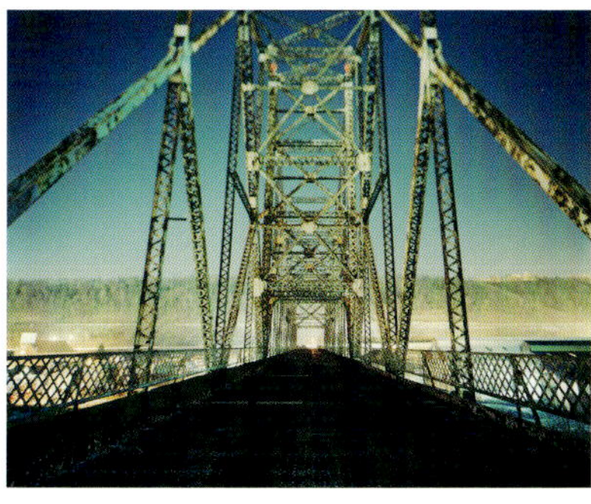

12
SG U #407, 2013
Inkjet print, 127 × 160 cm, 91.5 × 115 cm
Page 27

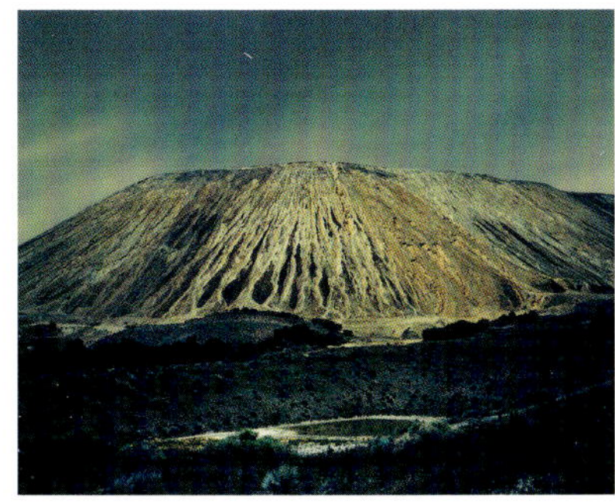

13
SG U #304, 2013
Inkjet print, 100 × 125.5 cm
Page 29

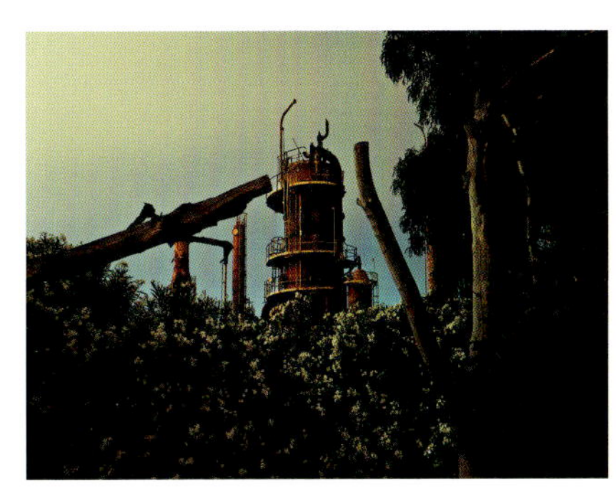

14
SG U #312, 2013
Inkjet print, 127 × 169 cm, 91.5 × 122 cm
Page 31

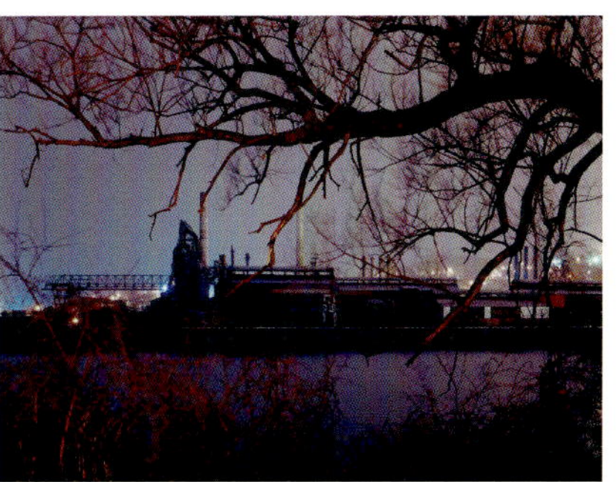

15
SG U #302, 2013
Inkjet print, 127 × 169 cm, 91.5 × 122 cm
Page 32

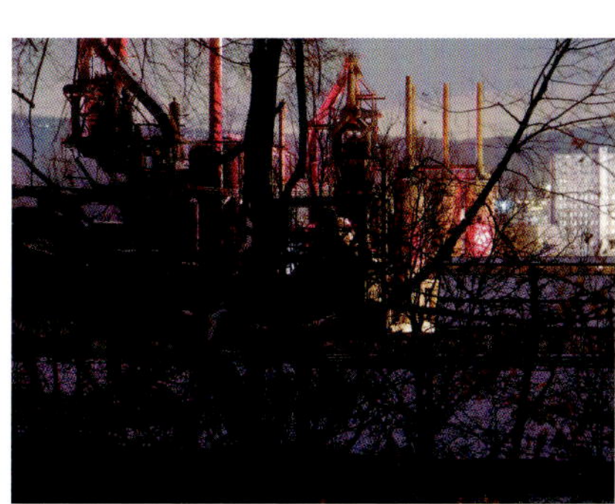

16
SG U #303, 2013
Inkjet print, 127 × 169 cm, 91.5 × 122 cm
Page 33

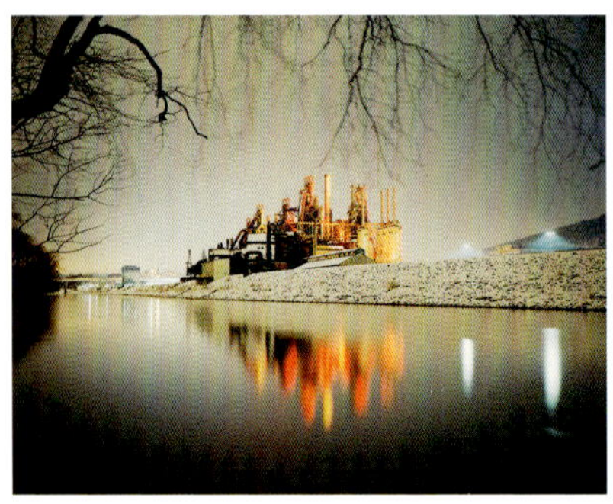

17
SG U #223, 2013
Inkjet print, 350 × 444.3 cm, 180 × 228.5, 127 × 161 cm
Page 37

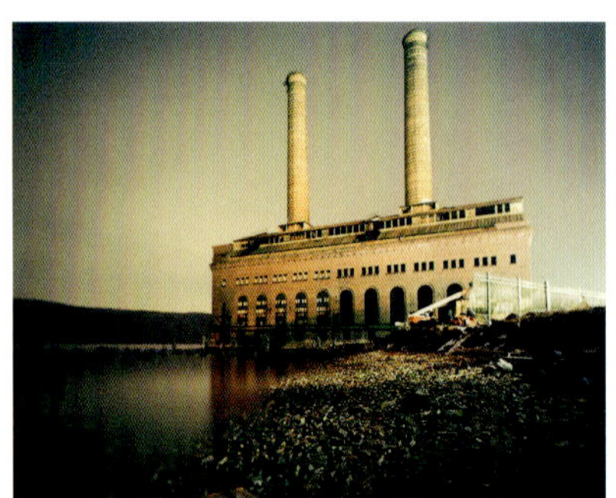

18
SG U #214, 2013
Inkjet print, 180 × 227 cm, 127 × 160 cm
Page 39

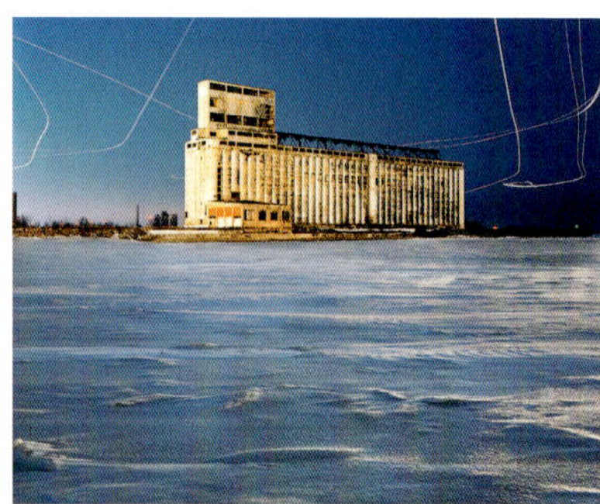

19
SG U #216, 2013
Inkjet print, 180 × 227 cm, 127 × 160 cm
Page 41

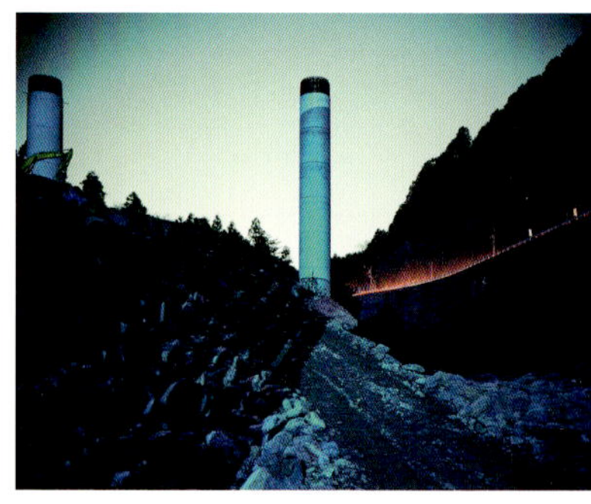

20
SG J #201, 2008
Inkjet print, 127 × 160 cm, 91.5 × 115 cm
Page 43

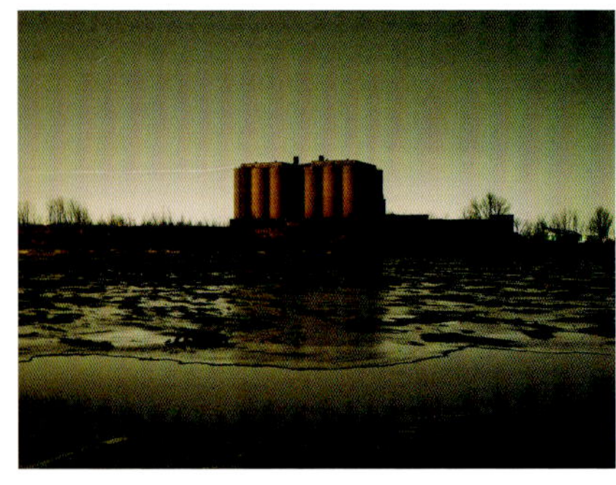

21
SG U #217, 2013
Inkjet print, 127 × 169 cm, 91.5 × 122 cm
Page 44

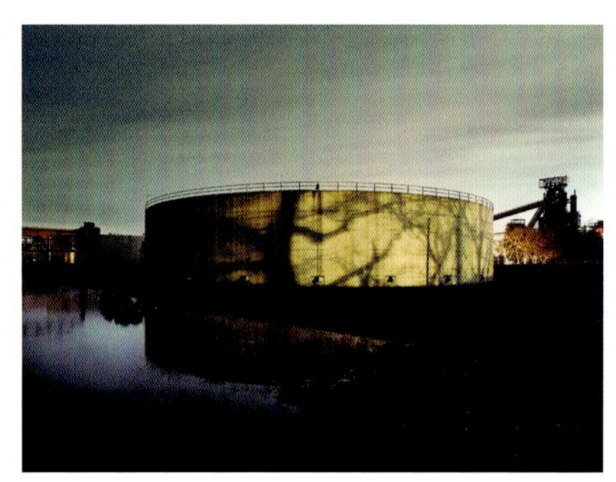

22
SG U #213, 2013
Inkjet print, 127 × 169 cm, 91.5 × 122 cm
Page 45

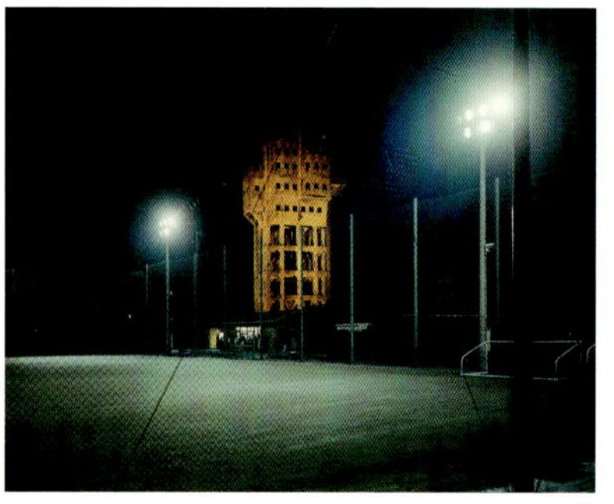

23
SG J #203, 2013
Inkjet print, 127 × 160 cm, 91.5 × 115 cm
Page 47

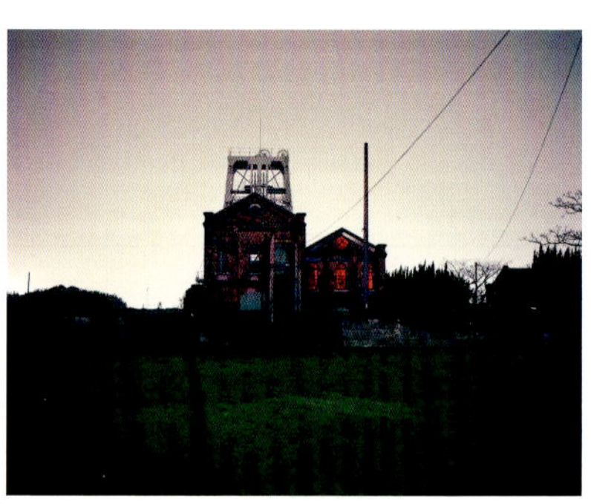

24
SG J #207, 2013
Inkjet print, 180 × 226 cm, 127 × 160 cm
Page 49

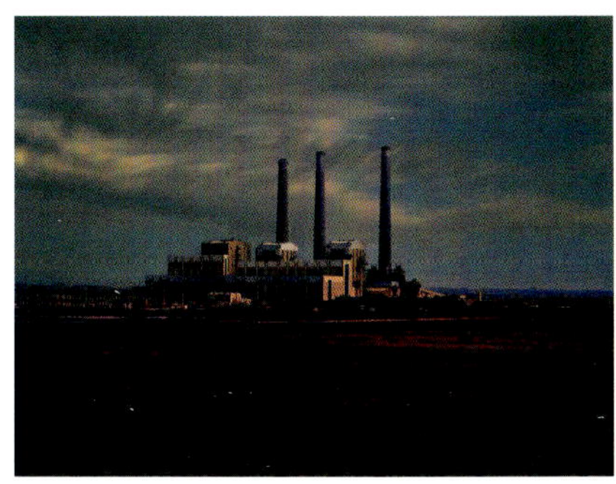

25
SG U #210, 2013
Inkjet print, 127 × 169 cm, 91.5 × 122 cm
Page 51

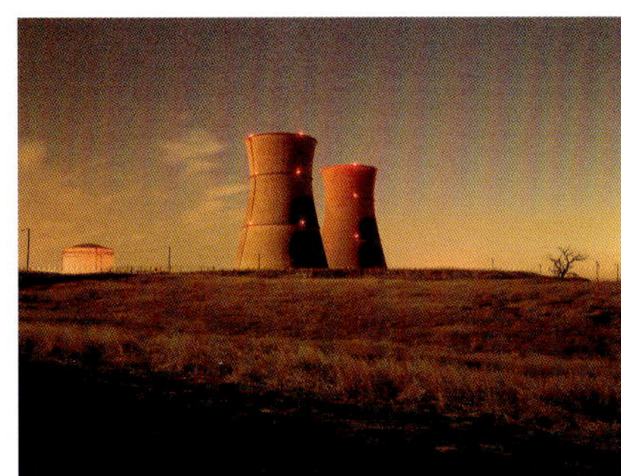

26
SG U #205, 2013
Inkjet print, 127 × 169 cm, 91.5 × 122 cm
Page 53

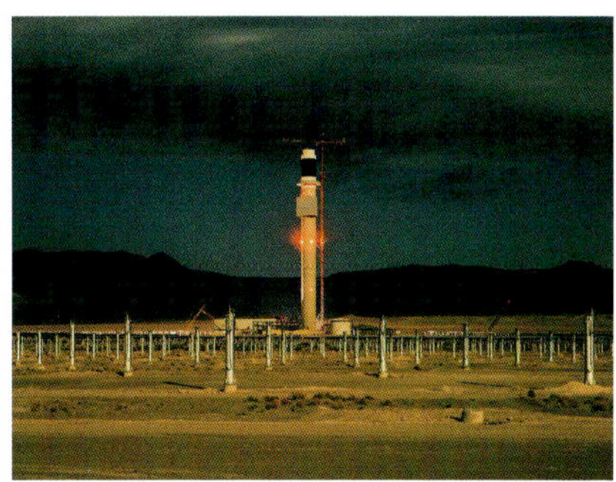

27
SG U #221, 2013
Inkjet print, 127 × 169 cm, 91.5 × 122 cm
Page 55

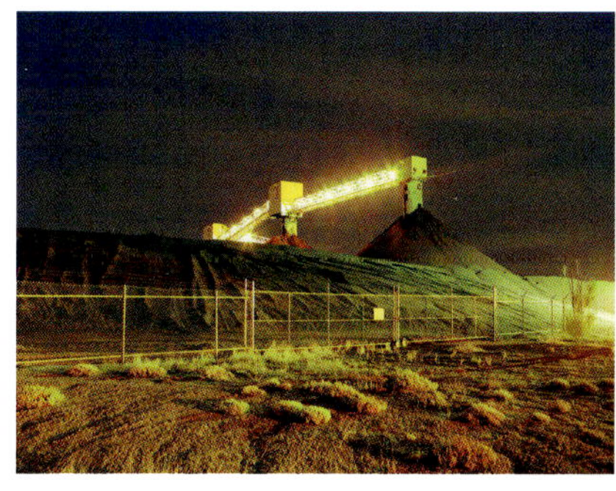

28
SG U #222, 2013
Inkjet print, 127 × 169 cm, 91.5 × 122 cm
Page 57

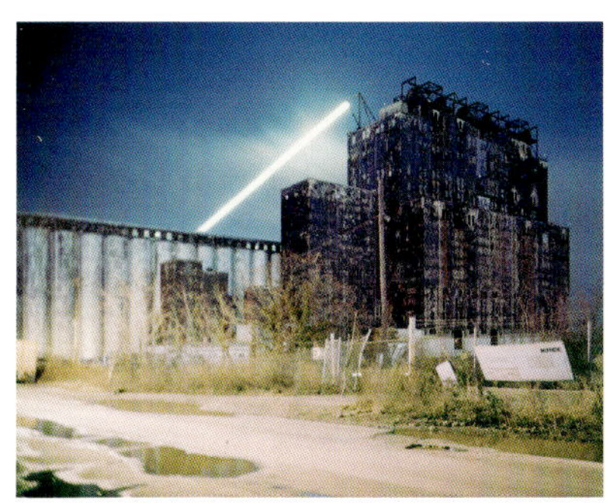

29
SG U #220, 2013
Inkjet print, 180 × 227 cm, 127 × 160 cm
Page 59

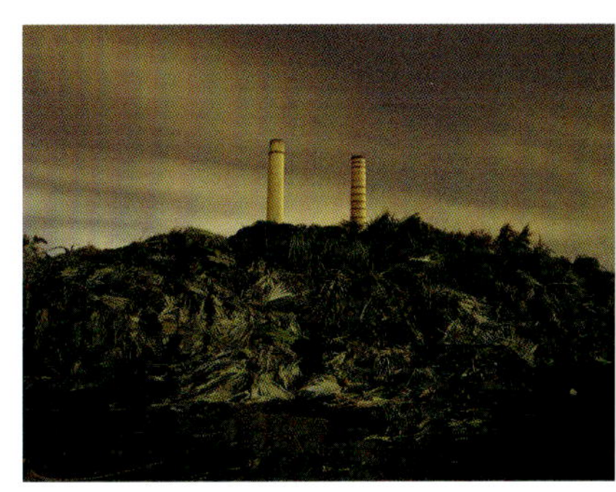

30
SG U #224, 2013
Inkjet print, 127 × 169 cm, 91.5 × 122 cm
Page 60

31
SG J #228, 2008
Inkjet print, 127 × 169 cm, 91.5 × 122 cm
Page 61

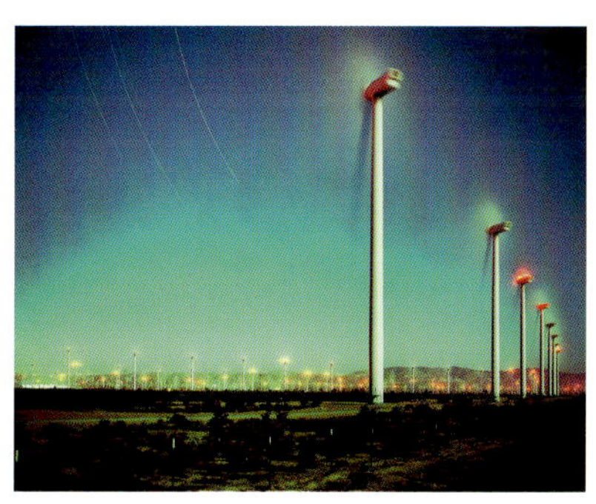

32
SG U #108, 2013
Inkjet print, 180 × 227.5 cm, 127 × 160 cm
Page 63

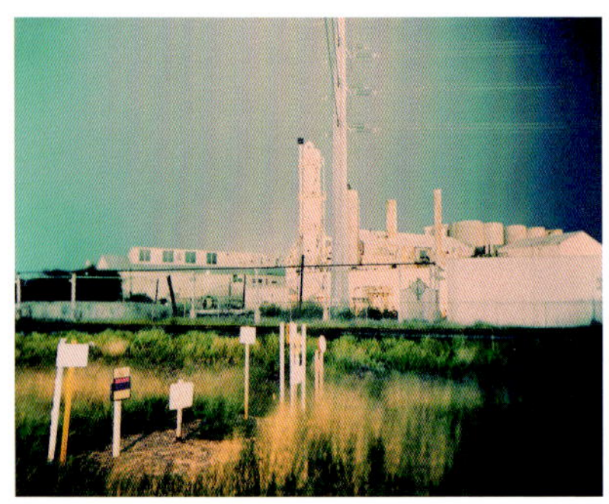

33
SG U #211, 2013
Inkjet print, 180 × 227 cm, 127 × 160 cm
Page 65

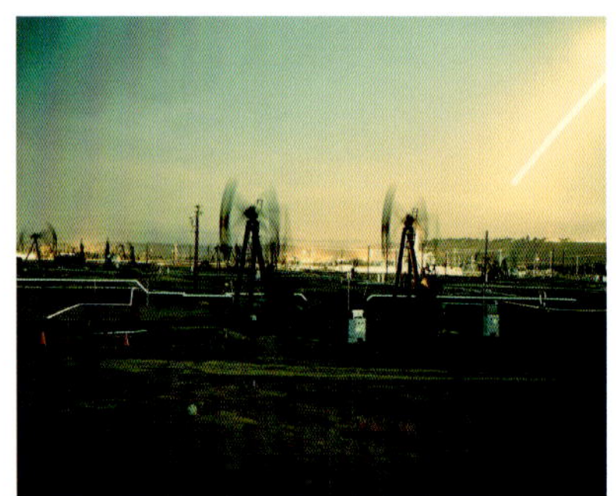

34
SG U #227, 2013
Inkjet print, 127 × 159 cm, 91.5 × 114.6 cm
Page 67

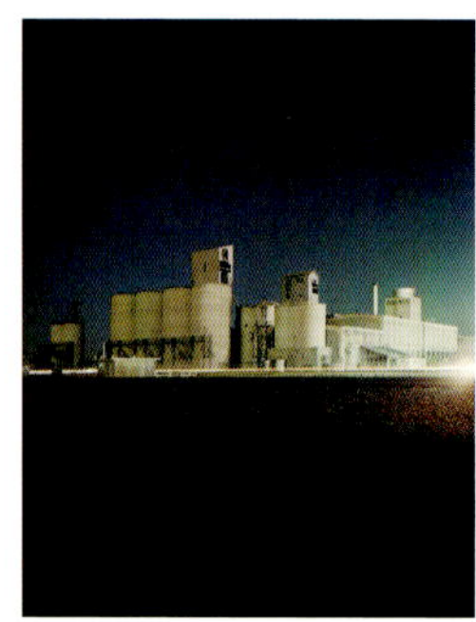

35
SG U #218, 2013
Inkjet print, 161 × 127 cm, 116 × 91.5 cm
Page 68

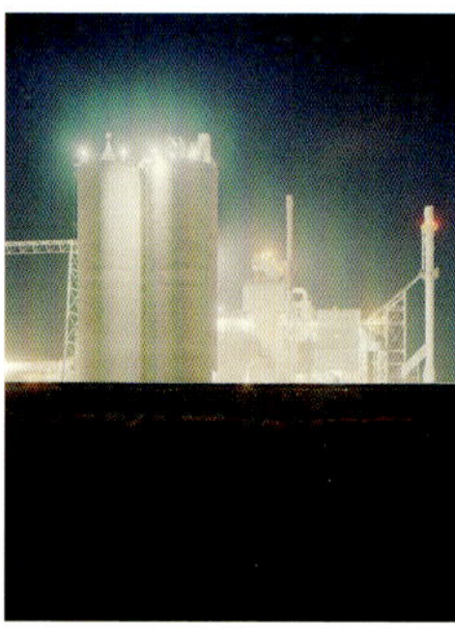

36
SG U #219, 2013
Inkjet print, 161 × 127 cm, 116 × 91.5 cm
Page 69

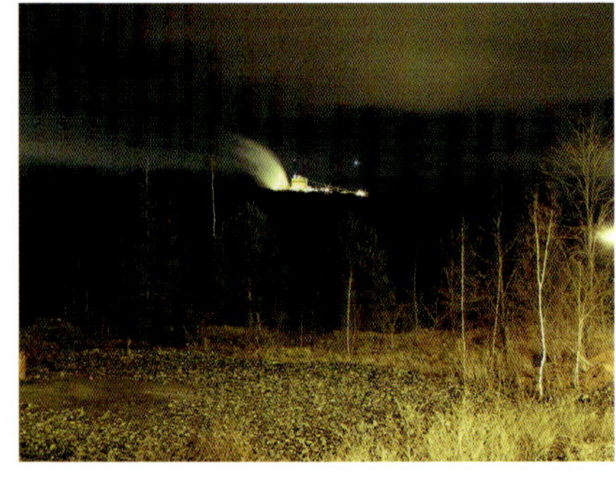

37
SG U #131, 2013
Inkjet print, 127 × 169 cm, 91.5 × 122 cm
Page 75

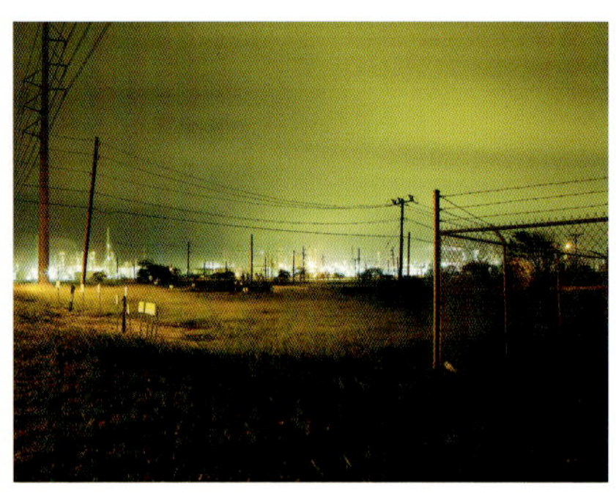

38
SG U #113, 2013
Inkjet print, 127 × 169 cm, 91.5 × 122 cm
Page 77

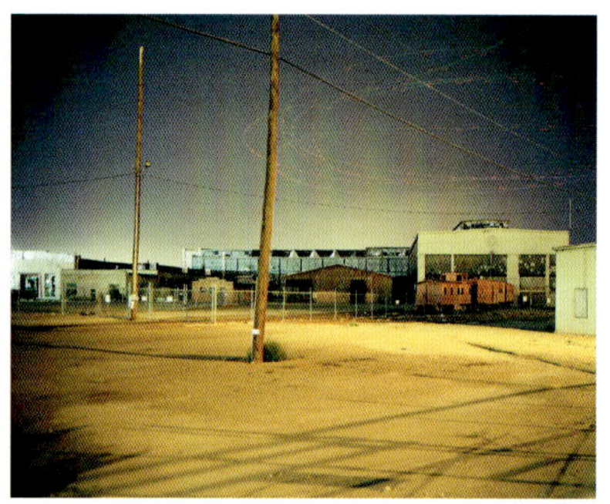

39
SG U #112, 2013
Inkjet print, 180 × 226 cm, 127 × 159.5 cm
Page 79

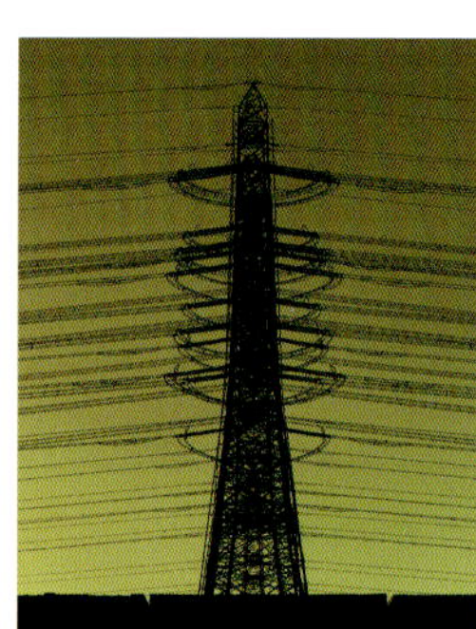

40
SG J #413, 2008
Inkjet print, 159 × 127 cm, 114.3 × 91.5 cm
Page 81

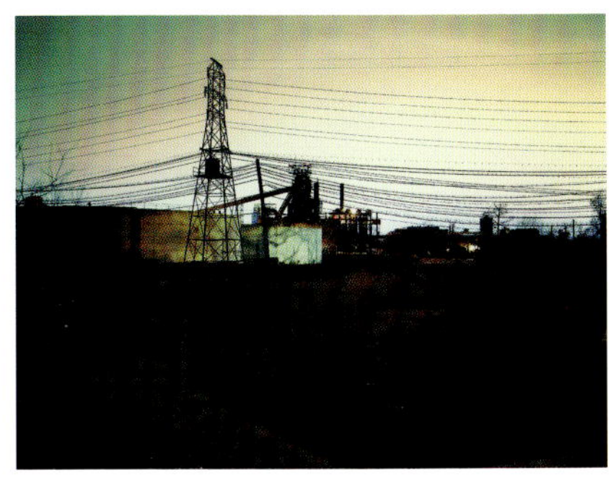

41
SG U #123, 2013
Inkjet print, 127 × 169 cm, 91.5 × 122 cm
Page 83

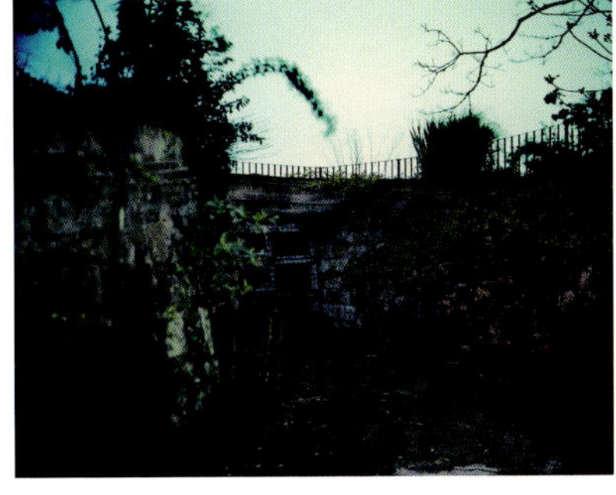

42
SG J #310, 2013
Inkjet print, 180 × 226 cm, 127 × 160 cm
Page 84

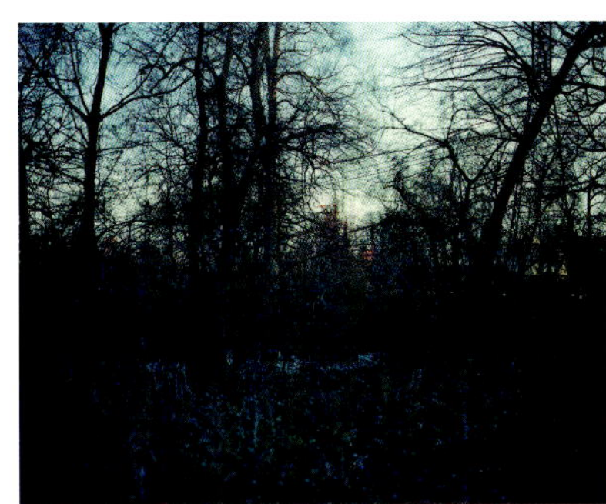

43
SG U #125, 2013
Inkjet print, 180 × 226 cm, 127 × 160 cm
Page 85

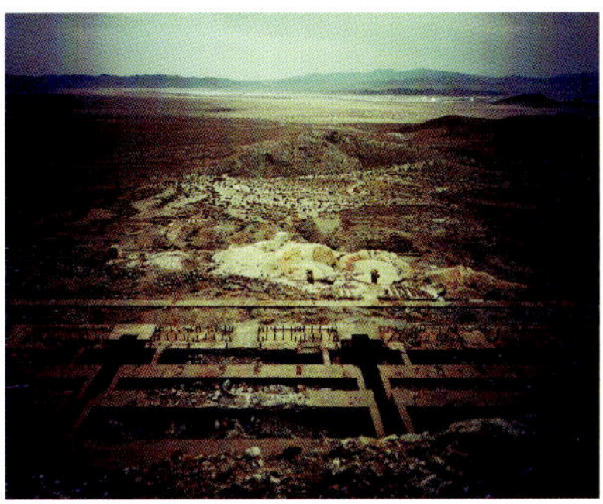

44
SG U #103, 2013
Inkjet print, 127 × 160 cm, 91.5 × 115 cm
Page 87

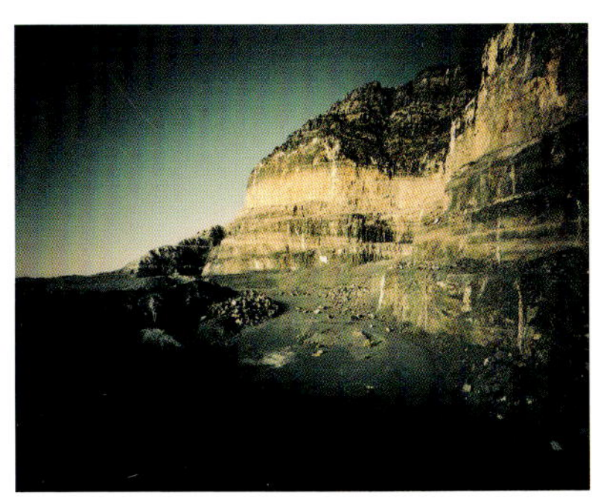

45
SG U #106, 2013
Inkjet print, 127 × 160 cm
Page 89

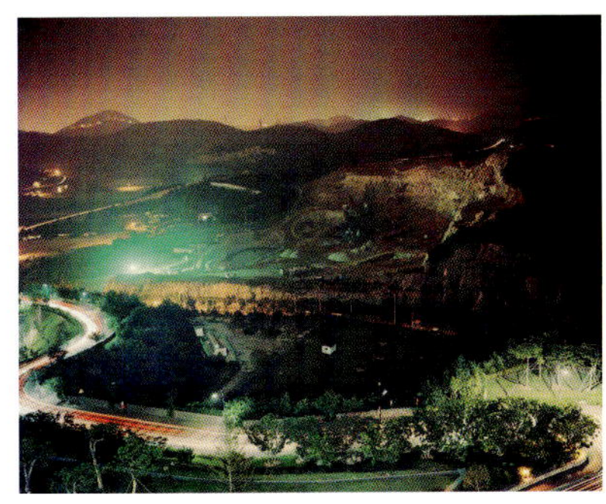

46
SG K #136, 2008
Inkjet print, 127 × 160 cm
Page 91

47
SG U #134, 2013
Inkjet print, 127 × 160 cm, 91.5 × 115 cm
Page 92

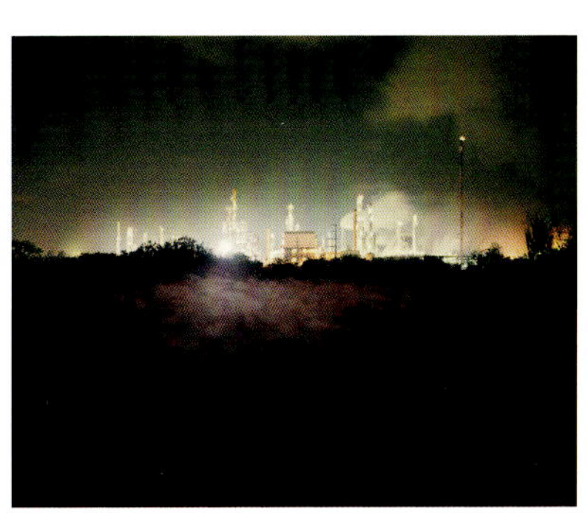

48
SG U #111, 2013
Inkjet print, 180 × 222.5 cm, 127 × 157 cm
Page 93

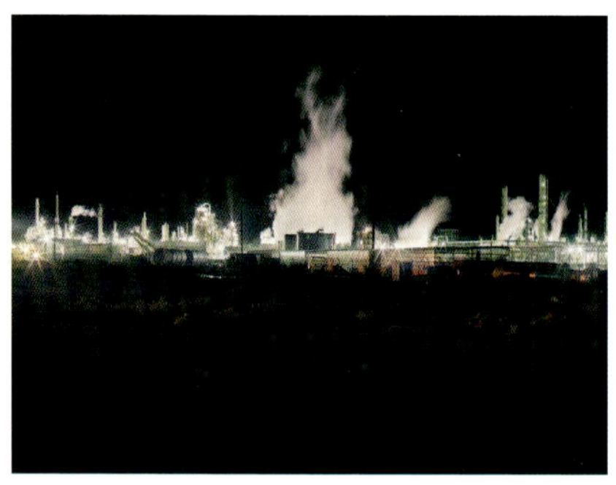

49
SG U #132, 2013
Inkjet print, 127 × 169 cm, 91.5 × 122 cm
Page 95

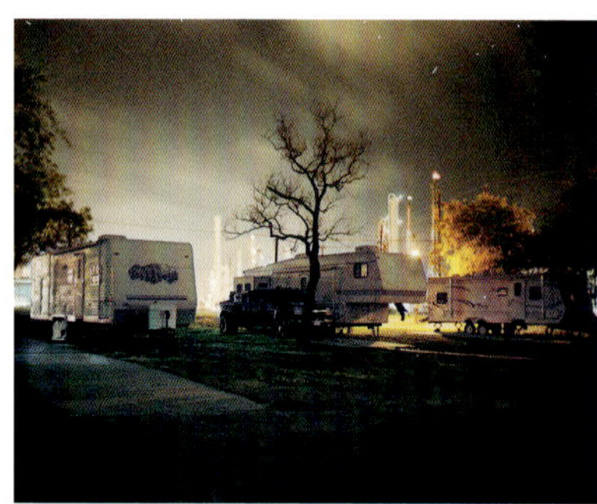

50
SG U #405, 2013
Inkjet print, 180 × 226 cm, 127 × 160 cm
Page 97

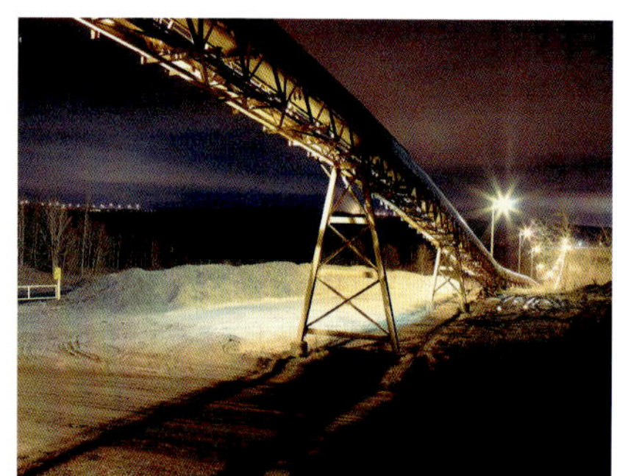

51
SG U #118, 2013
Inkjet print, 127 × 169 cm, 91.5 × 122 cm
Page 99

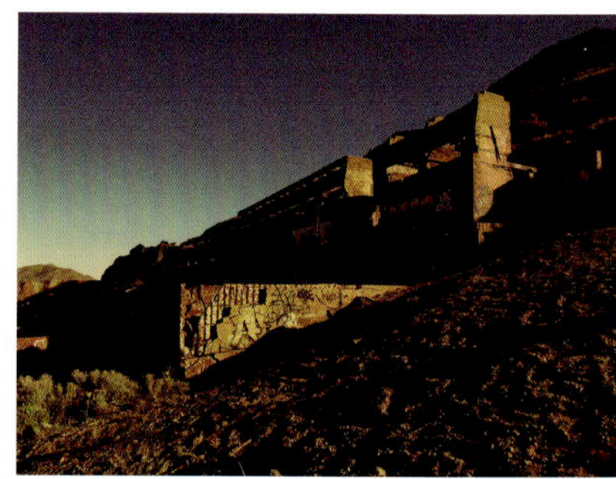

52
SG U #226, 2013
Inkjet print, 127 × 169 cm, 91.5 × 122 cm
Page 101

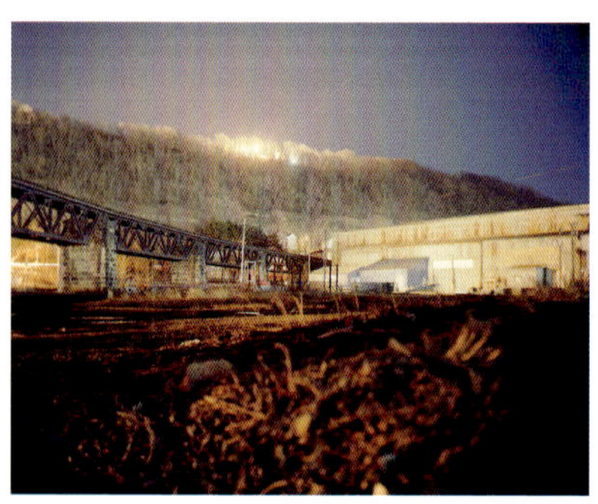

53
SG U #418, 2013
Inkjet print, 127 × 160 cm, 91.5 × 115 cm
Page 103

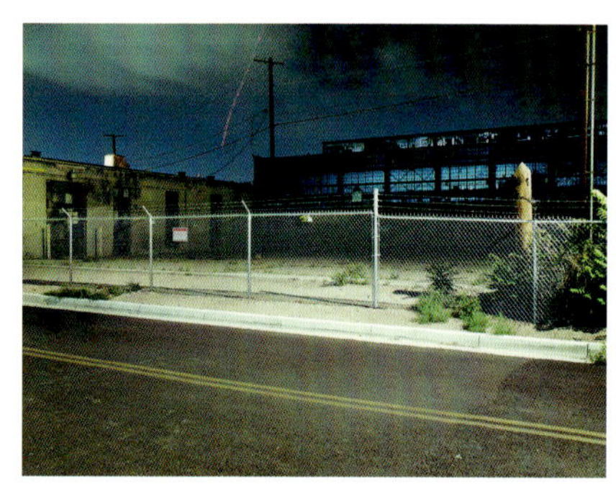

54
SG U #121, 2013
Inkjet print, 127 × 169 cm, 91.5 × 122 cm
Page 105

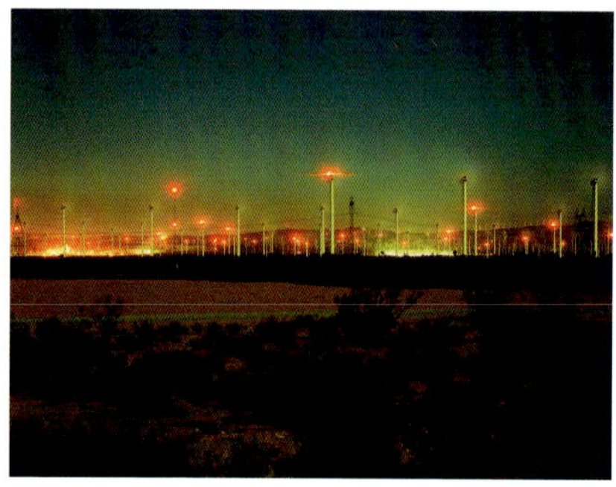

55
SG U #133, 2013
Inkjet print, 127 × 169 cm, 91.5 × 122 cm
Page 106

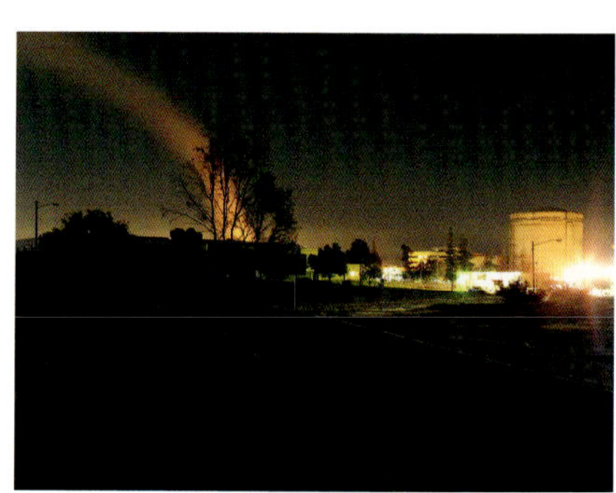

56
SG U #124, 2013
Inkjet print, 127 × 169 cm, 91.5 × 122 cm
Page 107

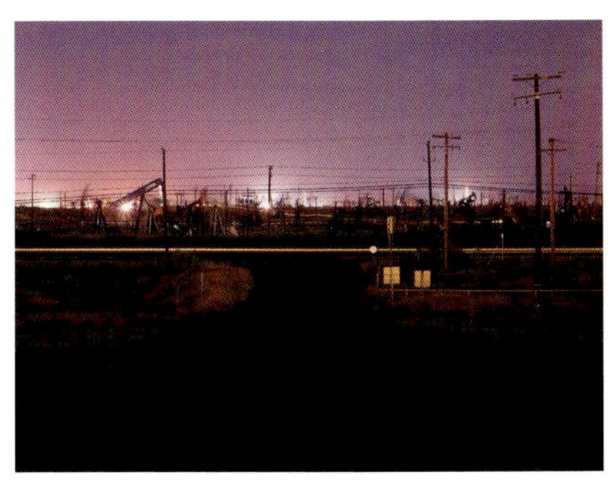

57
SG U #107, 2013
Inkjet print, 127 × 169 cm, 91.5 × 122 cm
Page 109

58
SG U #145, 2013
Inkjet print, 127 × 160 cm, 91.5 × 115 cm
Page 111

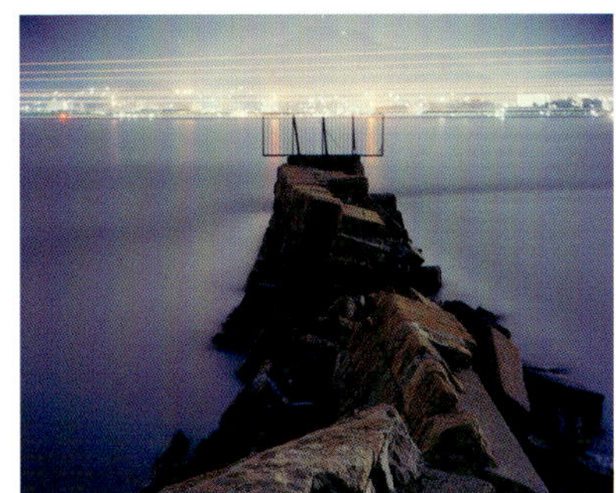

59
SG J #110, 2013
Inkjet print, 180 × 226 cm, 127 × 160 cm
Page 115

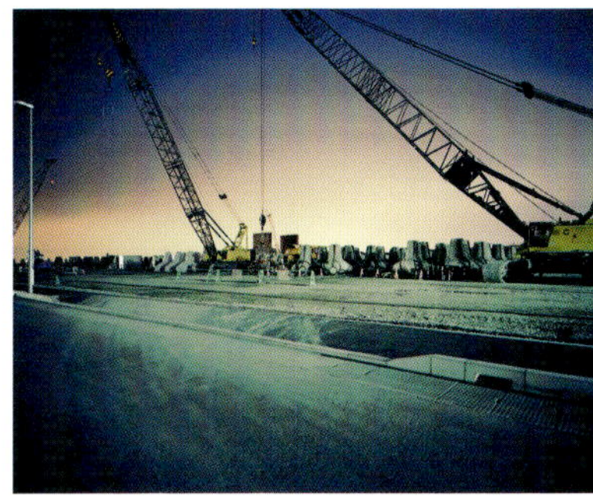

60
SG J #127, 2008
Inkjet print, 180 × 226 cm, 127 × 160 cm
Page 117

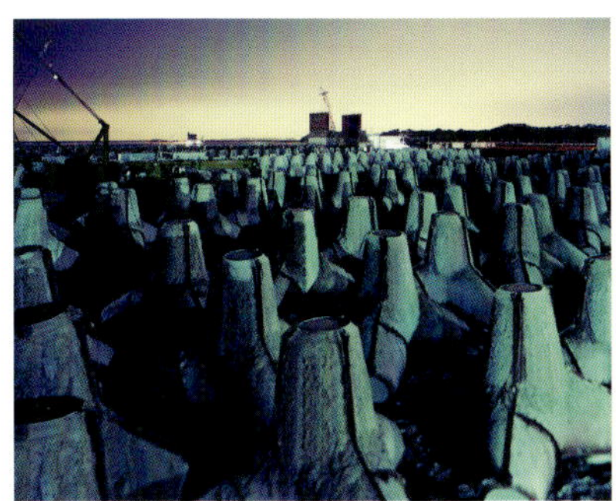

61
SG J #142, 2008
Inkjet print, 180 × 226 cm, 127 × 160 cm
Page 119

62
SG J #311, 2013
Inkjet print, 127 × 160 cm, 91.5 × 115 cm
Page 120

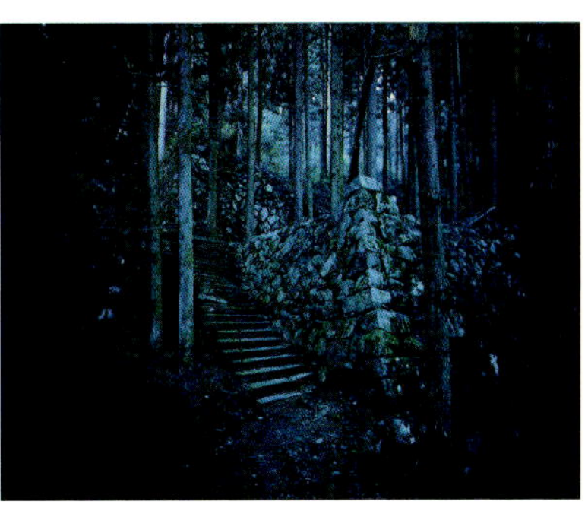

63
SG J #126, 2013
Inkjet print, 127 × 160 cm, 91.5 × 115 cm
Page 121

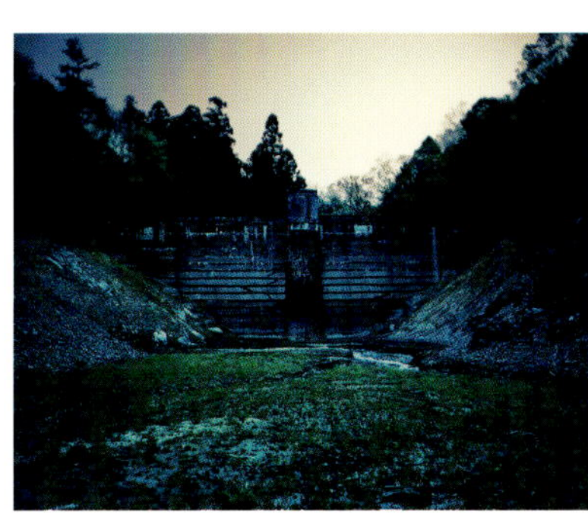

64
SG J #309, 2013
Inkjet print, 180 × 226 cm, 127 × 160 cm
Page 123

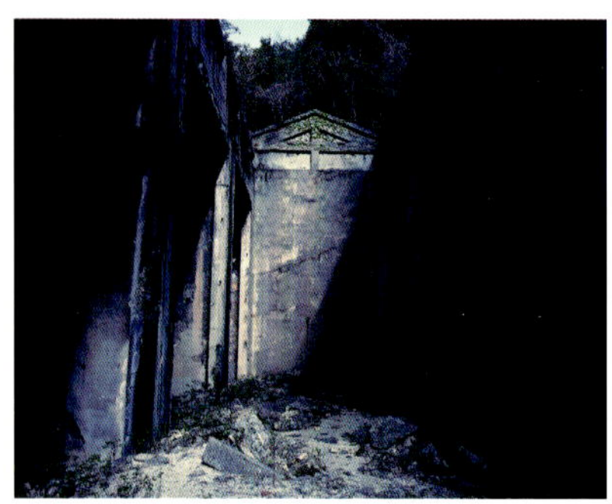

65
SG J #306, 2013
Inkjet print, 127 × 161 cm, 91.5 × 116 cm
Page 125

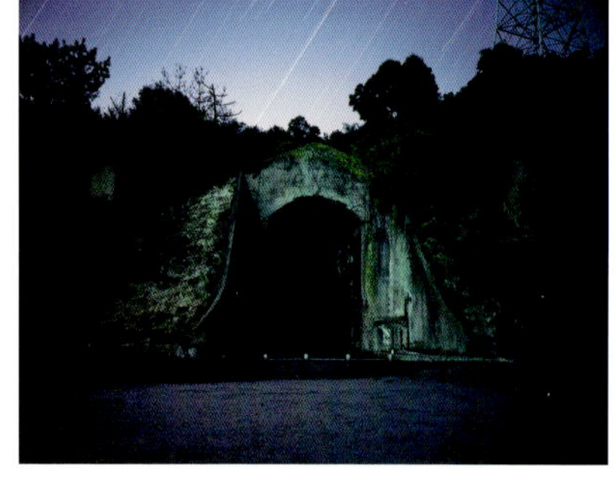

66
SG J #307, 2013
Inkjet print, 180 × 230 cm, 127 × 162 cm
Page 127

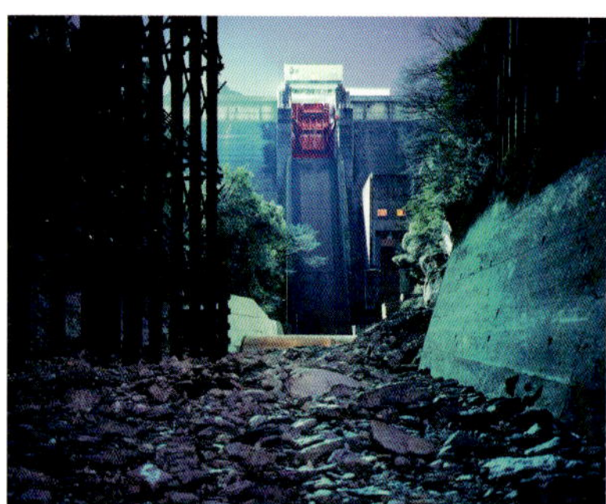

67
SG J #305, 2007
Inkjet print, 286 × 360 cm, 180 × 226.5 cm, 127 × 160 cm
Page 129

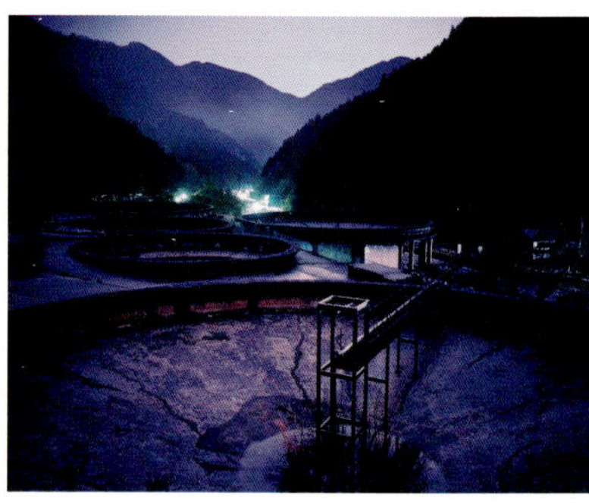

68
SG J #308, 2013
Inkjet print, 180 × 228.5 cm, 127 × 161 cm, 91.5 × 115 cm
Page 131

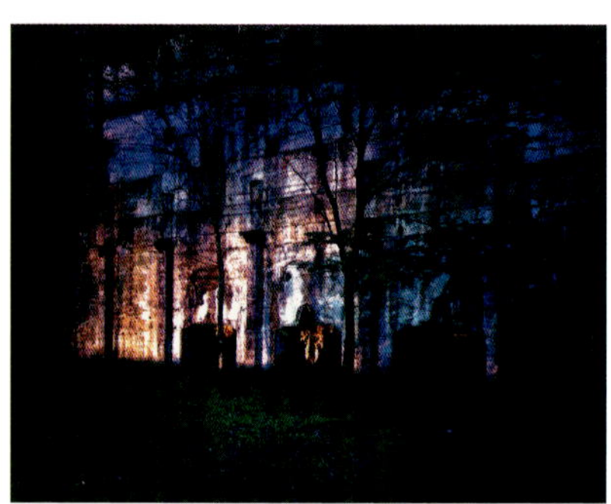

69
SG J #314, 2013
Inkjet print, 127 × 162.5 cm, 91.5 × 117 cm
Page 133

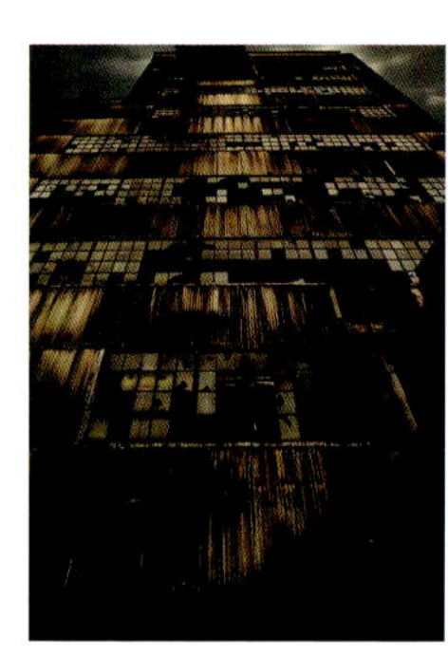

70
SG U #409, 2007
Inkjet print, 208.5 × 150 cm
Page 134

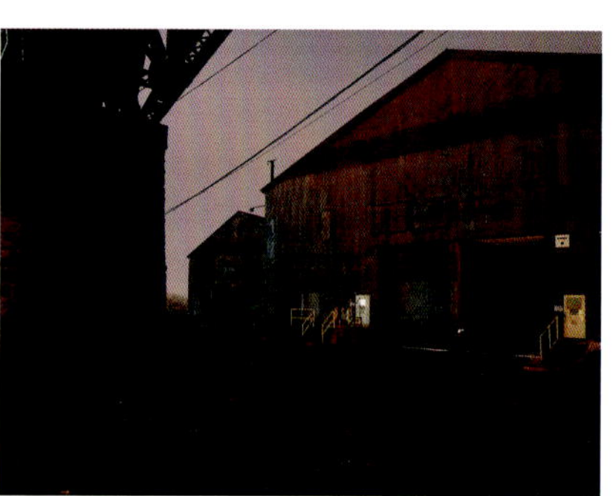

71
SG U #417, 2013
Inkjet print, 127 × 169 cm, 91.5 × 122 cm
Page 135

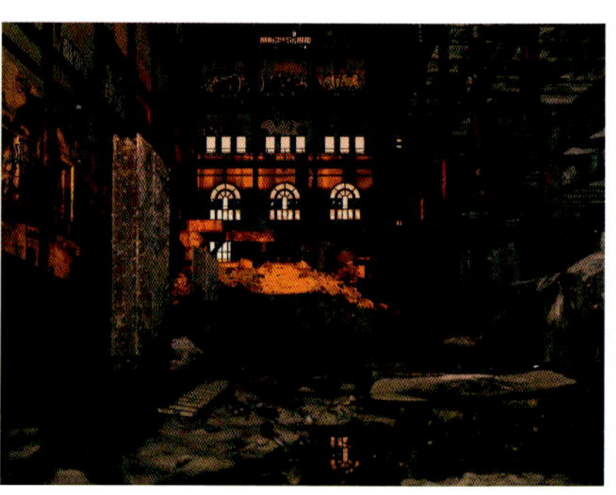

72
SG U #404, 2013
Inkjet print, 127 × 169 cm, 91.5 × 122 cm
Page 137

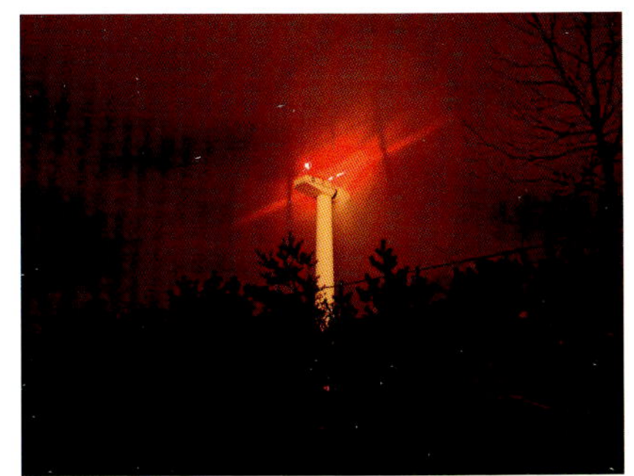

73
SG J #423, 2008
Inkjet print, 100 × 133.3 cm
Page 139

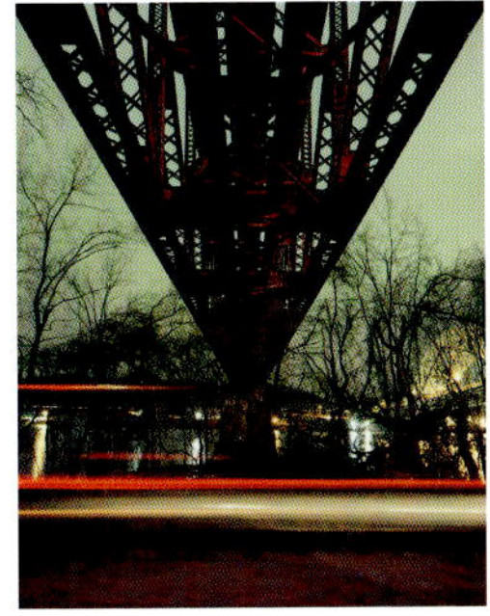

74
SG U #408, 2013
Inkjet print, 226.5 × 180 cm, 160 × 127 cm
Page 141

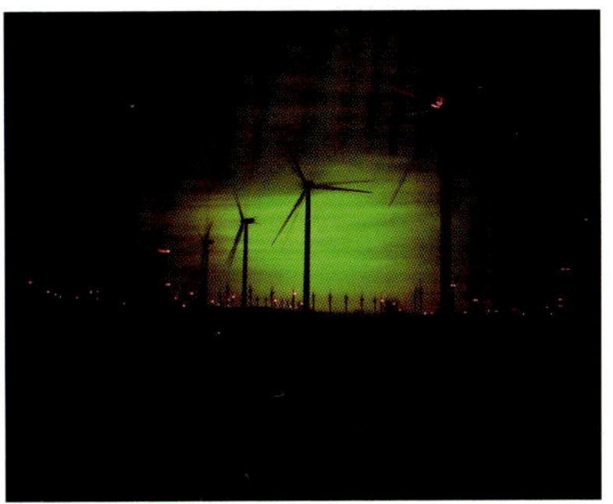

75
SG U #415, 2013
Inkjet print, 127 × 169 cm, 91.5 × 122 cm
Page 143

76
SG U #321, 2007
Inkjet print, 127 × 169 cm, 91.5 × 122 cm
Page 145

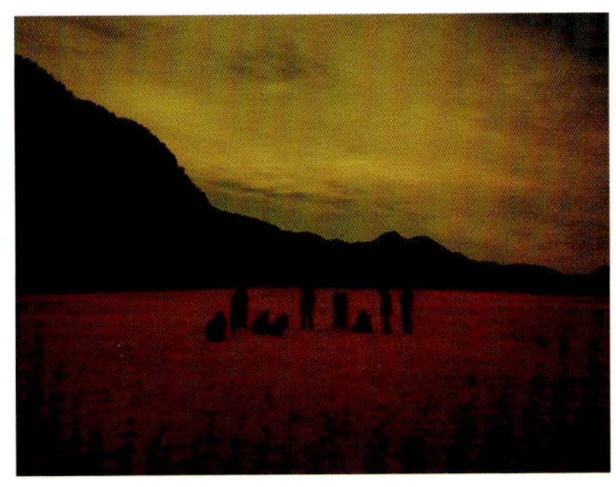

77
SG K #420, 2007
Inkjet print, 127 × 169 cm
Page 147

Taewon Jang

Born 1976 in Seoul, South Korea. Lives and works in Seoul and New York.

Education

Master of Fine Arts in Visual Art, School of the Arts, Columbia University, 2006

Bachelor of Fine Arts in Photography, School of Visual Arts, Chung-Ang University, 2001

Solo Exhibitions (Selection)

2012
Showcase, Ryu Hwarang, Seoul

2011
Generic Landscapes, ILWOO Space, Seoul

2010
New Work, Doosan Gallery, Seoul
New Work, Doosan Gallery, New York

2009
Collusion, Gana Art Gallery, New York

2007
Ooze, Heidi Cho Gallery, New York

Group Exhibitions (Selection)

2014
Photography and Media: 4 AM, Seoul Museum of Art

2013
Parallax: ASEAN Changing Landscapes and Wandering Stars, ASEAN-Korea Center, Seoul

Full Metal Jacket, INSA Art Space, Seoul

Two-person show with Michelle Forsyth, *Untitled*, University of Wyoming, Laramie

2012
ILWOO Photography Award Exhibition, ILWOO Space, Seoul

2011
Two-person show with Rinko Kawauchi, *Colloquy and Soliloquy*, Mountain Fold Gallery, New York

2010
Seconds of Life, 3rd Daegu Photo Biennale, Daegu, South Korea

The 10th Photo Festival: After 2010, Gana Art Gallery, Seoul

Urbanization and Globalization, Gana Art Gallery, New York

2004
Taewon Jang and James Woodward: Jack Goodman Award for Art and Technology, Rosenberg Gallery, New York

Oculus Photo Folio, UNM Art Museum, Albuquerque, NM

Oculus Photo Folio, Spark Contemporary Art Space, Syracuse, NY

2003
The Body: Visual AIDS, Gallerie Lelong, New York

Night of 1,000 Drawings, Artist Space Gallery, New York

Oculus Photo Folio, Tyler Gallery, Elkins Park, PA

Transgression, The Commons Gallery, New York

Awards

Seco Photo Award, Seco Group, 2012

ILWOO Photography Prize, ILWOO Foundation, Hanjin Group, 2010

LeRoy and Janet Neiman Fellowship, Columbia University, 2006

Kramarsky and Schafer Scholarship, Columbia University, 2006

Jack Goodman Award, New York University, 2004

Publications

Stained Ground, Hatje Cantz, 2014

Black Midday, IANNBOOKS, 2012

Taewon Jang's Self-Portraits, IANNBOOKS, 2010

Taewon Jang *Stained Ground*

Edited by Suejin Shin and Markus Hartmann

Copyediting: Leina González

Graphic design and typesetting:
Andreas Platzgummer, Hatje Cantz

Production: Nadine Schmidt, Hatje Cantz

Typeface: Thesis, The Sans

Reproductions: Jan Scheffler, prints professional

Paper: Galaxi Keramik, 170 g/m²

Printing and binding: DZA
Druckerei zu Altenburg GmbH, Altenburg

Published by
Hatje Cantz Verlag
Zeppelinstrasse 32
73760 Ostfildern
Germany
Tel. +49 711 4405-200
Fax +49 711 4405-220
www.hatjecantz.com
A Ganske Publishing Group company

Hatje Cantz books are available internationally at selected bookstores. For more information about our distribution partners, please visit our website at www.hatjecantz.com.

ISBN 978-3-7757-3784-5

Printed in Germany

Cover illustration:
SG U #223, 2013, page 37

Back Cover illustration:
SG U #132, 2013, page 95